A Kind
of Grace

A Kind of Grace

The Autobiography of the World's Greatest Female Athlete

JACKIE JOYNER-KERSEE

with SONJA STEPTOE

WARNER BOOKS

A Time Warner Company

B
Joyner - Kersee
Jo

Warner Books, Inc., 1271 Avenue of the Americas, New York, NY 10020
Visit our Web site at http://warnerbooks.com

w   A Time Warner Company

Printed in the United States of America
First Printing: October 1997
10   9   8   7   6   5   4   3   2   1

Library of Congress Cataloging-in-Publication Data

Joyner-Kersee, Jacqueline
   A kind of grace : the autobiography of the world's greatest female
athlete / Jackie Joyner-Kersee with Sonja Steptoe.
     p.   cm.
   Includes index.
   ISBN 0-446-52248-1   BT 23.00 | 12.24 10 | 97
   1. Joyner-Kersee, Jacqueline   2. Women track and field
athletes—United States—Biography.   I. Steptoe, Sonja.   II. Title.
GV697.J69A3   1997
796.42'092—dc21   97-14966
   [B]   CIP

Book design by Giorgetta Bell McRee

I dedicate this book to my mother, Mary Joyner, and my husband, Bobby. You are the two people I consider to be true friends. You both have been my strength when I was weak and a great source of light when times were dark. Because of you, I have developed into the person I am and I am able to do the things I do.

Momma, words cannot describe how much I miss seeing you, having our lengthy phone conversations that to me seemed timeless, and simply knowing that you were there for me. I never realized how much you taught me; and I am grateful that you gave me the gift of life. You told me to challenge myself and to be considerate of others. They are lessons I treasure. I love you and miss you dearly.

Bobby, my blessings and happiness have come from being married to you. Together, we shall move forward in life and face new challenges. You are my rock and my inspiration.

Acknowledgments

From Jackie Joyner-Kersee

There are so many people I want to thank and acknowledge for their support over the years.

To my many sponsors, GlaxoWellcome, Bob Ingram and Tim Tyson; Honda and Kiochi Amemiya; Nike and Phil Knight; Ray-Ban and Norm Sallk; McDonald's, Ken Barun, Jackie Woodward and Teddi Domann; and 7UP, John Albers and Warren Jackson. It was your commitment to me that paved my road to success. Thanks for sticking with me, whether I was healthy or injured.

To Elite Management: Thank you for securing corporate support and making life easier for me during the times I needed it most.

To my dad, Alfred: Thank you for providing us with shelter, food and lots of love.

To my siblings, Angie, Debra and Fret-fret: Our bonds will never be broken.

A special thanks to all of the people who played a significant role in my life as a young girl: George Ward, Tyrone Cavitt, Percy Harris, Puncho Hamilton, Big John and Tommy Dancy, Miss Mary Brown, Miss Wicks, Mr. Riggins,

Miss Walker, Miss Theodora Ash Smith, Miss Gillispe, Miss Hopkins, Mr. McDonald, Glover, Miss Stamp, Michelle Farmer, Joyce Farmer McKinney, Betty Young, the Slack family, Calvin Brown, Alan, Art and Brooks Johnson, and all the men on the corner of 15th and Piggott.

To my friends in the sports and entertainment industry who have supported and encouraged me throughout my career: Wilt Chamberlain, Bill Cosby, Louis Gossett, Jr., Michael Jordan, Dawnn Lewis, Ozzie Smith, Dawn Staley, Susan Taylor, Chris Webber and Terrie Williams.

To three very special ladies who inspire me to be a great person: Ruth Owens, Rachel Robinson and Betty Shabazz.

To the members of my foundation who help me in my dream to come back to East St. Louis and give hope to young people: Henry Brown, Bill Boyle, David Dandurand, Anita DeFrantz, Dave Dorr, Herb Douglas, Christopher Edley, Phil and Connee Freeman, Noel Hankin, Jim Koman, Earl Lazerson, Ann Moore, Jim Orso, Congress-woman Maxine Waters, Denise Williams, Russ Klein, Judson Pickard, Angela Roberson, Wayman Smith III and Judge Warton.

To Wallace and Debra Anderson: Thanks for allowing my sister and me to stay with you when we had no other place to go.

To Billie Moore, Dr. Judith Holland and Colleen Matsuhara: Thanks for recruiting me and making my dreams become reality.

To Coach Nino Fennoy: Thanks for being a great friend, mentor and dad. You are and always have been a great source of inspiration to me. I will always be in your debt for all of the support given over the years.

To Bob Forster and Dr. Rick Lehman: my career saviors. I owe a great deal of my injury-free years to your commitment and dedication.

Acknowledgments

To Dave Harris: Thanks for being there for me, and being a friend to the end to me and my husband, Bobby.

To my girlfriend Carmen: Thanks for being a friend, a sister and, sometimes, a mom. Our friendship is very special.

To Valerie Brisco: Thanks for letting me stay with you rent-free so that I could get my first car.

To Jeanette Bolden, Alice Brown, Sandra Farmer-Patrick, Flo-Jo and Gail Devers: I always believed we had a special connection that went beyond collecting medals. We are truly friends.

To Marie Kersee: I will always have a special spot in my heart for you because you always dropped whatever you were doing to help me. Thank you.

To Rhonda Harris: Even though you were only thirteen at the time, it was your and Sandra's encouragement at the 1993 World Championships that helped me stay strong through my illness.

To Joyce, Michelle and Percy: Thank you for helping Sonja and extending your "East St. Louis style" hospitality during her visit.

There isn't enough space to individually acknowledge each of the many contributors to this book. To all of those who assisted: Please know that in my heart I am grateful for your help.

Finally, to WILMA RUDOLPH: my hero, my friend, my idol. I miss you.

From Sonja Steptoe

Heartfelt thanks to:

My agent, Faith Hampton Childs, for her unwavering support and priceless wisdom.

My research assistant, Tracey Reavis, for her gold-medal reporting performance.

Photo editor Maxine Arthur Peacock for lending the picture collection her keen eye.

The *Sports Illustrated* library and computer operations departments for promptly answering my plaintive cries for help.

Nino Fennoy, Della Gray, Al Joyner and Joyce Farmer McKinney for supplying essential details and insights.

Jackie Joyner-Kersee's Athletic Record

1977: Wins Amateur Athletic Union Junior Olympics pentathlon, scoring 3,613 points
—national age group record
Wins 100-yard dash at AAU All-America City Relays
Wins 440-yard dash at AAU All-America City Relays
—meet record
Wins long jump at AAU All-America City Relays
—meet record

1978: Wins AAU Jr. Olympics pentathlon, scoring 3,817 points
—national age group record
Member of 1st place team at Illinois state high school track championship
—sets state girls' record in 440-yard dash, 56.75 seconds
—anchors winning mile-relay team
—runner-up in long jump
Averages 16 points, 17 rebounds for Lincoln High girls' basketball team
St. Louis Globe-Democrat Girl Athlete of the Year

1979: Wins AAU Jr. Olympics pentathlon, scoring 3,953 points
—national age group record
Wins AAU Jr. Olympics long jump, 20' 8"
—national age group record

Wins long jump at Illinois state high school track championship
—sets state girls' long jump record, 20' 7½"
—second best jump in the nation by a high school girl
—seventh best on U.S. girls' high school all-time list
Member of 1st place team at Illinois state high school track championship
Member of runner-up team in Illinois state girls' basketball championship tournament
—compiles 47 points, 26 rebounds, 8 assists in three tournament games
—named to All-Tournament Team
Illinois Track & Field News Female Athlete of the Year
Illinois Track & Field News Hall of Fame
Illinois Track & Field News Prep All-America
St. Louis Globe-Democrat Girl Athlete of the Year

1980: Wins AAU Jr. Olympics pentathlon, scoring 4,129 points
—national age group record
Wins AAU Jr. Olympics long jump, 21' ¾"
Wins long jump at The Athletic Congress Junior Track & Field Championships
Wins long jump at Jr. Pan Am Championships
Member of 1st place team at Illinois state high school track championships
—anchors winning mile-relay team
—wins long jump
Member of Illinois state high school girls' basketball championship team, Lincoln High, 31–0 season record
—named to All-Tournament Team

—named to All-State Team
—complies 59 points, 20 rebounds, 8 assists in three tournament games
Illinois Track & Field News Prep All-America
St. Louis Globe-Democrat Girl Athlete of the Year
Finishes 8th in long jump at U.S. Olympic Trials

1981: Runner-up in heptathlon at U.S. Championships
Finishes 3rd in heptathlon at Association of Intercollegiate Athletics for Women National Championships
Averages 9 points, 4.6 rebounds for UCLA women's basketball team
All-America, track
All-America, basketball

1982: Wins heptathlon at NCAA Championships, scoring 6,099 points
—sets NCAA record
Wins heptathlon at U.S. Championships, scoring 6,126 points
Runner-up in long jump at NCAA Championships
Averages 8 points, 6 rebounds for UCLA women's basketball team
Wins UCLA All-University Athlete Award

1983: Wins heptathlon at NCAA Championships, scoring 6,365 points
—NCAA record
Runner-up in heptathlon at U.S. Championships scoring 6,372 points
Finishes 4th in long jump at U.S. Championships
Finishes 3rd in long jump at NCAA Championships

Finishes 8th in 100-meter hurdles at NCAA Championships
Averages 9 points, 6 rebounds for UCLA women's basketball team
Wins UCLA All-University Athlete Award
Wins Broderick Award as nation's best college track athlete

1984: Wins heptathlon at U.S. Olympic Trials, scoring 6,520 points
Runner-up in long jump at Olympic Trials
Silver medalist in heptathlon at Olympics, scoring 6,385 points
Finishes 5th in long jump at Olympics
Finishes 3rd in long jump at U.S. Championships

1985: Highest individual scorer at NCAA Championships
—Finishes 3rd in 100-meter hurdles
—Finishes 2nd in 400-meter hurdles
—Finishes 2nd in triple jump
—Finishes 16th in long jump
Wins long jump at Grand Prix Finals
Wins heptathlon at National Sports Festival, scoring 6,718 points
—highest score in the world in 1985
—sets NCAA record
Sets American record in long jump, 23' 9"
1st team, All-Conference, women's basketball
Finishes 12th in scoring on UCLA all-time list, 1,167 points
Finishes 6th in rebounding on UCLA all-time list, 752
Wins UCLA All-University Athlete Award

Wins Broderick Cup as nation's best female collegiate athlete

1986: Wins heptathlon at Goodwill Games, scoring 7,148 points
—sets world record
—first woman in history to score over 7,000 points
Wins heptathlon at Olympic Festival, scoring 7,158 points
—sets world record
Wins long jump at U.S. Indoor Championships, 22' 10½"
—sets American record
Finishes 5th in 100-meter hurdles at Grand Prix Finals
Goodwill Games Outstanding Athlete award
Jesse Owens Award winner
Track & Field News Female Athlete of the Year
Sullivan Award winner as nation's top amateur athlete
U.S. Olympic Committee Sportswoman of the Year

1987: Wins heptathlon at World Championships, scoring 7,128 points
Wins long jump at World Championships, 24' 1¾"
Wins long jump at Pan Am Games, 24' 5½"
—ties world record
Wins heptathlon at U.S. Championships
—sets world heptathlon record in long jump, 23' 9½"
Wins long jump at U.S. Championships
Wins long jump at Grand Prix Finals
Overall Female Indoor Grand Prix Champion

Finishes 3rd in 55-meter hurdles at U.S. Indoor
Championships
Associated Press Female Athlete of the Year
Track & Field News Athlete of the Year
Jesse Owens Award winner

1988: Wins heptathlon at Olympic Trials, scoring 7,215
points
—sets world record
—sets American heptathlon record in 100-meter
hurdles
—sets American heptathlon record in high jump
—sets world heptathlon record in 200 meters
Wins long jump at Olympic Trials, 24' 5¼"
Gold medalist in heptathlon at Olympic Games,
scoring 7,291 points
—sets world record
Gold medalist in long jump at Olympic Games,
24' 3½"
—sets Olympic record
Finishes 5th in 55-meter hurdles at U.S. Indoor
Championships
Ties American record in 100-meter hurdles, 12.61
seconds
Sets American indoor record in long jump, 23' ½"
Sets American indoor record in 60-meter hurdles,
7.88 seconds
Women's Sports Foundation Amateur Athlete of
the Year

1989: Wins 55-meter hurdles at Millrose Games, 7.37
seconds
—Ties world record
—Sets American indoor record

Sets American indoor record in 60-meter hurdles, 7.81 seconds
Runner-up in 55-meter hurdles at U.S. Indoor Championships

1990: Wins heptathlon at Goodwill Games, scoring 6,783 points
Wins long jump at U.S. Championships

1991: Wins long jump at World Championships
Wins heptathlon at U.S. Championships
Wins long jump at U.S. Championships

1992: Wins heptathlon at Olympic Trials, scoring 6,695 points
Wins long jump at Olympic Trials
Gold medalist in heptathlon at Olympic Games, scoring 7,044 points
Bronze medalist in long jump at Olympic Games
Wins 60-meter hurdles in U.S. Indoor Championships
Runner-up in long jump at Grand Prix Finals
Sets American indoor long jump record, Yokohama, Japan, 23' 1¼"

1993: Wins heptathlon at World Championships, scoring 6,837 points
Wins heptathlon at U.S. Championships
Wins long jump at U.S. Championships
Sets American indoor record in 50-meter hurdles, 6.84 seconds

1994: Wins heptathlon at Goodwill Games, scoring 6,606 points
Wins long jump at U.S. Championships, 24' 7"

—sets American record
Wins 100-meter hurdles at U.S. Championships
Wins long jump at U.S. Indoor Championships,
23' 4¾"
—sets American indoor record
Wins long jump in Grand Prix Finals
Overall International Amateur Athletic Federation
Grand Prix Champion
IAAF Female Athlete of the Year
Track & Field News Female Athlete of the Year

1995: Wins long jump at U.S. Indoor Championships
Wins long jump at U.S. Championships
Wins heptathlon at U.S. Championships
Finishes 6th in long jump at World Championships

1996: Wins long jump at Olympic Trials
Runner-up in heptathlon at Olympic Trials
Bronze medalist in long jump at Olympic Games

CONTENTS

A Kind
of Grace

"I don't think being an athlete is unfeminine.
I think of it as a kind of grace."

—Jackie Joyner-Kersee
to Tom Callahan of *Time*,
September 1988

Prologue

A sense of nervous anticipation was building in the moist and muggy Atlanta air that late July morning. It was an hour before the heptathlon competition at the 1996 Olympic Games and the serious business of preparing for combat was well underway on the warmup track. Coaches reviewed strategy on the sidelines, while their athletes limbered up on the infield. Around them, competitors of every race, nationality and shoe company affiliation paraded around the jogging track, as television crews from NBC and CNN moved into position, angling for pictures and sound bites.

Sprinkled among the group were my opponents, the world's most versatile and gifted female athletes. They included Sabine Braun of Germany, Ghada Shouaa of Syria, Natasha Sazanovich of Belarus, Denise Lewis of Great Britain and Kelly Blair of the United States. Every four years, such a group gathered at an Olympic venue to contest the heptathlon, a two-day, seven-part trial of endurance and skill. To claim victory, a woman must outperform her competitors in negotiating 100 meters of track and hurdles, clearing the high-jump bar, throwing the javelin, sprinting 200 meters, leaping into the long-jump pit, putting the shot and running 800 meters. Her reward at the culmination of the grueling ordeal is an Olympic gold medal and the designation "World's Greatest Female Athlete."

Over the past thirteen years, the event had repeatedly tested my mettle. I had conquered opponents both human and inhumane: the East Germans, the Russians, drenching rains, extreme heat, pain, exhaustion, dehydration, asthma. Between 1984 and the beginning of 1996, I won every single heptathlon I completed, posting the six highest scores in the sport's history, setting four world records, winning two World Championships, and capturing two Olympic gold medals along the way.

Impressive as my record was, I didn't feel the least bit invincible that morning in Atlanta. Splayed on my stomach across a white bath towel on the infield grass, I thought only of my ailing right thigh. The fingers of my physical therapist, Bob Forster, furiously massaged the knot of hamstring muscle and scar tissue inside the thigh, still tender from the severe pull I'd suffered three weeks earlier. Gold medals and world records were far from my mind. Given the precarious condition of my leg, my goal was simply to survive the four events on the day's schedule.

My elaborate plans for a final Olympic heptathlon triumph were slowly unraveling. I'd chosen this occasion as the perfect opportunity for a swan song. I'd made my Olympic debut at the Los Angeles Games in 1984. Now, after achieving so much on foreign soil—a world record in Moscow, gold medals in Seoul and Barcelona, world championships in Rome and Stuttgart—I wanted to close out my participation in this event in my homeland, with the eyes of the world watching.

There were still a few springs left in my legs for long

jumping, my other specialty. But my days as a heptathlete were numbered. I still held the heptathlon world record, at 7,291 points, but the rigorous training and arduous competitions were taking a toll on my body, chipping away at my muscle mass and sapping my energy. As well, my chronic asthma condition was affecting me more and more on the track. I'd come close to dying *off* the track. I wanted to spend my final moment as a heptathlete on the medal stand, not on an ambulance stretcher.

I was drained emotionally, too. Dominance, I'd learned over the years, brings both adulation and attacks. No sooner had the "greatest female athlete" crown been placed on my head in 1988 than the efforts to knock it off began. I faced unfounded accusations of steroid use, heard unkind remarks about my appearance, and read hypercritical reviews of my performances. I tried to endure it all with good cheer. But in truth, the sniping hurt me deeply. If, as the critics kept saying, I was only as good as my last heptathlon performance, I wanted the final one in Atlanta to be my best of all.

But things started going awry in June at the Olympic Trials. I sprained an ankle, pulled my right hamstring, and battled a cold and an asthma attack during the meet and lost by three points to Kelly Blair, who performed magnificently as I struggled. It was my first defeat in twelve years. Then, just twenty-one days before the Olympics, the scar tissue gnarled around my right hamstring jerked away from the muscle while I was airborne over a hurdle. When the pain registered, I jumped and fell to the track, screaming in agony and rage. My leg had been obstinate since then. Each time I tried to blast out of the starting blocks or push across the shot-put ring in practice, the pain was excruciating. I hadn't been able to test the leg's strength, to employ it as I would have to in competition.

Now, with the moment at hand and my therapist's fingers furiously kneading that scar tissue and all the other tortured muscle fibers, I winced and wondered. Was my hamstring strong enough for the task ahead? How would it respond when I called on it to help me get over 100 meters of track and hurdles, to clear the high-jump bar, to provide the power to throw the javelin and, after all of that, to run 200 meters at world-class speed?

I had no idea.

As I walked into the packed Olympic Stadium, the sky turned gloomy. Raindrops dotted my legs and arms as we lined up in front of the blocks for the hurdle race. The drops became sprinkles and turned quickly into sheets of showers. The starter called us to the blocks and I insisted to myself that I was ready. Staring down my lane at the arrayed hurdles, I focused on starting strong and moving steadily forward, one step at a time.

I shot out of the blocks without pain. A good sign. I was in front heading into the series of hurdles. First, second, third, fourth. All cleared. So far, so good. Fifth, sixth . . . oh, God! The hamstring pulled as I stepped over the seventh.

"Keep going," I told myself. "Don't stop. It hurts, but there are only three left."

I gathered all my strength, and tackled the eighth. My cheeks puffing furiously, I gritted my teeth to cushion the pain as I landed. I pushed on to the ninth. Another deep breath, the jump, the wince, the exhale. One more. I gritted my teeth as I cleared it. Then, a grimace at the finish line. I made it! Not only was I still in the competition, I'd won the heat. Now, to get some help for my throbbing leg.

Dripping wet, I grabbed my gear and hobbled toward my husband and coach, Bobby Kersee. I was panting and in terrible pain, but I stopped on the way for a brief interview in the downpour with Cris Collinsworth of NBC, who held an umbrella over us. Between gasps, I told him, "I want to stay positive, take it one event at a time and let my physical therapist get in there and dig out whatever's in the muscle."

We went to the coaches' room, hoping to use one of the massage tables. But they wouldn't allow Bobby inside, even though he was my coach, because he didn't have the proper pass. So, the three of us, Bobby, Bob the therapist and I, climbed a flight of stairs inside the stadium to the concession area, where we found a little-used handicap-access ramp. I threw down a towel and stretched out on my stomach. Bobby and Bob went to work with ice packs and massaging hands to quiet the spasms inside my thigh. Spectators watching us from their seats applauded and shouted encouragement. "We love you, Jackie!" "You're the best!" "Good luck!"

Hearing them, I wished with all my heart that I'd be able to continue.

The spasms eventually subsided. And after an hour-and-a-half rain delay, the heptathletes were moving to the high-jump apron. The nice people who'd watched my therapy session cheered as I made my way down to the field. I took a practice jump at a very low height and knocked the bar down. I knew I was in trouble. But I refused to surrender. I walked across the track to the stadium railing, where Bobby was standing. "It feels like it's pulling," I said. "If I accelerate, I don't know what will happen. I'll try the next height and see."

I turned and walked away. As I crossed the track and reached the high-jump apron, I heard Bobby's voice over my shoulder. He'd jumped over the railing and was walking up behind me. "That's it, Jackie," he shouted. "I'm not going to let you do this."

I knew if he was on the track I was already finished in the

competition because he didn't have a pass. But I protested anyway. "No, Bobby, I want to try. Let me at least *try*."

He led me to the tent where the heptathletes had gathered. We sat on the grass. He looked at me and said, "I've watched you for twelve years give everything you've got. I'm no longer going to allow you to do this. It's time to go."

"Bobby, I just want to *try*."

"No, Jackie, this isn't a coach-athlete thing. This is your husband telling you it's time for you to go."

It was over. I sat there a good three to five minutes absorbing the impact, while Bobby told the officials I was withdrawing. I tried to hold back the tears, but they poured out of my eyes, down my cheeks. Bobby started crying, too. I leaned against him and put my head on his shoulder. He put his arm around me. We sobbed together.

Ghada Shouaa, a Syrian heptathlete, came over and hugged me. Then she kissed me on both cheeks. She also kissed Bobby. That was the greatest compliment a competitor could have paid me. Sabine Braun of Germany came over and patted me on the back. It was a touching gesture considering our tense rivalry. I gathered my paraphernalia and walked off the track with Bobby. None of the spectators knew what was happening, so there was no reaction. We walked past a wall of reporters. I was too upset to talk. If I had tried to open my mouth and speak, I would have burst into tears.

Bob, Bobby and I walked back to the hotel, just a few blocks from the stadium, in silence. With the track and field events underway, the streets around the stadium were deserted and deadly quiet. It was like being in a funeral procession. A funeral for my dead dream.

Within minutes our hotel room filled with our friends: my high school track coach, Nino Fennoy, and his friend

Toni; my aunt Della; my brother, Al, and sister-in-law, Florence; Bobby's best friend, Dave Harris, and his wife; my orthopedist, Dr. Rick Lehman; Bobby's sister Debra; Valerie Brisco, Jeanette Bolden and Valarie Foster, my assistant. Dave and his wife walked in wearing custom-printed caps that read, "JJK STILL NO. 1."

As each visitor came in and saw me, there was a new round of hugs, kisses and tears. The room was filled with warm affection. After what we'd just been through, it was the perfect tonic for Bobby and me. What began as the worst of days was ending as the best.

The phone rang nonstop, once the word got out that I'd withdrawn. Reporters wanted to interview us. I still couldn't talk about what had happened. Bobby agreed to go to the broadcast center for an interview with NBC's Dwight Stones. During the telecast, Tom Hammond and Dwight discussed my career, tracing the ups and downs. Their report showed scenes of Bobby yelling at me and comforting me, and replayed moments from my injuries and my victories.

Tom and Dwight said such wonderful things. For the first time in my career, I felt appreciated and respected for my accomplishments. "She is clearly the greatest female athlete of her day," Tom said. "If judged by her heart, then surely the greatest of all time." Tears came to my eyes.

Then Bobby's face appeared on screen. I could see how red his eyes were through his tinted glasses. As he described our conversation before I withdrew, he choked up and tears filled his eyes. In the hotel room we were all crying.

"Jackie Joyner-Kersee is very, very important to track and field," Dwight said in conclusion. "There's no argument that she is the greatest female athlete of all time."

Most people never get to hear such tributes, because they're bestowed after they die, at their funeral. I felt so privileged to hear them while I was alive. It was a shining moment for me at a time of darkness.

Bobby returned to the hotel room just in time for a call from Bill Cosby, our friend and trusted advisor for many years. Bill said he was thinking about us. Then, he teased me about the fight he figured Bobby and I were having about the decision to withdraw. It made me laugh. "I know you and Bob are going to get into it," he said. "But why don't you listen to your husband one time?"

Then he talked to Bobby and kidded him, "Try not to be so evil to your wife, man."

Flowers arrived throughout the day. One vase was from Aretha Franklin. Another arrangement arrived from Arsenio Hall. Lionel Richie also sent a bouquet. Late that night, we received a message that President Clinton was trying to reach us. He left a number to the retreat at Camp David, Maryland.

I was dumbfounded. To think that the President would take the time to call me and offer his support! I hadn't even won anything. Bobby called the number right after reading me the note. It was about 11:00 P.M. We worried that it was too late. But the President told us to call, so we did.

When Bobby handed me the receiver and I heard President Clinton say, "Hi, Jackie," I was speechless. He told me I'd done a lot to inspire the youth of the nation. Of all the nice things he said during the conversation, that compliment made me proudest. He also said he believed that Bobby had made the right decision in pulling me from the heptathlon, because it preserved my chance to come back for the long jump. I smiled as I listened to him, but I was tongue-tied. All I could manage was "thank you, Mr. President."

The question on everyone's mind after my withdrawal was whether I had a realistic chance of making it back to the track for the long jump. I had four and a half days to rest, but the hurdle race had further weakened the muscle. Subjecting it to additional stress would be like playing Russian roulette. It could rip the very next time I tried to run hard. That would surely end my athletic career, and possibly maim me for life.

But in my mind, the decision came down to this: I couldn't let that tearful withdrawal stand as my final Olympic act. Though my entire athletic career might be at risk, I knew what I had to do. It was time to reach deep into the core of myself, to call on the voices from my past— alternately sympathetic, challenging, even derisive—that had urged me on over thirty-four years of living and competing. At the appointed hour, I would show up at the long-jump pit, and hope and pray I could respond one last time.

1

My Roots

The night in October 1960 when Alfred Joyner and Mary Ruth Gaines eloped, they told their grandmothers they were going on a date. Ten months earlier, in January of that year, Mary had given birth to a baby boy, Alfrederick. Mary's grandmother, Lena Rainey, didn't approve of teenage pregnancy, but she allowed Mary and her baby to continue living with her. Mary didn't dare tell her about the marriage. She was just sixteen. Her groom was only fourteen.

Mary was my mother, one of four children born to Estella and Sylvester Gaines. Momma and her younger sister Della were born in Ruleville, Mississippi, and were raised there from birth by Estella's mother, Lena. When Lena moved from Ruleville to East St. Louis, Illinois, she brought my mother and Della with her.

By the time she was a teenager, my mother had blossomed into quite a beauty, standing 5' 6" and weighing about 130 pounds. Alfred, my father, was just entering puberty at the time of their marriage. But A.J., as Daddy was known in the neighborhood, looked and acted like a man.

He ran track and played football. He was tall and handsome and had an athletic build, reaching 6' 2", 190 pounds before he stopped growing. Wary parents in the neighborhood called him, and boys like him, "mannish."

After taking their vows, Momma and Daddy went back to their separate homes. Two years later, my mother was pregnant again. When my great-grandmother found out, she hit the roof. And when she discovered that Alfred was also her grandson-in-law, she tried to hit my father. She chased him out of her house and all the way down the street. Then she stormed back into her house and kicked my mother and her baby son out.

Lena considered herself a devout Christian. But I guess she was too mad at my mother to care that she'd be giving birth soon or that she and her baby son had nowhere to go. Fortunately, Daddy's grandmother, Ollie Mae Johnson, took in Momma and my brother, Al. Ollie Mae told her neighbors, "I won't have my great-grandkids raised on the street or in some stranger's house."

My father's mother, Evelyn, worked and lived in Chicago and visited East St. Louis on holidays and weekends. She was home for the Christmas holidays in January 1962, a few months before the second baby was due. John Kennedy was president at the time, and grandmother Evelyn told my mother, "If it's a girl, name her Jacqueline because she's the first Joyner girl and someday she'll be the first lady of something!"

Three months later, on March 3, 1962, I was born.

My sister Angela was born eleven months after me, in February 1963. Debra arrived the following year in June. While Momma stayed home with the babies, Daddy finished high school and found a job after graduation. They were kids raising kids.

The six of us lived with my great-grandmother Ollie Mae in her small, six-room, wood-frame house. The house wasn't spacious or opulent, but it was home to us. My mother treated our living room furniture like fine antiques. She kept plastic slipcovers on the couch and upholstered armchairs, and wouldn't allow us to sit in the room unless visitors came over. Space was at a premium. The house had one tiny bathroom. I shared the room off the kitchen at the front of the house with Debra, on the other side of the wall from the family room. By day, the family room was the gathering place for meals and TV watching. At night, it was the bedroom for my other sister and great-grandmother, who slept on the fold-out sofa. My parents' bedroom was across the hall from the kitchen. Al took the room at the back of the house.

Except for Al's space and the bathroom, the house didn't have interior doors. We walked right out of one area into the next. As soon as fall began to turn into winter, my father turned on the furnace. As the feeling of warmth circulated through the house, we gathered around the door frames with armfuls of blankets. Daddy stood on a chair with a hammer and a pocketful of nails. Holding the satiny hem of the blankets to the top of the frame, he drove in the nails. The makeshift insulation trapped heat within our bedrooms, and kept Al out in the cold, literally. His room could have doubled as a refrigerator.

All of our efforts to trap the precious warm air came to nothing when the furnace broke, a frequent wintertime occurrence. At those times, the kitchen stove was our heater. My mother kept the oven door open day and night. For most of the winter, the kitchen replaced the den as the family gathering spot.

On the coldest days, I'd walk in after track and basketball practice, and before removing my coat, run into our toasty kitchen. With the aroma of simmering pork chops and gravy wafting through the air, I stood in front of the stove with my long arms outstretched toward the inside of the oven. After my bones were good and warm, I removed my coat and hat and returned to the kitchen and took a seat beside my sisters on the floor.

Leaving the oven on for so long wasn't safe, but it was either that or freeze. The stove so bathed the kitchen in heat, I hated to go into the other parts of the house, where it sometimes got so cold I could see my breath when I talked. At night, that heated kitchen floor was our mattress. We covered the brown linoleum with blankets and sheets and slept in front of the open oven. Even Al, who usually craved privacy, camped out with us.

The other virtual certainty during winter was that the water pipes would freeze and burst. After the first episode, which resulted in a sinkful of dirty dishes, an unflushable toilet and no bathwater, my mother devised a backup plan. On fall Saturday mornings, I stood at the sink, filling a dozen plastic milk jugs with tap water while Debra and Angie stacked them against the wall.

East St. Louis, Illinois, is twenty miles across the border and the Mississippi River from St. Louis, Missouri. Our home sat on Piggott Avenue, between 14th and 15th Streets on the south end of town, in the center of a rough-and-tumble precinct. Tiny, wood-frame shotgun houses with painted cement porches lined both sides of our block, except for a fifty-meter stretch of assorted businesses directly across from our front porch.

For a certain kind of man, those enterprises catered to almost every need. He could grab a haircut, shave and shoeshine at the barbershop, then walk to the corner convenience store for a pack of cigarettes before joining his buddies in the poolhall for a cold beer and a few games. Or he might lay down a bet on someone else's cue stick and listen to the blues playing on the jukebox. After that, he could fill his tank in the tavern next door and grab a fifth for the road at the liquor-sales counter. The Swahili Club, a bar and lounge just around the corner on 15th, catered to the velvet-banquette-and-tablecloth crowd. Ruby D's, another lounge in the vicinity, had similar ambience.

The entire one-block radius around our house was a magnet for assorted winos, pimps, gangsters, ex-cons and hustlers. But we always said hello to the men who called the spot headquarters. Two of them, who were known to everyone in the neighborhood as Squirrel and Doug, were around so much they seemed like neighbors. My father had grown up with them. They practically adopted Al, who worked in the barbershop shining shoes for 35 cents with the kit Daddy had given him as a Christmas present. In addition to Squirrel and Doug, I vividly recall three other men whose nicknames were Slick, Dick and Bubba. They wore sunglasses, wide-brimmed hats, shiny alligator shoes, brightly colored suits with bell-bottom pants and open-necked print shirts. And lots of gold chains. Slick, Dick and Bubba were reputed to be the biggest gangsters in town—men who'd actually committed murder, according to local legend. The men greeted Al the same way each time they walked into the barbershop. They extended an open palm and waited for my brother to slap it, a gesture known as "givin' 'em five." "Hey little A.J., what's up, man? Anybody messing with you?" they'd ask him during the ritual.

Al pulled his box over, shined their shoes and listened to their war stories. When he was done, they gave him fives—bearing Abraham Lincoln's picture. I walked out on the porch one afternoon and found them sitting on the steps with Al, helping him put his train set together. During my brother's senior year in high school, Slick, Dick and Bubba were ambushed late one night and gunned down, gangland style. When Al heard about it, he cried as if a member of our family had been killed.

I never feared the men who hung out on the corner and

in front of the liquor store. Whatever bad things they did, they didn't do them around us. When our parents weren't around, these men were our protectors.

During the day, things were quiet, except for occasional joking and friendly arguing. As the sun descended, the action heated up. Cars abruptly pulled up to the liquor store and poolhall, or came screaming around the corner. Men and women climbed out and entered the clubs and taverns. Sometimes they ran back out, shouting over their shoulders at someone inside. When arguments turned ugly, with curse words or murder threats, Squirrel and Doug usually warned us to get off the street and go inside. At other times, events exploded without warning.

That's how it happened the night my sister Debra narrowly missed being shot. Al was stooped over, shining someone's shoes near the doorway of the barbershop. My great-grandmother was on the porch talking to our neighbor, Mrs. Newman. Two men burst out of the tavern screaming and cursing at each other. One of the men turned to walk away and the other pulled a gun out of the front of his trousers. At the same time, Debra, oblivious to the altercation, was darting across the street toward our front yard.

The unloading gun chamber sounded like Fourth of July fireworks. Debra didn't realize what was happening or how close she was to the line of fire until the victim dropped dead on the sidewalk practically at her feet. If any of those seven bullets had missed their target, she would surely have been hit. She stood there, looking at the dead and bleeding body, stunned.

Al ran across the street, the shoeshine rag still in his hand, and rushed my great-grandmother and Debra inside. When they told Angie and me what had happened, we jumped up. We were eager to run out and see the corpse.

But my brother wouldn't let us. He said the sight was too gruesome.

Another night, we were all outside when a guy nicknamed Bird was shot as he came out of the tavern. He survived and filed charges against his assailant. A month later, he was shot and killed late one night inside Ruby D's, along with Ruby the tavern owner, her security guard and another man. The men in the barbershop told Al that the police caught the man who did it, thanks to a clue left by Ruby. She wrote his name in her blood before she died.

The violence and intrigue fascinated us. We were too young to perceive the danger. But my mother deplored it and tried to shield us from as much of it as possible. She didn't want us playing in the street or peeping out of the windows to see what was happening. "One of these days you're going to look out that window at the wrong time and whatever's out there is gonna get you," she warned me.

Eventually, the violence did hit home. It changed forever the way I regarded murder and drug abuse. My parents got a call from the police in Chicago telling them that my grandmother Evelyn, who wasn't yet fifty, had been murdered in her sleep by her boyfriend. A chilly silence engulfed our house for days. My parents never explained the circumstances of her death, but from the whispering I overheard, I surmised that it had been drug-related. First the men and women in the neighborhood, now Evelyn. I was still in elementary school, but I was old enough to make the connection. It seemed that every time someone I knew died violently, drugs or alcohol were somehow involved. No one had to tell me to stay away from them after that.

2

Momma and Daddy

Because my parents were so very young and weren't well educated when they married, the odds were against us from the start. Our lives were an almost constant struggle. It's remarkable that Momma and Daddy were able to provide for all of us and hold our family together.

When I was very young, our lives were happy and mostly tranquil. The whole family ate dinner together, with my father at the head of the table, my mother at the other end and two kids on each side. No one raised a fork until we entwined our fingers in front of our plates, bowed our heads and said grace.

Even when there wasn't a lot to eat, our meals were always tasty. Daddy had an extra helping of neckbones each time Momma served them. On Fridays, we looked forward to fried fish and spaghetti.

Despite the shortages and problems, my parents never allowed us to think of ourselves as disadvantaged or as victims. While they wanted us to strive for more, they also taught us to be grateful for what we had. I always sulked while walking home at the end of a day spent with my friends who lived in housing projects. Our house was several blocks from the village of high- and low-rise apartment buildings and I felt isolated, living so far from my playmates. One day, I walked into my house and said to my mother, "I wish *we* could live in the projects."

Momma stopped what she was doing, whipped around and looked at me as if I'd cursed. "Jackie, have you lost your mind?" she asked. Her voice became more passionate: "You should be glad you have a house to live in. People live in projects because they don't have anywhere else to stay."

The nights my parents went to the movies or to dinner were always exciting. Daddy walked into the living room, smelling of cologne and looking razor sharp in his wide-brimmed hat, polyester slacks, print shirt and shiny crocodile shoes. "How do I look? Good, huh?" he'd ask. We all eagerly nodded.

Looking at the photo on the wall of him in his Lincoln High football uniform, I could see he'd gotten heftier over the years. My father wasn't a football standout, but he'd been one of Lincoln's best hurdlers. Indeed, he might have been able to earn an athletic scholarship in track after graduation. But he honored his responsibilities to his wife and growing family and went to work.

From where I sat watching him put on his overcoat, he looked ruggedly handsome. The combination of his deep voice, dark complexion, full head of hair and high cheekbones reminded me of singer Lou Rawls and the great NFL defensive end Deacon Jones.

My parents were an attractive couple. Momma was beautiful. She had gentle eyes and caramel-colored skin. I thought she looked just like Diahann Carroll, who starred in the TV show *Julia*. Of course, Momma had added pounds since high school, but they'd settled in all the right places. She had an hourglass figure, which she maintained with a combination of daily housework and nightly exercises. Debra, Angie and I giggled whenever she stretched out on the floor and started doing sit-ups to the crooning of Al Green on the stereo. "Laugh if you want to, but just wait," she'd say, between deep breaths and crunches. "Someday you'll have to do the same thing."

Having a pretty mother was fine when she went out with my father. But I got tired of people asking me if she was my sister. Her visits to school for awards ceremonies were more annoying than joyous. The boys who passed us in the hall treated her like she was a pretty new classmate. As we walked down the crowded corridors, me in braids, jeans and a T-shirt and my mother in a perfectly coiffed pouf, sweater and slacks, bug-eyed stares and whistles followed us. One boy ran up to me after she left and exclaimed, "Wow, your mom's a fox!"

When I came home, I indignantly reported the comment to Momma, who by now had donned her familiar flowered housecoat and slippers. Her eyes never left the pot she was tending on the stove as she shrugged and said, "I'm not thinking about those mannish boys."

When my father wasn't home to dictate, Al and I argued about what to watch on TV. My brother wanted *Bonanza*. I wanted anything else. On nights when *Good Times* and *Sanford and Son* aired, we were in accord. On Sunday evenings, the whole family watched *The Ed Sullivan Show*. The night the Jackson 5 performed, I sang along with every song and swooned over Randy Jackson, the youngest brother. Al always danced whenever soul or rock-and-roll singers appeared on the show. As James Brown performed one evening, Al spun and slid around the room, doing a somewhat more manic imitation.

The one thing we didn't do as a family was go to church. My father wasn't big on church services, but my mother roused Al, my sisters and me early every Sunday morning to dress for Sunday School and church. "You can worship everything else during the week, but on Sunday, you'll worship God," she'd say whenever one of us balked at getting up early or begged to stay home.

Donning our Sunday best—pressed dresses, white knee socks, patent leather shoes, gloves and purses, and for Al, a suit and shined shoes—we walked single-file down the street. Angie was first, Debra was behind her, then me, followed by Al. Momma, clad in nylon stockings, a suit, pillbox hat and gloves, brought up the rear. We looked like a gaggle of geese with their Mother Goose as we marched the two blocks down 15th Street to St. Paul's Baptist Church.

Like most kids, I dreaded sitting through the services. Sunday School wasn't so bad. Not because of the stories we read and the lessons we learned, but for the chance to whisper and giggle with my friends while the teacher conducted class. As I grew up, my mother instilled in me a reverence for God. Before going to bed every night I knelt on the side of the bed, closed my eyes and recited the Lord's Prayer, as she'd trained me to do. The ritual ended with a good-night kiss on her cheek. As I got older, I decided I was too big to be kissing her. One night I went straight to bed after praying. The next day, Momma wanted to know why I hadn't kissed her.

"It's too baby-fied," I said.

"Have you stopped praying at night?" she asked. "Is some boy telling you you're baby-fied?"

"No ma'am. I just think it's childish."

She looked hurt. "I see. So now you're too grown to kiss me good night."

I felt so guilty, I dutifully gave Momma her kiss after saying my prayers that night. And I did it every night afterward until I left home for college.

My parents did their best to keep us out of harm's way.

My mother outlined a code of conduct and strictly enforced it, to try and protect us. But her rules served an additional purpose. She was determined to put us on the path to a better life by teaching us to be disciplined, hardworking and responsible.

The complete list of her rules would fill this book. But here's a sampling: No gifts from strangers. No playing too far from the front yard. No playing outside after dark. No playing outside until your household chores are done. No playing at all if your report card has Ds or Fs. No makeup. No long phone conversations. No boyfriends until age sixteen. No dates past 10:00 P.M.

We didn't have closets full of clothes. Each of us had one or two outfits and a pair of shoes for church and special occasions. The few pieces composing our school wardrobes, along with a pair of shoes, which we received at the beginning of the term, had to last the entire year. And because we couldn't afford the luxury of going to the laundromat every day, our clothes had to stay as clean as possible between washings. My mother insisted that we change out of them immediately after school. And she made us wear the same outfits two days in a row, which I just hated. I was confident and outgoing at school. But down deep, I felt embarrassed and self-conscious. I was sure everyone noticed I'd worn the same clothes the day before. At the time, it seemed like the worst social offense in the world.

I tried to negotiate. "Why can't I wear a dress on Monday and wear it again on Friday?"

"Because I said you can't, that's why," Momma said sternly. "And as long as you're the child and I'm the adult and you're living in this house, you'll follow my rules."

I loved getting clothes from my aunt Della and my cousins, all of whom also wore a size 8. Their clothes were hip and cute. But when Momma made me wear outfits she bought at the secondhand store, it was humiliating. They looked so old-fashioned. The dresses were all below the knee and dark-colored. The frills, puffs and long hemlines were a dead giveaway that they weren't new. After all, it was the 1970s and the other girls at school wore psychedelic prints, short dresses and tight skirts.

"A girl at school today asked me if I wore long dresses because we were sanctified," I told my parents one night during supper. "Sanctified," was a term we used to describe people who were highly religious and wore very conservative clothes. "Nobody else dresses like me," I complained. "Everyone else wears short skirts and bright colors, not ugly old-lady dresses like mine. Carmen Cannon had a really pretty sweater on today. I wish I had one like it—"

"Stop right there," my father said. "Don't tell me what other people are doing. We're not trying to keep up with the Joneses."

I know that all those years of not having nice clothes or any say about what I wore explains why I'm a clotheshorse and shopaholic now. When I visit a foreign country, I find myself shopping rather than sightseeing.

We never received birthday presents or had parties. But at Christmas, my parents made up for the absence of luxuries by giving us everything on our Christmas gift lists, no matter what sacrifices had to be made. By the time the gift wrap was ripped and the boxes were open, the living room was awash in bicycles, musical instruments, walkie-talkies, train sets, electric football games, board games, Easy Bake ovens, stacks of new clothes and Barbie dolls.

Those Barbie dolls were my prized presents. Over the years, I amassed the whole gang: Barbie, Ken, P.J., Skipper and Barbie's black friend, Chrissy. Actually, I'm still a Barbie fan. It's a way of linking with my childhood, I guess, but I've taken to collecting them the way others collect baseball cards and stamps.

• • •

Despite the occasional whippings he got from my father, my brother, Al, got away with murder when we were growing up. With the generous gratuities he received, my brother made a small fortune from his shoe-shining job. But he never saved a dime of it, spending it all on wacky gadgets advertised in the back of comic books. Neither of my parents said a word about it. But when I took a summer job selling concessions at a movie theater in downtown St. Louis, Momma insisted that I fork over half of every check to her and that I deposit a big chunk of the other half in a savings account. She said I had to learn financial responsibility. When I complained about the double standard, she replied, "Boys can take care of themselves."

I pouted about it all summer. But I now realize that my mother was teaching me the value of money and the importance of managing it wisely.

Her other priority was keeping me away from "those mannish boys." Better than anyone, my parents knew what a pitfall teen pregnancy could be for young black people. They drilled it into my head that they didn't want me to repeat their mistake, and they did everything in their power to see that I didn't. As a result, I was never in serious danger of becoming pregnant in high school.

My aunt Della was less strict than Momma. I spent a lot of time at her house on weekends and used her phone to talk as long as I liked. Della also let me invite boys over. Somehow my mother found out about it and chastised Della. "How am I supposed to maintain discipline if you let them do whatever they want?" she huffed. That was the end of good times at Della's.

When I turned sixteen, I fell for a boy on the basketball team who was two years older than me and in the same homeroom as Al. My brother reassured my parents that he was a nice guy and a good athlete, which also helped my father warm to the idea, after the boy got off on the wrong foot with him.

Without warning, the boy had appeared at my front door one night at 9:30. Al answered the knock and was shocked to see his classmate standing there. The boy asked if I was home. Daddy was sitting nearby, and Al, realizing what was about to happen to the poor guy, just chuckled.

"Who did he say he wanted to talk to?" my father shouted.

"He said he wants to talk to Jackie!" Al hollered back.

Hearing this, I ran into the room. Daddy got up off the sofa, stomped over to the door and stood behind my brother. "Boy, do you know what time it is?" he asked. "Don't ever come to my house at no nine-thirty at night and ask to see my daughter!" He slammed the door in his face as Al's laughter filled the house.

It was humiliating—for me and for my friend. But we eventually started dating. He was on the basketball team and we shot hoops together at the Community Center. I liked him because we shared a common interest in athletics. My mother grew to like him because he was courteous and obeyed her rule that I be home by 10:00 P.M. after our dates. She called him a "gentleman."

But as his graduation approached in the spring, the guy wanted to start a sexual relationship, which I promptly reported to Momma.

"No, no, no," she said, vigorously shaking her head. "We are *not* making any babies in this house. If he wants sex, he can get it from someone else. You have too much to do in life. You don't have time to bring any babies into this world now."

I was head over heels for the guy. Still, I wasn't ready for anything serious. He said he wanted to date other girls, which I didn't like, but felt powerless to prevent. Several months later I heard that the girl he was seeing was pregnant. That night I sat in my bedroom and cried. Although we'd broken up, his actions felt like a betrayal. Momma came into my room and sat beside me. I told her what happened as she wiped away my tears. "I know it hurts now," she said in a soft voice. "But the pain will go away and you'll see that you made the right decision."

After work each evening, my father stopped in front of the liquor store and tavern across the street from our house to get the lowdown on the day's developments from Squirrel and Doug. Inside the house, we heard his deep baritone chuckle as the group traded laughs, gossiped and argued about sports. Then he walked across the street carrying his lunchbox, waved to our neighbor, Mrs. Newman, and climbed the porch steps to the front door.

Daddy had a reputation as a quick-tempered, tough guy around the south side of East St. Louis. A lot of men feared A. J. Joyner because he followed the code of the street: Hit me, and I'll hit you back harder. It wasn't just talk. A drunk stumbled out of the tavern late one night and tried to break into our house. My father scared him away before he could steal anything or do any damage. The next day, however, Daddy found the man and, according to street legend, badly beat him up. No one messed with A.J. or his family.

My father had a tender side he rarely revealed. One of the first, and few, times I recall seeing it was early one fall morning when I was a second-grader. Al had come into my bedroom and said it was time to get dressed for school. Though it was still dark outside, at that age I believed everything my big brother told me. I got dressed and went into the kitchen for breakfast. Daddy had just come in from work. "What are you doing up? It's three in the morning!" he demanded.

"Al told me it was time to go to school," I explained helplessly.

"Come over here and let me teach you to tell time so he won't fool you anymore," he said.

He hoisted me onto his knee and, pointing to the clock on the wall, explained all about the hours and minutes and short hands and long hands.

My father also had a childlike, playful streak. Several times a year, he gave my mother a breather and drove Al, Debra, Angie and me to the Six Flags amusement park in St. Louis. He enjoyed the rides as much as we did, especially the roller coasters. He read comic books along with Al. And he relished any opportunity to poke fun at us. He taunted me about my long, skinny legs and gave our baby sister, Debra, the nickname "Hog" because of her jowly cheeks. At the dinner table, I teased Al about being a weakling and called him "Olive Oyl" when he wouldn't eat spinach. That always made Daddy throw his head back and roar.

My father's favorite pastime was watching sports on TV. On fall football Sundays, he prayed for a San Diego Chargers victory, and whenever their games were televised, he was riveted to his easy chair. He felt a kinship with the Chargers, he said, because his "cousin" Charlie Joiner was the starting wide receiver. One day, after listening to Daddy's familiar speech about Cousin Charlie's inherited athletic brilliance, I pulled my chair close to the TV and noticed the spelling of the name on the back of his jersey.

"Daddy, his uniform says J-O-I-N-E-R! That's not the way we spell our name. How can he be our cousin?" I asked him.

"He's a distant cousin," my father replied confidently. "His side of the family spells it differently, but we're all kin."

He was dead serious and no one could challenge him. Questioning my father's word about anything, even something as trivial as Charlie Joiner's relationship to us, was considered talking back—a most serious transgression. That's when we saw the side of his personality that made people fear him.

The summer before I entered the eleventh grade at Lincoln High, a boy from our rival school, East St. Louis High—a name that we shortened to Eastside in conversation—invited me to a Jackson 5 concert. Ordinarily, Eastsiders and Lincoln students didn't mix. But during the summer, we ran track and played basketball together on a community-league team that competed in Amateur Athletic Union meets around the Midwest. I'd met the boy at track practice and we struck up a casual friendship.

I was dying to go to that concert. My friends and I knew every word to every one of the Jackson 5 songs. Those concert tickets were like pieces of gold. I would have accepted his invitation on the spot, but I knew I had to get permission.

"Ask your Daddy," Momma said. I knew I was doomed.

"A concert in St. Louis?" Daddy asked. "Who is this boy?" He made it sound like St. Louis was on another continent.

"He goes to Eastside . . ."

"Nope. You're not going out with anybody from Eastside. I went to Lincoln High, you go to Lincoln. We don't deal with people from Eastside, period."

I rolled my eyes. "Here we go with that again—"

Before I finished mumbling, the back of Daddy's massive hand stung my cheek.

"Don't you talk back to me, girl! The answer is no and that's the end of it."

During the 1960s, East St. Louis was a prosperous place, an all-American city with low unemployment and a bustling economy. We had a Sears store, big grocery stores, a big Woolworth's store—complete with a luncheonette and a long counter—banks, several hospitals and a clutch of locally owned businesses.

To the strains of "Burn, baby, burn," the city was rocked by black militant protests, vandalism and arson during the late 1960s. White residents fled the city for outlying suburbs. With their customer base shrinking and their assets threatened, local businesses closed. Eventually, Sears left, too.

The manufacturing companies with operations in town, including the glass works, the steel mill, the rubber and tire company, the railroad and the stockyards, followed. They relocated to areas where labor costs were cheaper. The moves threw people in my neighborhood, most of whom were union laborers like my father, out of work in droves. By the mid-1970s, East St. Louis's economy was nosediving. Between 1974 and 1975, the already high unemployment rate skyrocketed from 12 percent to 17 percent. As unemployment rose, crime exploded. Pretty soon, parts of East St. Louis looked like shelled-out war zones and the city suffered from a terrible national reputation.

For many years, Daddy made a good living, first as an airplane assembly line worker at McDonnell Douglas. After he was laid off by the aircraft company, he did manual labor at a manufacturing company. The mood around the neighborhood at the time was tense and grim. My father frequently came home with news of another plant or store closing or more firings someplace. He held on for a while, but finally the ax fell on him, too. He was out of work for a long time, doing odd jobs like mowing lawns before he was hired as a switch operator by a railroad company in Springfield.

Conditions were tough. Our meals became skimpier and portions were smaller than in the past. Instead of hamburger and pork chops, we ate chicken, Spam, canned Vienna sausages and luncheon meat. When that ran out, we ate peanut butter and jelly sandwiches. Sometimes, the only thing in the house to put between bread slices was mayonnaise. So we ate mayonnaise sandwiches.

Eventually, my mother found a job to help make ends meet. The morning before she left for her first day as a nurse's assistant at St. Mary's Hospital, she gathered Al, Debra, Angie and me around her to explain why she had to leave us on our own. Dressed in her pale blue uniform, white stockings and white shoes, she looked each of us in the eyes as she spoke. "I'm not going to be here to help you get ready for school, to make sure you do your homework and to cook your supper every night, because I have to go to work now," she said. "I hope you understand. It doesn't mean I don't care about you anymore."

I know Momma hated not being at home with us. But entering the working world improved her self-confidence and gave her a sense of independence. She was in her late twenties and had been a housewife since she was sixteen. She'd never even learned to drive, so one of her co-workers picked her up every morning and dropped her off every afternoon. Momma's main responsibility was bathing patients on the south corridor of the fourth floor, in the surgical ward. She enjoyed her job and gained a reputation for being efficient and conscientious. And she made lots of friends. She learned to bowl and joined her girlfriends on their Wednesday night trips to the alley. Her very best friend was Joyce Farmer, the head nurse on one of the surgical wards. Momma and Joyce were inseparable. They went shopping together on weekends. On paydays, they treated themselves to the lunch special at Woolworth's—a hamburger on rye bread with cheese and onions. My mother and her friends also conspired to find eligible bachelors for Joyce to date.

When my father found the railroad job in Springfield, 100 miles away, he rented a room and lived there during the week, returning home on weekends. Heart-to-heart conversations were Momma's specialty, but before Daddy left for Springfield that first time, he talked to us the same way my mother had the morning she started work at St. Mary's. "I'm not abandoning you," he said. "So, while I'm gone, don't give your Momma a hard time because I'll be back every weekend and I'll get a full report."

It would have been easy for my parents to lose hope and give in to wayward temptations, the way so many other people did in East St. Louis. But they never became dejected or hopeless. They never blamed anyone for their predicament. They never considered doing anything illegal. No matter how hard the times were, they kept plugging away, working hard and doing the best they could with their limited resources. The beliefs they held and examples they set counteracted the negative forces at work on the streets of our neighborhood. Their unwavering commitment to the work ethic and their sound values informed my life from childhood into adulthood.

3

Inspirations

With work keeping my parents away from home, most days our aging and sickly great-grandmother was the only adult around. We were virtually on our own, and my brother and I constantly squabbled about who was boss. Al was the oldest and in junior high. Debra, Angie and I were in grammar school.

Every morning, the script was the same. At 7:00 A.M., about an hour after my mother had gone to work at St. Mary's, I jumped out of bed, roused Debra and Angie, and prepared for the moment I relished. Rubbing my hands together, the sleep still caked around my eyes, I took the short walk down the hall to the room at the back of the house. I burst through the door, and with all my might, gave the slumbering lump on the bed a violent shove. "Wake up, Al! It's time to get up!" I shouted to my older brother.

He jumped up, swinging his arm at me. "Touch me again and I'll pop you!"

"You gotta get up *now*!"

"Get out of my room, you old buckethead!"

As I left, I laughed and shouted back over my shoulder, "You better get out of that bed!"

Al and I took different approaches to just about everything. I was diligent and responsible. He was undisciplined and happy-go-lucky.

At the start of each school year, Momma asked each of us: "What do you want to be when you grow up?" One year my answer was a Broadway dancer, the next a teacher, the next a physical therapist. The answer wasn't so important. She just wanted us to always think about and plan for our future.

When he was thirteen or so, Al told Momma he wanted to be a pimp when he grew up. She slapped him on the side of his head and reported the comment to Daddy. Then, Al confessed that he didn't know what a pimp was. He was only repeating what his friends said. Daddy explained to him that it wasn't a job he should seek. Furthermore, Daddy said, "If you don't stop running with that bad group, you're going to end up right where pimps end up— dead or in jail."

Al didn't like school and was frequently suspended for fighting in elementary and junior high school. My father whipped him with an extension cord every time it happened, but Al's behavior didn't change. Those mornings before school were sometimes the only time my sisters and I saw Al until the evening, just before Momma got off work. We were all supposed to come directly home after school, but with no one at home to enforce the rule, Al never did.

Before long, my brother was skating on thin ice with Momma and Daddy. He was caught behind the wheel of a friend's car, driving without a license. The police officer who stopped him knew Daddy, so he let Al go without a ticket. But when Daddy found out, he grabbed the extension cord, stormed down to Al's room and closed the door. All we heard was the sound of repeated lashings.

Al was following a group of boys who were older and more streetwise than he was. They enjoyed throwing rocks at the windows of passing cars. One day while Al and my mother were at a relative's house, someone spotted his buddies breaking more car windows and called the cops. The police combed the neighborhood, rounding up them all. That close brush with an arrest and the thought of what Daddy would do to him scared Al. He never went near that gang again.

I, on the other hand, loved school and hated to miss a day. But in the fifth grade, I was having trouble with arithmetic. I just couldn't figure out long division. Unfortunately, the students who performed poorly on tests got whippings with a ruler, and I became Victim No. 1. It got so bad, I dreaded going to school.

I went to my mother in tears one morning and told her I didn't want to go. She knew something was wrong. When she saw the bruises on my leg, she walked to school with me. She met with the teacher and demanded that he stop the whippings. With the pressure off, I relaxed and was able to concentrate. I sweated over my math homework every night for several more days, reviewing the examples in the book over and over again, trying to decode the process. Finally one night, it all clicked. I had mastered long division. I called Momma at work to tell her. She was as excited as I was. My self-esteem soared.

Growing up, I could always count on Momma to be my champion. Her constant encouragement formed my deep well of inspiration. I wanted to prove to her and everyone else that I had the ability to excel. I have approached every endeavor since then—athletic and otherwise—with that same sense of purpose.

After school and on weekends, I spent hours playing in our front yard with my sisters, cousins Gerald and Sherrell, and the youngsters from the Cole family who lived next door: Kim, Felicia, Michelle, Phyllis, Renee, Keith and Craig. We made up games that reflected our yearning for the things we didn't have.

One of my favorites was called "first star." At dusk, we stood in the yard and twirled around with our heads back and noses pointed at the sky, searching for the evening's first star. The person who spotted it got to make a wish and, we told each other with conviction, it was guaranteed to come true. I always wished for a big house and good food to eat.

During the day, after a round of tag or a race around the block, we rested on the porch, fantasizing that the passing cars were ours. By then, our family car was an old jalopy that didn't always run. The other kids knew a lot about cars and could spot the various makes and models from a distance. But, when it was my turn, it didn't matter to me what kind of vehicle came by, as long as it was new, shiny and running.

Every Fourth of July evening, Al, Debra, Angie, the Coles and I took turns climbing the oak tree in our front yard to stare west and watch the fireworks exploding above the St. Louis Arch. The edifice was called "the Gateway to the West." Glimmering against the backdrop of those sparkling bursts of red, green, blue and silver, the Arch to me was a gateway to the whole world, a bright and shiny symbol of life beyond East St. Louis. As I watched the show, I yelled down to the others, "I can't wait for our field trip to the Arch next spring."

"I went last year," somebody said. "It's great up there. When you look out the windows, it's like you're in the sky, standing on the top of the whole world. You can see all over!"

The words made me tingle inside. Aside from a few family trips to my father's relatives in Toledo, Ohio, I hadn't traveled far away from home. Everything was so drearily familiar in East St. Louis. I wanted to know what the rest of the world looked like. I stared at the Arch. I just had to get up there and see things for myself.

When the elevator doors opened that spring morning, I ran to a window and soaked up the view. All around me were pathways to the rest of the world, the Mississippi River, the highways and the bridges. Seeing it all stretched out before me made the possibility of finding that other world real. I remembered the words of a man who had spoken to our class earlier that year. Our teacher had invited him to tell us about his life and to offer some advice. He was successful, but he said his life had been difficult initially because he was lazy and didn't work hard. Once he turned his life around, he said he had vowed to give every task his very best effort because he didn't want to look back with any regrets.

Although I was just eleven, I took the advice to heart. Standing at the top of the Arch as a wide-eyed sixth-grader, I just knew that if I followed those roads leading out of East St. Louis, I wouldn't regret it. I knew they would lead me to better things.

One Kind of Grace

With so few role models and symbols of success available as I grew up, I gathered tiny drops of incentive whenever they came my way. In time, the city of East St. Louis broke ground on a project that made the task a little bit easier.

The dump trucks, cement mixers and bulldozers carrying hard-hatted workmen rolled through our neighborhood early one summer morning in the late 1960s. They clustered at the corner of 15th and Piggott and began digging at the entrance to Lincoln Park.

As I watched them, I recalled how, after school, on weekends and during summers, that grassy tract across the street from my house had beckoned my friends and me. We romped across it while playing tag and turning backflips. When we were exhausted or just bored, we stretched out on it and studied the clouds in the sky. And we ran through it on our way to the swimming pool and the sandbox. Farther back, near 17th Street, was a baseball diamond and another grassy field, bordered by a round cinder track.

We were sorry to lose our playground. But when the

construction crew began pouring the foundation and as-
sembling the skeleton of a big building, our mourning
ended and we began speculating on the project's purpose.

The structure became an obsession to me. I was six years
old. As the building took shape over the months, I sat on
my porch railing and gazed across the street, lost in my
daydreams. I tried to guess what it was going to be. We
were intrigued by the dome-shaped structure in the center
of the two square ones. We'd never seen anything like it.

Occasionally, a group of us ventured over to the site and
stood bright-eyed with our faces pressed to the fence,
watching the construction crew's every move and jabber-
ing away.

"You think it's a place to play?" I asked.

"I think it's a theater," someone responded.

"Maybe a skating rink," another voice suggested.

"Can you skate?" another asked.

Once the cinder block exterior was complete, the crew
put the finishing touches on the interior. Before the complex opened in 1969, a security guard kept watch outside
to deter the local vandals. Weary of our persistent questions
about what was inside, he let us in one day for a sneak peek.

It was more fantastic than anything I imagined. It was
big, beautiful, air-conditioned and, best of all, free of
charge. It smelled of new wood, fresh paint and varnish.
The windows, the glass, the walls and the rest rooms were
shiny and clean. The guard said they were going to name it
the Mary E. Brown Community Center, after a woman
from our city who had made contributions to the community.

During our quick tour, we discovered to our delight that
the domed part was the recreation area. It featured a basketball court and bleachers. A library and rooms for arts
and crafts, dancing and meetings occupied one of the
square-shaped buildings adjacent to the dome. Administra-

tive offices would fill the other one. The three buildings were connected by big glass double doors.

All the kids from the neighborhood spent time at the Center, but I practically *lived* there. On summer and Saturday mornings, I woke up at first light and got my two sisters out of bed, anxious to be across the street. Because of my mother's rule about my sisters and me going and coming together, I had to bribe Debra to accompany me in the mornings and to stay at the Community Center until closing time. The price of her cooperation typically was either a candy bar or a dime, which I gladly paid. Angie was much more agreeable, doing whatever I asked.

We dressed and perched on the Center's front steps to await the arrival of Tyrone Cavitt and Percy Harris, the recreation directors. They unlocked the double doors and we followed them inside. I helped them erect the Ping-Pong tables and then laid out the balls and paddles. Initially, I did it for free, but eventually they paid me a few dollars to help them set up every morning and clean up every night.

The Community Center provided the closest thing to culture in East St. Louis. To see the ballet or a Broadway show, or to hear symphony orchestras and Jackson 5 concerts, we had to pay a lot of money for tickets and make the twenty-mile trek across the state line and the Poplar Street Bridge into St. Louis.

The Center revealed a whole new world to me, teaching me things I wouldn't have learned otherwise. I was a human sponge, soaking up as much as I could. Every day at story time, I sat on the floor and listened to an adult read the story of Black Beauty or Rapunzel. I made black ashtrays and green planters in ceramics class and cotton-candy-colored Styrofoam waste baskets from egg cartons in crafts class. Much of my handiwork became Christmas and birthday presents for Momma.

I attended lectures on all kinds of subjects. One night an official from the Nation of Islam headquarters in Chicago spoke. He wore a dark suit, stiff white shirt and a bow tie and spoke forcefully about the evils of eating pork and the benefits of the Muslim faith. He taught us some Muslim expressions and passed around copies of the *Muhammad Speaks* newspaper. Afterward, he circulated a sheet of paper and asked everyone to list their name, address and phone number if they wanted more information. I was fascinated by what he said and wanted to know more. So, I signed the list.

The next day, as my mother mopped the floor and hummed the words to a Teddy Pendergrass song playing on the stereo, someone knocked on the front door. It was the same man who'd spoken the night before at the Community Center, dressed in the same suit and bow tie. He started telling Momma what a nice little girl I was and how happy they'd be to have me join the faith. As he talked, Momma became more and more agitated. He was the latest in a long line of people who'd called our house or appeared at the front door to follow up on some interest I'd expressed at the Center. She interrupted him when he started explaining the daily prayer schedule, politely explaining that I'd been baptized in the Baptist Church and wouldn't be joining the Muslims. After shutting the door, she told me if I didn't stop putting our address and phone number on every Center list that was passed around, she'd make me stay home.

She didn't object when I signed up for modern dance class, however. She and everyone else seemed to think I was clumsy and could use some grace. I was always tripping or stumbling over something. One winter morning I'd pranced out of the house, slipped on the ice-covered sidewalk and landed on my butt as the school bus approached our house. It wasn't really clumsiness—just a case of being too eager to show off. Someone had just given me a pair of black leather boots and I was so intent on modeling them for everyone, I forgot about the ice. The kids all had a good laugh while I died of embarrassment.

I thought dance lessons would improve my coordination. I loved to dance, but could never get the hang of the popular dance steps as fast as Al and Debra. Al was the best dancer in school and won every contest he entered. He could mimic Michael Jackson and James Brown. But Elvis Presley was his favorite and his specialty. After the dances, with the guitar he got for Christmas slung over his shoulder, he did his Elvis routine while people threw him money. The girls screamed and swooned as he strummed the strings, gyrated his hips and spun around the floor, singing the words, "You ain't nothin' but a hound dog."

The dance classes turned out to be one of the most enriching experiences of my childhood. Our teacher, Mr. Wilson, was a devotee of the Katherine Dunham technique. Ms. Dunham is an internationally renowned dancer and choreographer whose style incorporates elements of African and Caribbean folk cultures. She was one of the first African-Americans to have a professional, touring dance company. Alvin Ailey and Debbie Allen studied her technique. On Saturdays, our class met at the Dunham Center, instead of the Community Center.

Ms. Dunham and Josephine Baker were famous, successful women whom girls in East St. Louis could relate to, because they were from our hometown. I read about how they performed all over the world and lived glamorously. Josephine Baker resided in Paris. But Ms. Dunham continued to live in East St. Louis, which gave me a sense of pride.

When she was in town, she came to our Saturday classes and talked to us about dancing and self-expression. She was an exotic, elegant woman. Her dresses were loose, long and flowing and made of colorful fabrics. She wore the most beautiful scarves tied around her head. Her voice was soft. Her diction was perfect. As she spoke, her expressive hands moved gently through the air, decorating each phrase. I sat cross-legged on the floor in my leotard, looking up at her, mesmerized and hanging on every breath she took. Those were thrilling moments.

Ms. Dunham was my first truly accessible role model—a woman I was able to admire up close and in person. She still lives in East St. Louis, and over the years she and I have become close friends. She writes to me from time to time when she's traveling, and I visit her when I'm at home.

The Dunham method influenced not just how I danced, but how I carried myself. Mr. Wilson said that Dunham dancers had a distinctive elegance. "They don't walk, they glide," he explained. "To be a true Dunham dancer, you must point your toes, hold your heads up and your stomachs in."

I took him seriously. At home in the mirror, I practiced walking just as Mr. Wilson had shown us. He was challenging me to learn something that would help me improve myself. I wanted to meet that challenge.

Unlike the bus stop, the hustle and the other dances we did to the music on the radio, the more classical dance movements Mr. Wilson taught us came easily to me. "You have talent," he told me after class one day. "Your legs are long and powerful. That's what a good dancer needs." His words made my heart leap.

"Could I be a Broadway dancer?" I asked.

"Yes, if you keep practicing and taking classes," he said.

No one had ever complimented me for having long legs. With Daddy and Al constantly teasing me about being tall and skinny, I had become self-conscious about my height. But Mr. Wilson made me proud of my body. I now thought of my long legs as an asset. A powerful asset.

Because of Mr. Wilson's encouraging words, I began fantasizing about being a performer on Broadway or an actress. I liked glamour as much as any other little girl. And I thought entertainers were the most glamorous people of all. I started imagining myself dancing on stage in a glittery costume under bright lights. For a while, I believed I might be discovered, too. As silly as it sounds, I had this idea that someone from Hollywood puts hidden cameras in houses and that's how stars are discovered. And so I stood in front of the big mirror in my parents' room for hours at a stretch, putting on a show—mimicking scenes from TV shows, doing voice imitations and rehearsing my dance routines—just in case the talent scouts were watching.

Although dancing was just a hobby to me, I probably would have continued taking lessons if Mr. Wilson hadn't died. He was shot to death, allegedly during an argument over drugs. After the incident, the classes stopped and so did my interest in dance.

Losing Mr. Wilson as a mentor shattered me. I admired him a lot. He was the first adult, other than my parents, who took an interest in me and tried to help me develop my talents. The news about his murder and the fact that drugs might have been involved devastated me. I didn't know what to believe in after his death. He and other adults who gave speeches at the Community Center talked to us about doing the right things, not taking drugs and staying out of trouble. To find out that this man—whom I associated so strongly with dancing—might have been involved in drugs, soured me on dance as an ambition.

5

Seeking an Identity

Without dancing, I was adrift. I wandered around the Community Center for weeks, looking for something that sparked my interest, something in which I could excel.

While I searched, I diverted a portion of my considerable energy to cheerleading for the boys' basketball and football teams. I was captain of the squad, which also included my sisters, Debra and Angie; my neighbor Kim Cole and a few other girls. I was pretty bossy, expecting the others to perform to perfection the routines I made up. Everyone obeyed me except Debra. She either ignored my orders or talked back. I expelled her from the squad several times.

My two sisters are a study in contrasts. Debra has always been strong-willed and outspoken, very much like my father. She must do things her way. In school, Debra was the eye of the hurricane. A social butterfly with tons of friends and charm, she loved going to dances and being the life of the party. But there was also a mischievous, troublemaking streak to her personality. If she were a soap opera character, Susan Lucci would play the part.

I remember the day she single-handedly started a major ruckus at school. She went to the boyfriend of one of her girlfriends and told him the girl was messing around with another guy behind his back. She did this to her own girlfriend! The two boys fought about it and the girl wanted to kill Debra. I asked her how she could do something like that. She just thought it was great fun.

Angie, on the other hand, was shy and introverted. Growing up, she had a habit of gnawing the skin on the side of her hand when she was nervous. At parties, while Debra and Al held center stage, Angie hid on the sidelines, a real wallflower. She was so cooperative, acquiescing to anything anyone suggested. Left to her own devices, Angie probably wouldn't have spent much time at the Community Center. She would have been content to stay at home. Angie wasn't the baby of the family, yet she held tightest to my mother's apron strings.

Both of my sisters were good athletes. Each were standouts on their respective junior high basketball teams. But only Debra continued playing sports in high school. She was on the Lincoln basketball team when we won the state girls' championship. She also ran track and played volleyball. She eventually attended Arkansas State on a volleyball scholarship. Angie was a late bloomer who made the dean's list at Southern Illinois University at Edwardsville before dropping out to start working. Debra has two children, Antoinette and Anthony. Angie has a daughter, Sherrell.

As a cheerleader, I was a real "jumping Jackie," if you'll pardon the pun. The dance exercises—knee bends, squats and stretches—made my legs stronger. When the others were breathing heavily and slowing down, I was still jumping and kicking. My favorite stunt was to jump up in the air into a spread eagle, touch my toes, and land on the ground in a split, while the others did a less daring jump and slid into a split. The people in the bleachers cheered and applauded every time we did it.

Our sponsor, Mrs. Johnson, disapproved of it, though. She thought it was vulgar and dangerous. "You girls are going to hurt something doing that routine," she said, frowning and shaking her head every time I went up in the air. She didn't like our dances, either. I overheard her tell another woman that she knew I was going to get pregnant before I finished high school because I was so "fast." "Fast" was to girls what "mannish" was to boys. It was a derogatory term, used to describe girls who liked to show off and flirt and who often did end up pregnant before graduating.

"The nerve of her!" I told my mother after repeating what I'd heard. I wasn't showing off or flirting or doing anything bad. Of course, I was happy that the crowd enjoyed my performance. But I danced and cheered because I enjoyed it and felt I was good at it. I didn't understand why an adult would criticize me for that.

"Don't pay any attention to it. That's just the way some people are," my mother comforted. But I've never had an easy time ignoring negative comments—particularly unjustified ones. I've always been sensitive to them, allowing them to upset me more than they should.

Looking back on it, all the time I was cheerleading, I never considered it a marketable skill. Cheerleaders were just cheerleaders. Cheerleading scholarships, which many colleges now offer, were unheard of then. And we didn't have a Paula Abdul, the L.A. Lakers' cheerleader who became a dancer, choreographer and singing star, to emulate. It just goes to show how much times and attitudes have changed. And it illustrates the power of role models. Had I known I could possibly parlay cheerleading into a career in entertainment, my occupational arena might have been a theater stage rather than a track oval.

• • •

One day, in 1972, when I was ten, a sign-up sheet for girls' track appeared on the bulletin board at the Community Center. "If my legs are strong enough for dancing and jumping, maybe I can run fast, too," I thought to myself. I printed my name on the first line.

A bunch of girls, including Debra, Angie and me, showed up for the track team on a sunny afternoon in late May. We were dressed in T-shirts and shorts and we squinted and cupped our hands over our eyes to shield them from the sun as we looked up at our coach, Percy Harris. He explained that practice would be held every afternoon and that we had to run around the cinder track behind the Center to prepare for our races. He pointed to the area.

"All the way around there?" one girl said after she turned around to see where his finger was pointing. She turned back to Percy wearing a frown. "It's hot out here!"

"That's far!" another complained.

It did look like an awfully big circle, which grew wider as we got closer to it. But I kept my thoughts to myself. Momma and Daddy told us never to talk while adults were speaking. Besides, I wanted to see if I could make it all the way around. I was ready to run.

That circular track, which still exists at the back of Lincoln Park and became a fixture of my teenage years, is unconventional. It measures about 550 yards around, roughly a third of a mile. A standard track is oval-shaped and measures 400 meters, a quarter-mile. Those of us who completed the lap were panting hard by the time we reached the end. We bent over and put our hands on our knees when we finished. The other girls had stopped running and were walking. Percy said we had to run around two more times without stopping to get in a mile workout. Some of the girls mumbled and rolled their eyes. I took off around the track.

Each day, fewer and fewer girls showed up until finally the track team consisted of the three Joyner girls, two of whom were there under protest. At that point, Percy gave up the idea of forming a team. But I wanted to continue running, so he introduced me to George Ward, who coached a half-dozen girls at Franklin Elementary and brought them to Lincoln Park in the summer to practice.

"I don't know if I'm good," I said shyly when Mr. Ward said I could join his team.

"Don't worry about that. We're just having fun. If you win a ribbon, good. If not, that's okay, too," he said. I breathed a sigh of relief.

The practice sessions with Mr. Ward's group were a lot of fun. Suddenly I had six new friends. I didn't know Gwen Brown or any of the others from Franklin Elementary because I attended John Robinson Elementary and the schools were in different parts of town. Most of the others had been training with Mr. Ward for over a year and, as I would soon discover, were already very strong, fast runners.

The first race I ran for Mr. Ward was the 440-yard dash, now called the 400 meters. He lined us up opposite two bent steel poles. Then, stopwatch in hand, he walked around to the other side of the circle and stood on the board 440 yards away. From there, he yelled, "On your mark, get set, go!"

The rest of the girls charged ahead. I ran as hard as I could, but I couldn't catch them. I finished last. Once I caught my breath, I was disappointed. I couldn't believe how fast the others were!

"What can I do to get faster?" I asked Mr. Ward.

"Just keep coming to practice, you'll get better," he assured me.

I finished last or nearly last in every race that summer. But Mr. Ward stuck with me. When school resumed, he picked me up every afternoon at home in the spring and drove me to track practice at his school. I looked forward to it all day. I was eleven. I would rush home after school, cram down a few oatmeal cookies or a bag of potato chips, quickly do my geography, math, spelling and science homework and then do my chores—or pay Debra to do them—so that I was ready when his car pulled up. I waved good-bye to Momma, who was getting home about the time I left, and hopped in Mr. Ward's car.

The practices were pressure-free, but there were rules. We weren't supposed to talk while running. But I chatted away with my new friends. Every time Mr. Ward caught me, he stopped us, pulled me out of the group and scolded me. As punishment, he made me run in the opposite direction from the others. I didn't mind. I was so happy to be out there with the others. With a smile on my face, I ran clockwise while the others ran counterclockwise.

One day I got sick and started throwing up while running. Mr. Ward asked me what I'd eaten. When I told him about the oatmeal cookies, he shook his head. Junk food was a no-no, he said. My punishment that time was three extra laps, all in the opposite direction. He said he wanted me to feel how eating junk food would affect my endurance. But it didn't bother me. I felt as if I could run forever. I just wasn't very fast yet.

After several more races and no ribbons, however, I became discouraged. "Am I ever going to win anything?" I asked.

He gave me a consoling pat on the back as we walked to his car. "You will if you keep working hard."

I wasn't crazy about running the 440-yard dash. But it

was a challenge. I wanted to catch those other girls. My real love was jumping. But I was too shy to tell Mr. Ward. At the time I didn't know anything about the intricacies of the long jump. I just knew my legs were strong and I was a good jumper, based on my cheerleading and dancing performances.

For weeks, I watched Gwen Brown run down the long-jump track and leap into the air, like a plane taking off. I bit my lower lip as she practiced, yearning for just one chance to run down the dirt path and jump into the shallow sand. When I returned home that afternoon, I got a brainstorm. I found potato chip bags and convinced my sisters to go over to the sandbox in the park, fill the bags and help me bring the sand back to our house. Over the next several afternoons we secretly ferried sand from the park to the front yard, where I made a small sand pit. On the days when I didn't go to practice, I hopped onto our porch railing, which was about three feet high, crouched down with my back arched and leaped into the sand. The feeling was so satisfying and so much fun, I did it over and over again for about an hour.

One afternoon after all the other girls had left practice, while I waited for Mr. Ward to drive me home, I walked over to the runway. It was nothing more than a long strip of grass, marked off with a strip of tape at one end and a shallow hole with a thin layer of sand at the other end. The sun was ready to set, but the air remained hot and thick. I was tired after running sprints and conditioning drills in the oppressive heat. But standing there, looking down the long-jump lane for the first time, I was energized. I mimicked what I had seen Gwen doing. I charged down the lane as fast as I could, planted my right foot and jumped up as high as I could. I kicked my legs out in front of me and pushed myself forward.

What a feeling! It was like flying. I stood up, content

with myself and feeling daring. I smiled as I dusted the sand off my shorts and legs. Mr. Ward ran toward me. I was afraid he was going to be mad. But there was an excited look in his eyes.

"Do that again!" he shouted.

I trotted back to the starting line and repeated the process: charge, plant, push, kick, fly. His jaw dropped.

"I didn't know you could jump!" Mr. Ward said when I emerged from the sand.

"Oh, I love to jump," I said. "My legs are strong from cheerleading. I have wanted to try jumping for the longest."

"Starting tomorrow, come to the long-jump pit and I'll work with you and Gwen together," he said.

I was delighted. When he dropped me off, I skipped through the yard, bounded up the steps and ran inside to give everybody the news.

Mr. Ward was volunteering his time to the after-school track program. In coaching young girls, he and Nino Fennoy, a teacher at Lilly Freeman Elementary who had organized a girls' squad at that school, were exploring uncharted territory and exposing themselves to criticism. No one in town had ever tried cultivating athletic interest among girls. While boys had high school and junior high teams, Little League baseball and Pop Warner football, girls in our community had no organized sports activities whatsoever.

Congress had recently passed Title IX, the federal legislation requiring public schools to give girls and boys equal opportunities to participate in athletics. Mr. Ward and Mr. Fennoy used the new law to develop opportunities for girls in sports. The combined Franklin-Freeman Elementary School team competed against other schools during the academic year. In 1974, when I was twelve, the two men organized a track squad of male and female athletes from all the schools in town that competed in summer Amateur Athletic Union (AAU) track meets. The squad was called the East St. Louis Railers.

Although I didn't realize it at the time, my participation on the Railers squad set me on a course that would lead far beyond Piggott Avenue and the Arch, into a world full of life experiences both painful and joyous.

6

My Guiding Light

People have always assumed I succeeded at sports because I was a natural talent. Not quite. I had talent and determination, but I needed someone to help me develop it. Nino Fennoy was that person. He encouraged me to imagine myself doing great things and worked with me to turn my fantasies into reality.

I met Mr. Fennoy on a spring day in 1973. Mr. Ward piled the girls he'd been coaching into his car and drove us to the field at Hughes Quinn Junior High, some eight blocks from my house. Every evening Mr. Fennoy worked with a group of boys and girls from Lilly Freeman Elementary at the Hughes Quinn playground. The two men had decided to divide the coaching duties of the Franklin-Freeman squad, with Mr. Ward taking the boys and Mr. Fennoy the girls.

To determine our skill level, they asked us all to run 120 yards, then circle around and run back, and repeat the drill several times. I did it easily. I still wasn't the fastest, but after almost a year of training with Mr. Ward, I had lots of stamina. I stood about 5' 5" tall and weighed a lean 120 pounds—all arms and legs.

"What else are we going to do?" I asked the two coaches when we were done. Mr. Fennoy looked at me and smiled.

The longer I worked with him, the stronger and faster I became. But I still wasn't in the front of the pack at the end of the races—my 440 time was well over a minute. In my first race with Mr. Fennoy as my coach, I didn't finish last, but I was well back. I hoped he wouldn't be disappointed and drop me from the team.

"I tried," I said, shrugging my shoulders apologetically afterward.

He responded with a reassuring smile: "That's all I ask."

Over time, lots of girls started the Railers track program. But as training drills intensified, sessions lasted longer and the temperature rose, many of them dropped out. A group that included Gwen Brown, Deborah Thurston, Carmen Cannon, Tina Gully, Danette, Cindy and Mona Onyemelukwe, Devlin Stamps, Pat Riggins and me stuck it out that summer and all the seasons thereafter. We formed the core of the girls' athletic program on the south side of East St. Louis. That program included volleyball, basketball and track squads. Most of us played two sports. I was one of the few who played all three. In summers, we competed as East St. Louis Railers. During the school year, we competed for our respective junior high teams, and later, as Lincoln Tigerettes in senior high.

Mr. Fennoy, the son of an East St. Louis political leader, was a high school classmate of Daddy's. After an undistinguished athletic career at Lincoln, he realized his future was in coaching, rather than competing. He studied physical education in college and earned a master's degree from Southern Illinois University. He got the idea of using sports to help the youngsters in East St. Louis after administering the President's Physical Fitness Test to a group of

Lilly Freeman students early in the school year. When they scored in the top percentile, without any preparation or coaching, he knew he'd found the seeds of a potentially fruitful program. The influx of federal funds to East St. Louis for educational and recreational programs in the 1970s, coupled with passage of Title IX, provided the fertilizer.

Mr. Fennoy was only about 5' 7", but his ideas were lofty. The skin beneath his afro, mustache and beard was the color of parchment and he dressed like many of the other thirtysomething men in town. But he spoke like a wise, old man—a combination sociologist, philosopher and motivational speaker. With his index finger jabbing the air and his hazel eyes staring intently at us, he peppered his speeches at team meetings with phrases like "making maximum use of minimal resources" and "the parameters of acceptable behavior."

He had a broad vision of what he wanted to accomplish through the track program. He encouraged us to work hard in practice, as well as in class. With a solid foundation in athletics and academics, he told us, the possibilities were unlimited—college scholarships, graduate school, good-paying jobs and productive lives.

In one of his first speeches to us after practice when we were still in elementary school, he explained that success in sports could open doors for us and set us on the path to broader success. "Doing well in sports is fine. But in order to compete and get any portion of what this country has to offer, you have to have an education. You can't get a job if you can't fill out an application."

Like my parents, he stressed that there was a world beyond East St. Louis and that life in that world wouldn't be a struggle if we were properly prepared. "You have alternatives," he said. "You don't have to just be housewives. You don't have to settle for staying here."

Other than my parents, Mr. Fennoy was the major influence on my attitudes and outlook. He inspired me to make the most of my talent, to withstand peer pressure and to avoid the traps into which others fell.

He was a constant force in our lives, serving as our AAU coach from elementary school through junior high. By the time we entered Lincoln High, he was the head track coach there as well. He got to know us almost as a parent would—sometimes even better. Beginning in junior high, he asked us to record everything we were thinking and doing and eating in a daily journal. I recorded my times on sprint and endurance drills, as well as my long-jump distances. I reviewed the day's activities at school. I wrote that I hated typing class and that I was flunking home economics because I couldn't cook. I described how excited I was to be involved in the History Club's program to bring Donald McHenry, the United Nations ambassador and Lincoln High alumnus, back to campus for a lecture to the student body. I also related my experiences with my boyfriend.

Every week until my senior year, Mr. Fennoy reviewed what I wrote and discussed it with me. Nothing got by him. After hearing about my ex-boyfriend's new girlfriend being pregnant, I was melancholy and uninspired. Mr. Fennoy talked to me about it away from the others.

"What's wrong?" he asked.

When I told him, he said, "I figured that was it. You shouldn't be upset. Breaking up with him was the best thing that could have happened to you," he said. "Now, let's get back to work."

As protective as my parents were, they allowed me to go to out-of-town meets with Mr. Fennoy because they knew I was in good hands. He was like a father away from home. Mr. Fennoy always seemed to know what we needed, without our having to ask. He gave me my first pair of track shoes and never asked for any money.

When it was time to travel to meets out of state or across country, we sometimes raised the money for travel expenses by holding bake sales and raffles. But Mr. Fennoy often turned down huge donations from people in town, even though expenses could run as much as $5,000 when several of us and a coach had to travel out of town. We heard about some of the offers and asked why he'd refused them. "You never want anyone to think you owe them something," he said. Also, he reminded us, eligibility rules prohibited gifts to high school and college athletes.

Mr. Fennoy, assistant coach Arlander Hampton and Mr. Ward drove us to meets in their cars when the Railers were first organized. After the program became successful and our victories were publicized, the school board agreed to fund the summer track program. From that point on, we rode to meets in chartered buses and rented vans.

On one of the first trips I took with the Railers, I didn't have money for lunch. My father wasn't working and my mother said she just didn't have anything to give me. If I went, she said I'd have to wait until I got back home that night to eat. When the van carrying us pulled into the McDonald's parking lot at lunchtime, my mouth watered and my stomach gurgled. I'd exerted myself all morning and I was starving. But when it was time to get off the bus, I was too embarrassed to say I didn't have any money, so I told everyone I wasn't hungry.

While my teammates rushed inside with bills clutched in their hands, I waited on the bus. No sense torturing myself by going inside and smelling the french fries. Mr. Fennoy walked back to the bus and asked why I wasn't inside. I told him I wasn't hungry. Without inquiring further, he said, "Come on inside with me and order what you want."

"Thanks!" I said, flashing a big, grateful grin. We walked in side by side.

After that, whenever Momma was running short and a trip was approaching, I saved my lunch money during the week or bought candy bars at the store for a nickel and sold them at school for a dime. At mealtime after the meets, I rolled down my socks, pulled out the ball of money hidden there and walked in with everyone else, carrying a fistful of money.

With Mr. Fennoy, I got a taste of life away from East St. Louis. It was, at times, a bittersweet experience. But he tried to insulate us from the most painful aspects. In most cases, the only way white schools would agree to compete against us was if we traveled to their schools. East St. Louis had such a bad reputation, people were afraid to come into town. One white coach told Mr. Fennoy he was afraid his bus would be vandalized. It made me sad to hear what people thought of the place I lived.

Some of our trips took us to remote towns in Illinois and Missouri. Without explaining why, when the driver stopped for gas in those places, Mr. Fennoy said we should stay on the bus. Whenever a ticklish situation arose at a meet that indicated prejudice or a racial bias, Mr. Fennoy handled it diplomatically and taught us to do the same.

During the preliminary round of an AAU meet in Poplar Bluff, Missouri, in 1976, when I was fourteen, I landed a jump in my last turn during the qualifying round, which should have been long enough to put me in the final round. But the official failed to record it. As a result, I was out of the competition. At the time I thought it was a deliberate oversight. The disappointment was all the more bruising because I had to finish in one of the top three spots to advance to the AAU Regional competition, and to have a chance at ultimately competing in the AAU National meet. When the official told me I'd failed to qualify, tears welled up in my eyes and my body stiffened. I was ready to yell at someone. Mr. Fennoy saw my face and called me over.

"It's not fair . . ." I started to rant.

"Don't say another word," he ordered, pointing his finger at me. "Let me handle it. And you better not cry, either."

He didn't make a scene. He huddled with the officials, discussing the issue calmly. Then he walked back over to me and told me the decision was final. I wanted to scream about the injustice of it all. I felt as if someone had stolen something from me. While he was gone, I had overheard some of the chaperones say that Mr. Fennoy had run into trouble with one of the judges at the meet in the past. The conversation made it sound like it was a racial issue. When I asked him about it, he said whether the oversight was racially motivated or not wasn't the point.

"Rather than looking for someone to blame or to be mad with, let's learn from this," he said. The idea of blame and anger appealed to me more, but I listened.

"From now on, after every jump, always make sure that the judges have recorded your mark. And let's work harder on your jumping so that next time, one jump won't mean the difference between qualifying and not qualifying."

The lessons stuck with me. Watching Mr. Fennoy, I learned to handle controversy and adversity calmly. And at each long-jump competition I enter, I walk by the judges after every jump and, while pretending to look at the standings, make sure they've recorded the result.

7

A Consuming Passion

Mr. Fennoy has told people that when he was coaching me, I acted like I was on a mission. In a way, he's right. There is something about seeing myself improve that motivates and excites me. It's that way now, after six Olympic medals and five world records. And it was that way when I was in junior high, just starting to enter track meets.

For me, the joy of athletics has never resided in winning. Don't get me wrong, I love every one of those high school championships, gold medals and world records. But I derive as much happiness from the process as from the results. I don't mind losing as long as I see improvement or I feel I've done as well as I possibly could. If I lose, I just go back to the track and work some more. That's why those losses when I was just starting out didn't bother me so much. I knew I'd given my very best.

There has been within me a driving force to be the best I could be, to run faster, jump higher, leap farther for as long as I can remember. When I started long jumping, nothing was better than the feeling of flying farther and farther down the pit and watching my coach's tape measure get longer and longer as he measured my jumps. When I first started leaping, I jumped 15 feet routinely. But with coaching and practice, I improved steadily. I calculated that I gained almost a foot in distance each year.

I got so motivated by my progress, I started to daydream about jumping farther and farther. When I was fourteen, my personal best was 17' 1¾". After practice one day, I sat down and plotted just how far I might go. I figured that if I was jumping 17 feet at age fourteen and I was adding a foot in distance each year, I should be jumping 18 feet at age fifteen. At sixteen, I would jump 19 or 20 feet. And by the time I was nineteen, I saw myself jumping 23, or maybe even 24 feet! Those projections became my targets.

It sounded crazy, but I was serious. Mr. Fennoy had taught me to believe in myself. I was young and enthusiastic, and I just didn't think there were any limits to what my body could do if I kept working hard. Although I learned differently as I got older, I never lost that youthful optimism and determination.

I began competing in the pentathlon at age fourteen. It wasn't something that was part of any grand plan. It was an afterthought. But in retrospect it made perfect sense. Mr. Fennoy had me competing in a slew of individual events—sprints, hurdles, middle distances and long jump—and said I might as well compete in the one that put them all together. The pentathlon consisted of five events: the 100-meter hurdles, the high jump, the long jump, the shot put and the 800 meters. I wasn't good at some of them and I didn't like others. But I didn't complain or refuse to try.

I could handle the long jump, shot put and 800 meters. And though my hurdling was ragged, I knew I could run fast. So I ran fast and hopped over them. It wasn't the proper technique, but it worked. I also didn't know if I could high-jump; but I knew I could jump high. After a three-step run up to the bar, I would plant my left foot, take a big jump and—while keeping my legs bent and my head up almost like a baby in the fetal position—hurl myself up over the bar. My rhythm was simple: one, two, three, launch, jump.

The pentathlon wasn't contested at high school meets in Illinois. So I only competed in it during summer AAU competitions. Athletes in multi-events compile points based on the results of each event. The points are awarded based on how the athlete performs in each event compared to an arbitrary standard established by the judges. The competitor with the highest total score after the last event wins.

I didn't know exactly what the running and jumping I was doing on the track could lead to until I watched Bruce Jenner win a gold medal in the decathlon at the 1976 Olympic Games in Montreal. His performance was inspiring. I hadn't yet made a connection between what I was doing and the "real" Olympic Games. After watching the Montreal Games on TV, I could relate my training with Mr. Fennoy at Lincoln Park to something bigger and better. I realized that athletics might take me somewhere. Also, a part of me was still hoping to be discovered and get on TV!

"They're doing the same things I do," I told Al while sitting on the porch one day after the Olympics ended. "I'm going to try for the Olympic team. I want to be on TV."

I announced my plans to Mr. Fennoy after our next practice. "You think I could get to the real Olympics?" I asked.

"Let's try and see," he said.

My training for the individual events during the school year helped my performance in the pentathlon. Right off the bat, the results were encouraging. A year after I first tried the pentathlon, I qualified for the AAU Junior Olympics.

My Railers teammate Deborah Thurston also was a pentathlete. I usually finished ahead of her in competition. But by the summer of 1977, when I was fifteen, we both were among the best in the nation, on our way to the AAU Junior Olympics. The meet was held in Yakima, Washington, about as far from East St. Louis as you could go and still be in the continental United States.

To raise the $5,000 for the trip, we held sock hops, bake sales, car washes, and went door-to-door soliciting contributions. It was discouraging at times. A lot of people wanted to see us do well and happily put big bills in the envelope when Deborah and I knocked on their doors and explained why we needed a contribution. But others didn't. One man said we were wasting our time. As we stood there, shocked and insulted, he told us he didn't think athletics was important and didn't see how it could lead to anything worthwhile. We turned on our heels and walked away, grumbling about how mean people could be.

Despite it all, we raised enough money to go to Yakima. Mr. Fennoy had to attend another meet, so Coach Arlander Hampton went with us. At the St. Louis airport, we met Bill Cosby. We told him it was our first time flying and he just laughed. It was unreal. He talked to us for a long time. He was so nice to spend so much time with us. Seven years later, after the 1984 Olympics, I met him again and, to my surprise, he remembered that airport meeting. We've been good friends ever since.

In Yakima, we stayed at a hotel that had an indoor pool. It was the first time I'd seen one and I was dying to jump in. But our coaches never let us swim until after a meet was over. They said the chlorine might drain our bodies. Also, they wanted us to take care of the business at hand and remain focused. "First things first," Mr. Fennoy always said.

Deborah was good in the high jump and 800 meters, but I was faster, and a better long jumper. I usually built up a lot of points in the long jump and 100-meter hurdles and was far ahead by the time we got to the 800, the last event and her best. So in the past I never really had to run hard in the 800. But in Yakima, I didn't hurdle well and my high jump was off. So although I beat her in long jump, we were close in points, because we ran close in the hurdles and put the shot about the same distance.

It came down to 800 meters, the event I dreaded. It's two laps around the track at a pretty fast pace and it always wore me out. Deborah was an expert distance runner. She was rail thin and seemed to have lungs made of steel and legs made of rubber. She just never got tired. On top of all that, I was already pretty worn out. We'd done all the events in one day with a break in the middle, instead of doing them over two days as we did at most meets. Coach Hampton knew that when he sat the two of us down during the break. He explained that by his calculations, Deborah would probably win. My best 800 time was around 2 minutes and 26 seconds. Deborah's was 2:19. He figured I had to run 2:19 to beat her, which I had never come close to doing before.

It was a challenge. But I wanted to win badly. It came down to me either running 2:26 like I usually did, or going for it. I was going for it. As we walked back to the track after lunch, I told Deborah, "I'm gonna beat you. I don't care what Coach says." I meant every word.

After one lap, I felt good. Still no problem along the backstretch. As I made the final turn and headed for the finish line, I was in the lead, but Deborah was at my heels. I held on and finished first. She crossed the line right behind me. I knew I was under 2:20; I could feel it. In fact, I had run 2:19.7 exactly—my lifetime best. The gold medal was mine. Not only had I won, I scored a total of 3,613 points and set a national age group record. I was elated and felt like jumping for joy. But I also felt bad that my teammate had finished second, with 3,404 points. I knew she was disappointed. I had the urge to apologize for winning. But I caught myself before I did. There was nothing to apologize for, I realized. It was all a part of competition.

I felt a kind of high. I'd proven that I could win if I wanted it badly enough. I knew Deborah should have beaten me. The 800 was her specialty. But I'd won because I wanted it more than she did. That win showed me that I could not only compete with the best athletes in the country, I could *will* myself to win. *Sports Illustrated* ran my picture along with a summary of my performance and the record in its "Faces in the Crowd" section. Then the East St. Louis paper, *The Monitor*, ran a story about the *SI* story. I tried to keep it all in perspective.

8

Championship Seasons

Our practice sessions in junior and senior high were prime examples of Mr. Fennoy's philosophy of making maximum use of minimal resources. After school the boys and girls teams jogged to Lincoln Park's irregular-shaped track and makeshift long-jump pit. The track was a 36-inch-wide strip of black cinders sprinkled amid the rest of the dirt and grass. We called it the bridle path because that's what it looked like. We ran over, around and through the potholes, rocks, glass and tree limbs that littered the track. We dodged line drives hit into the outfield during baseball games being played while we ran. We also had to keep an eye on the discus throwers and shot putters working on the cement slab in the center of the field. Each day after school we ran around and around that track at the park. After practice, we jogged another two or three miles around the neighborhood to complete our workout.

In winter, when it was too cold to practice outside, we trained inside the Lincoln High building. Every afternoon after school and at 9:00 every Saturday morning, the team of twenty-five girls split into groups on the two floors and ran along the brown concrete corridors. When it was time for hurdling drills, Mr. Fennoy set up hurdles in the center of the hallway on the second floor, and put us through our paces. We sprinted and leaped past the doors to the math and science classrooms. We ran to the end of the hall, turned around and repeated the drill in the opposite direction.

On the first floor, we ran the 440 much like outside, the only variation being the scenery. Instead of ball players and motorists, we ran past the trophy case, lockers, bulletin boards and classrooms before circling through the auditorium at the end of the hall and heading back toward the trophy case at the other end. The hallways were about 110 meters long, so two trips through the auditorium were roughly equivalent to 440 yards. Mr. Fennoy stood along the hall eyeing his stopwatch as we passed, hollering out the time. We had to run ten of those 440s without stopping, each one in less than 63 seconds. I was also on the mile relay team. Those drills began as soon as the 440 work ended. Up and down, up and down. Again and again and again for an hour.

The running drills, exhausting as they were, eventually paid off. In 1977, between the ninth and tenth grade, I developed booster rockets and cut an astonishing four seconds off my 440 time. I surged to the front of the pack in practice heats. By the time we entered Lincoln High as tenth-graders, I was the fastest 440 runner on the team. The last was—at long last—first.

It was like an overnight miracle. One day I was a tortoise, the next, a hare. Some might attribute my transformation to the laws of heredity, the inevitable development of fast-twitch muscle fibers that were part of my genetic makeup as the daughter of a former sprint hurdler. But I think it was my reward for all those hours of work on the bridle path, the neighborhood sidewalks and the school-house corridors.

Our home track meets were held at Parsons Field, a stadium owned by the city school district that sat fifteen minutes away from my neighborhood and the high school. The Parsons Field track was by no means plush, but compared to the park's bridle path and the school's cement floors, its red cinders felt like cotton when we raced there.

The East St. Louis Relays were held there over a spring weekend each year. Everyone in the city anticipated them because of the athletic talent on display. All of the schools in the area competed—the three elementary schools, four junior high schools and the three high schools. Spectators crammed into the galvanized-steel-covered stadium, which looked just like the one in that famous scene with Glenn Close in the movie *The Natural*. The overflow spilled out into the adjacent uncovered stands, then down along the fence line, all around the track, and into the portable bleachers on the opposite side of the field.

The meet was held in late April, and the weather was always extreme, either searing heat or pouring rain. But the crowd was always huge and enthusiastic. Even in downpours, the fans sat and stood in the open air to watch the competition. Rivalries were intense and occasionally fights broke out between the Lincoln and Eastside factions. The aroma of cooking hot dogs, popping corn and spinning cotton candy wafted onto the field during those meets, testing my resolve not to eat junk food.

As we ran, particularly in sprint events, the cinders kicked up and created clouds of dust in our wake. By the end of the day, the dust and dirt pellets were in our afros and cornrows, under our fingernails and in our eyes and mouths. When we sweated, the heat baked the dirt into our pores. Afterward, I had to scrub hard in the shower to get rid of the gritty feeling. When it rained, our feet sank into the ground as we ran. By the end of the meet, our feet and ankles were covered by the stuff. And our shorts and jerseys and the backs of our legs were splattered with little reddish brown dots, marking the places where the muddy cinders landed after shooting off our spikes.

An announcer in the matchbox-sized press box on the roof kept everyone abreast of names, times, standings and records. Whenever I did something noteworthy, the crowd cheered and applauded. But above the cheers could be heard a baritoned roar: "Jaaaaaaaackieeeeeeee!" It was Daddy. He screamed out my name whenever I came to the starting blocks, as I rounded the turn for the finish and after I landed in the long-jump pit. It made me cringe with embarrassment. I know he was proud and excited; but his cheers drew more attention to me, which I hated. Preferring to be low-key, I wanted my performances to speak for themselves. But that was impossible with Daddy shouting out my name all afternoon. I asked my mother to tell him to stay home. But he hardly ever missed a meet or a basketball game.

His voice was also a painful reminder of the problems brewing at home between my parents. Daddy had started coming home drunk and arguing with Momma. His temper was getting shorter, making the atmosphere in our house unpleasant and very tense. Because the track was my refuge from the turmoil, his presence in the stands was an unwelcome intrusion.

The meets held at white schools took us to a wholly different world. Instead of cinders, we ran on soft, cushy rubber tracks.

Competing against Palatine, in a wealthy suburban Chicago school district, gave us an eye-opening look at how the other half lived. While circling the brand-new rubber track, we passed a big elementary school complex that consisted of several buildings. Beside it was the three-story, white marble high school. It had shiny, tinted windows and a three-court gymnasium. My teammates and I were awestruck. The schools were so immaculate and so big, they didn't look real. The whole complex looked like a palace compared to our squat, cramped schools and our grungy facilities.

But Mr. Fennoy wouldn't let us lament the advantages others had. He told us to exploit them for our own benefit, pointing out that the softer surfaces should shave a half-second off our sprint times and as much as a second off our 400 times.

We soundly beat Palatine that day and I was voted athlete of the meet. We got on the team bus for the ride home and sang and cheered all the way, while munching on the Hershey bars and oranges the coaches passed around to help replenish our energy.

Those bus trips were unforgettable and educational. As we rode through the Ozark Mountains in Missouri, we gawked out the windows at the sights below. We marveled at how quickly the sky changed from sparkling blue to white to gray as the bus collided with rainstorms, then turned back to brilliant blue as we moved farther down the highway. On a trip to Miami for an AAU meet, we walked along the shore in shorts and T-shirts and frolicked on the beach, collecting seashells and screaming as the waves sent seawater rushing up our legs. It was the first time any of us had ever been that close to the ocean. The palm trees were like nothing we'd ever seen. The sight of them at night, the long tapered fronds silhouetted against Miami's neon lights, dazzled all of us.

On one of those trips, we decided to give ourselves nicknames. Someone suggested Jazzy Jackie for me; but I didn't think it fit my personality. I picked Joker because I loved playing practical jokes on people. Nothing mean or painful. Just silly, harmless fun to keep the mood light and make people laugh. Like the time I told my teammates that one of our best sprinters had broken her leg. They gasped and cried "No!" I started laughing and said, "Just joking!"

Devlin Stamps, whose mother came along as our chaperone, got her nickname on that trip to Miami. She realized she'd left her shoes in the hotel as we were about to board our bus one morning. She was in such a hurry to retrieve them that she ran into a plate glass window. She cut her leg, but wasn't seriously hurt, thank goodness. To commemorate the disaster, we called her Freda Payne—as in window and ouch.

All of the running and pounding eventually took a toll on my legs. I ran almost every afternoon in fifth and sixth grade and competed in the hurdles, the 400 meters, sprint relays, long jump and pentathlon on summer weekends. In junior high and high school, I ran and practiced six days a week, year-round, first for volleyball from August to November, then basketball from November to March, followed by track from spring to summer's end. The cycle began again each fall.

The first few times I felt stinging sensations up the front of my leg, I just ran through them. Eventually, the pain in my shins became a dull ache every time my foot hit the ground. I had been able to bear it in junior high, but my first season at Lincoln High had worn me down. I played a full season in volleyball, then the basketball team went all the way to the sectional finals. By the time I got to the spring track season the shin splints were so severe, I was, at the ripe old age of sixteen, perilously close to having stress fractures, according to Dr. Stan London, the St. Louis Cardinals team physician who examined my legs.

When he heard the diagnosis, Mr. Fennoy shook his head and apologized. "You haven't had a day off since the fifth grade, have you?" From that moment on, he said, I would take two weeks off between seasons.

That was fine for next season. The problem was what to do about the remaining weeks in this track season. The team needed my contribution in the mile relay, the 400 and the long jump to qualify for the state championship meet. The doctor showed Mr. Fennoy how to wrap the leg to minimize further damage.

Heading into the sectionals—the qualifying meet for state—the situation was bleak. At practice I was sluggish in the 440, running it in 60 seconds. That would never do. We figured the time to beat at state would be nearly three seconds faster. I was inconsistent on the long jump. One minute I looked like the best in the nation. The next, I looked like a novice. I told Mr. Fennoy I could bear the pain; but I was discouraged by my performance in practice. "Just stay confident," he said. "Everything else will fall into place."

He consulted with Mr. Ward about my long-jump troubles. Mr. Ward came to the track the next afternoon with a stopwatch and helped me settle into a consistent groove down the runway. He clocked me as I ran down, planted and jumped. As I stood beside him panting after a couple of attempts, with my hands on my hips, he talked me through the run and pinpointed the spot where I needed to accelerate before planting my foot and leaping. I nodded after each instruction. Thirty minutes and a few jumps later, I had the rhythm down and my confidence up.

At sectionals, we performed well enough to qualify for state. During the weeks leading up to the state meet in late May, I stayed off my legs completely, the only stress coming when I gingerly hobbled up and down the two flights of stairs at school.

At the state championships, the Lincoln Tigerettes went about their routine as if it were just another meet. We set up our camp on the infield or in the parking lot just outside the stadium gates. Before the competition began, we all gathered and joined hands with our coaches and prayed. Then we organized our equipment and supplies: shoes, warmup clothes, water bottles, ice, pillows and blankets. Other athletes roamed around, laughing and talking and cutting up with friends. But the Tigerettes always stayed together at our camp—a mass of orange and black. Staying together allowed us to support and encourage each other and helped us stay focused. Meanwhile, Mr. Fennoy nervously roamed between our camp, the coaches section and the track, watching the races, yelling out encouragement as we ran past him, and staying abreast of the team standings.

The track at Eastern Illinois University, the site of the state championship meet, was made of Tartan, a synthetic material softer and squishier than rubber. When I burst out of the blocks, I felt as if I was running on feathers! I finished second in the long jump, with a leap of 19' 2¾", which pleased Mr. Fennoy and me. My leg felt fine. I ran the first leg of the 880-yard medley, equivalent to the 800-meter relay, and our team placed second. Then I anchored the mile relay and finished in a dead heat with the girl from Eastside. We both set a state record, with a time of 3 minutes, 55.27 seconds. By the 440-yard dash, my shins were screaming. But I fought through the pain, hitting the tape first, in 56.75 seconds. It was my fastest time ever. When the times were announced, Mr. Fennoy looked at me in amazement and embraced me. We won the meet with a total of 37 points, the most ever accumulated by a team in a state girls' meet. We were 1978 state champs, the first girls' sports title for Lincoln High. We held on to the track championship for the next two years.

I rested my legs for the next few months. To help the shins heal and to stay in condition, I ran in the pool at Lincoln Park. The AAU Junior Olympics were coming up in

August and I desperately wanted to compete for another pentathlon gold medal, this time in the fifteen to sixteen age group.

Because of the injury, I had to miss the regional qualifying meet, which on first impression appeared to disqualify me from further competition. I was crushed. But Mr. Fennoy found a loophole in the rules permitting the automatic entry of the defending champion. My legs healed and I came back from Lawrence, Kansas, with my second Junior Olympic pentathlon gold medal and another age group scoring record, 3,817 points. In Bozeman, Montana, the next year, 1979, I improved to 3,953 points. I won again at the 1980 games in Porterville, California, with 4,129 total points. I also won the long jump in Santa Clara with a leap of 21' ¾".

The more awards I collected, the more pressure was put on Al to join the track team. My father came home one night, picked up a newspaper article about one of my track victories and said, loud enough for all of us to hear, "I thought my son would be the one bringing trophies into the house, but I guess my daughter will be the one upholding the family name in track and field."

Everyone told Al he was the spitting image of Daddy as a teenager and probably a natural athlete, just as Daddy had been. Al was over six feet tall, broad at the shoulders, narrow at the waist, with skinny legs. He weighed about 150 pounds, almost none of it fat. Mr. Fennoy told him repeatedly that his build made him ideal for the sport. All he needed to do was train to build up his strength and speed.

But Al had other ideas. Like me, he dreamed of athletic success. And just like mine, his dreams were fueled by watching the Olympics. But unlike mine, they didn't involve running on the track or jumping on the field. He was a great swimmer and passed the lifeguard exam on the first

try, when he was fifteen. He idolized Mark Spitz, who won
seven swimming gold medals in 1972. But when he
watched Phil Boggs win the springboard diving competition in 1976, his fancy turned to that sport. He thought he
could learn to dive and walk on to Indiana's team after
graduating from Lincoln in 1978. But the pool at the park
wasn't Olympic-sized and it had neither a 3-meter springboard nor a platform on which Al could practice. Also, Al
didn't have a Mr. Fennoy to help him develop and train
properly.

I didn't have much sympathy for him, though. Another
reason Al resisted track was that he knew it was hard work
and he was lazy. And he was obnoxious about it. He'd
never spent a second on the track working out. Yet, one
summer day in 1976, after I'd done well at a meet, he and
some of his school friends came by our house and started
speculating about whether he could beat me in a race. Al
was sixteen, about to enter his junior year; I was fourteen,
a rising freshman.

"Yeah, she think she's bad but I can beat her easy," Al
crowed.

"Bet you can't," one of his friends said, taunting him.

"I'll race her right now and show you!" Al said, standing
up and sticking out his chest.

I ignored them and continued talking to my girlfriends.
I wasn't going to dignify any of it with a comment.

"Come on, Jackie, let's race now and settle this," Al demanded, beckoning me to the street.

I was so sick of hearing him boast that I agreed—just to
shut him up. "Okay, let's race from the front door of the
Community Center to the mailbox in front of the tavern."

"Fine, let's go."

Like a scene out of the *Little Rascals* series, Al and I
walked out of our yard and marched up the street, surrounded by a group of neighborhood kids. We walked the

fifty meters to the front door of the Center. Our spectators, about ten boys and ten girls, gathered around the mailbox, the finish line. It wasn't quite a battle of the sexes, though. In addition to all of the girls, some of the boys were cheering for me. The men in front of the tavern watched, but didn't choose sides.

At the starting point, Tyrone Cavitt yelled, "On your mark, get set, go!" The kids all screamed—but Al couldn't stay with me. I beat him by several steps. Everyone surrounded me and patted me on the back, laughing and cheering. Al looked deflated. Word of the race results spread like a forest fire the following day at school. Al's friends teased him mercilessly. I felt sorry for him, but I had to teach him a lesson. I never heard another word of trash from him after that.

The defeat prompted him to go out for track and get in shape. Confirming Mr. Fennoy's prediction, Al was an instant sensation, qualifying for the state championships in the sprint hurdles his first season on the team in the spring of 1977. In his senior year, the coach asked him to try the triple jump and he won the district championship with a leap of 47' 9¾", the second-longest in district competition that year in Illinois. He finished third at the state championships. At the AAU Nationals a month after he graduated from Lincoln in 1978, he triple-jumped 51 feet on his first attempt. The meet officials and everyone in the crowd watched his leap in stunned silence. Amid wild cheering, the officials scurried around, trying to devise a method for measuring the distance. Their tape measures didn't extend past 50 feet! Up in the stadium, Daddy kept yelling, "That's *my* boy!"

Later that summer in Lincoln, Nebraska, Al won the AAU Junior Olympic triple jump with a leap of 50' 2½". Everyone in town was ecstatic, and for his part, Al reveled in his notoriety and welcomed the spotlight. Like his hero,

Elvis Presley, he'd burst onto the scene from nowhere and left everyone breathless with his performance. He turned down several scholarship offers from good track programs, including Illinois and Missouri, to accept one from Tennessee State. The school had a respected women's track program and Al believed the coaches were going to build a men's team around him. Unfortunately, he arrived in Nashville to find that his scholarship was really a tiny student loan. He was always strapped for money, enduring one semester without textbooks. So, after a year, he transferred to Arkansas State. In Jonesboro, he continued his athletic progress, breaking a number of collegiate triple-jump records. But with no scholarship and only loans, his college career was a financial struggle.

A yellow school bus carried a big crowd from East St. Louis, including Della and Daddy, to the state track championships when I was a junior. Momma didn't attend many of my competitions. She felt it was her duty to stay at home with my ailing great-grandmother. The people from my hometown all sat together in a clump, surrounded by the 5,000 other spectators.

When the long-jump competition began and I stepped up to the line, the crowd was buzzing. "Aw, she's gonna do it, you watch," someone shouted. "Here she goes!" someone else yelled out as he pointed to me on the field. Then I heard the familiar, "Jaaaaaaaackieeeeeeee!"

I got the signal and I took off. I pumped as hard as I could, running faster, faster, faster, down the runway. I took the last three steps, slammed my right foot down on the board and leaped. As I extended my arms and legs through the air, I knew I'd popped a big one. I'd never been in the air so long. I was floating. I came down in the dry, undisturbed part of the sand pit, far down from the section they'd raked and watered after everyone else's jumps.

In unison the crowd roared. Everyone was standing as I landed. I got up, looked back at the pit to see how far down I was and stepped out. I smiled and dusted myself off. The whole place was buzzing again, in anticipation.

"She got it! She got it," said a man who was not my father.

The officials were still measuring as I walked back to our camp and put on my sweatpants. I'd set a state record in the qualifying round with a jump of 19' 9¼". And though I'd never experienced a 20-foot leap, this one felt like it was way past 20. I'd never landed that far down the pit before.

When they raised the three standards—one at a time—to show my mark and the first number was a 2, the crowd exploded. I'd set a new record. The only mystery was how far I'd gone. Next came a 0, then a 7½. It was 20' 7½". The moment was as electric as the instant the 0.00 flashed on the scoreboard in Montreal during the 1976 Olympic gymnastics competition, signifying that Nadia Comaneci had received a perfect score on the uneven parallel bars. People who were there still talk about that afternoon at Eastern Illinois University in Charleston and the feeling they got watching that jump and seeing the numbers.

"Jaaaaaaaackieeeeeeee! That's my girl! Jaaaaaaaackieeeeeeee!" Daddy was beside himself.

I smiled modestly, raised my hand as far as my forehead, and gave a little wave in the direction of the stadium.

With that leap, I became one of the best long jumpers in the nation in both the junior and senior divisions. It was the best jump in Illinois by a high school girl and the second longest among female junior-division competitors in the country that year. I ranked eighth among all female long jumpers in the nation at the end of that year. For the second consecutive year, I was named the Illinois Girl Athlete of the Year by the *St. Louis Globe-Democrat*. I was also named a Prep All-America by *Illinois Track & Field News*. I repeated as the Girl Athlete of the Year the following season, and as a Prep All-America.

I thought I'd reached the height of celebrity in November 1979 when a big picture of me long jumping during the AAU Junior Olympics appeared on the cover of *Women's Varsity Sports* magazine. When I saw my picture, all I could do was grin. I couldn't believe it was me on the cover of a magazine.

With two state track championship trophies already in the case at school, I returned to Lincoln the following fall with one goal—winning the state basketball championship and adding that trophy to the case. It was senior year, the last chance for Deborah Thurston, Barbara Gilmore, Devlin Stamps and me to make history by being the first squad to win a girls' basketball title at Lincoln, and to see all our work during the previous years pay off.

We'd gotten close enough to taste it the year before, losing the championship game to Skokie-Niles West. As the team's cocaptain, I took it upon myself to keep everyone focused and motivated. Whenever our enthusiasm or energy level sagged in practice, I yelled out to my teammates, "Remember how it felt to lose in the finals and to watch that other team get the championship trophy, cut down the nets and celebrate? If you don't want to go through that again, we have to keep working!"

We went undefeated that season. Our only close game was against Marshall, the perennial powerhouse team from Chicago. It was late in the season and we were playing them on their home court in Chicago. Marshall's mascot is the Commando and they were in command of this game. We hadn't lost all season but we were trailing 59–61 with just a few seconds left. My teammates and I refused to believe we'd lose to any team that season. We didn't feel desperate or despondent. In the huddle at the bench during the last timeout, we told each other we'd find a way to win the game. Still, things looked bleak. Marshall had the ball and the clock was running down.

Justine Moore, our quick point guard, stole the ball and scored: 61–61. Marshall brought the ball upcourt again. All they had to do was hold it and let the clock run out. We had to make something happen. I saw the point guard's eyes shift and I anticipated a pass. As she turned to throw the ball, I jumped out and intercepted it. My heart was in my throat as I dribbled downcourt to our basket. The rushing footsteps behind me sounded like a stampede. The pro-Marshall crowd was screaming. I focused on making the shot. I put it up and watched it fall in. A millisecond later, the buzzer sounded. Lincoln 63, Marshall 61. My ecstatic teammates rushed me and I whooped. We tumbled to the floor, giddy and relieved. We didn't come close to losing again en route to the finals where our opponent was none other than Chicago Marshall. A rematch.

"They'll want revenge," I told my teammates in the locker room before the game. I was standing in front of them, my game face decorated with braided pigtails and an orange sweatband. "We can't let them have it. We've worked too hard to get it. We have to *want* this title more than they do to win."

The game was played inside Assembly Hall on the University of Illinois campus. The place holds 11,000, but only 4,000 seats were filled, most of them by fans from East St. Louis. They had carpooled or ridden in one of the school buses as part of the caravan that arrived in Champaign-Urbana on Thursday night for the Friday-Saturday tournament. Our team bus, an air-conditioned charter, had led the caravan. With so many fans in the stands, it felt like a home game at Lincoln High gym.

We were up by just six points in the third quarter when Deborah Thurston jumped up for a rebound and came down on the side of her ankle, twisting it. Gut check time. We all knew we had to play with more intensity to compensate for Deborah's absence under the boards. Debra Powell replaced her and started hitting shots from everywhere on the court. I banged the boards and snatched every rebound I could. We applied a full-court press that finally wore Marshall down. We pulled away and won 64–47. We now had a gold medal to go with the silver one each of us had received the previous year.

We mobbed each other at center court. Then we got a ladder, walked over to our basket and cut down the net, which we draped across the championship trophy. On the bus ride back home, we sang our theme song, the Kenny Loggins tune "This Is It." We were delirious. When Deborah Thurston and I helped the track team win a third straight track championship, it was the perfect way to finish our high school careers.

9

My Feminine Mystique

There was no jealousy or animosity between the boys' and girls' squads at Lincoln. The boys respected our talents and always congratulated us after we won a meet or a basketball game. During our first basketball season at Lincoln, while the girls' and boys' coaches bickered over which squad would practice first in the gym after school, the boys on the team volunteered to let us start first, at 3:30, so that we could get home before dark.

A few of the male long jumpers treated me as a rival, albeit a friendly one. Even though I rarely jumped farther than they did, they kept close track, as a matter of pride. They didn't mind being beaten by other boys, but they were determined not to be outjumped by a girl. At joint meets, they wandered over during the competition and stood beside the pit to watch my jumps. At school, on Mondays following weekend meets out of town, they rushed to me in the hall to ask about my performance. They always looked relieved when I told them. "Oh, that's good," they said. "As long as we can still beat you we're happy."

The backhanded compliment rolled right off my back. Their insecurity and grudging respect was amusing to me. I wasn't interested in competing with or comparing myself to boys. But they certainly were worried about me.

Although no one came right out and said it, I sensed that the idea of my playing sports didn't sit well with my parents at first. Partly, they were concerned for my safety. They wanted to know the names of all the adults involved before they allowed me to run track. However, once they heard the names Ward and Fennoy—men they knew and trusted—they gave me permission to join the Railers.

Daddy wasn't troubled by the idea that I'd be running and jumping in track and field events. But he and my mother were skeptical about the basketball team. When I first broached the idea, Momma and Daddy looked at each other uneasily and said, "We'll have to think about it."

It was such a touchy subject, they didn't discuss it in front of me. They went into the bedroom and when they came out, they told me they didn't think it was a good idea. The reason: With track, my studies and my household chores, I was already spread too thin.

But the truth is, while they were comfortable with the notion of girls' track, they associated basketball with men and boys and didn't think girls should be playing it. It was a new concept and they hadn't accepted it yet. Unlike other school districts around the country, East St. Louis had never before offered competitive basketball for girls.

I'm embarrassed to admit it, but my parents thought if I played basketball, I'd become a lesbian. Along with most of the other people in the community, they were unenlightened. Sports were fine for other girls, but not *their* girls. When Mr. Foster, the gym teacher at John Robinson Elementary, decided to start girls' sports teams at the school, he recruited girls from another school! Then the coach had the audacity to ask me and the other cheerleaders to cheer for them.

"Cheer? Why can't we be on the team?" I asked him.

"I didn't know you wanted to play; I thought you all just wanted to cheer," he said.

"I love being a cheerleader, but I want to play."

I was annoyed and I didn't care if I got in trouble for talking back. I wasn't going to stand on the sidelines cheering while people kept me from doing something I knew I could do well. However, I didn't play on a girls' basketball team until I was in junior high, when the school district began to sanction the teams and games. The school's supervision of the activities reassured my parents.

The usual hobbies for girls in my hometown at the time were cheerleading, baton twirling, dancing, cooking and sewing, and dating. The most esteemed extracurricular activity was making a debut. The debutante cotillions were the social events of the year in East St. Louis. My classmates talked of nothing else between November and January. But by the time I was old enough to be involved, I was interested solely in athletics. So while we sweated inside the practice gym at Lincoln High in shorts and T-shirts, the debs were either in St. Louis department stores, trying on expensive, beautiful dresses, or sitting at home addressing fancy, printed invitations to their balls.

Afterward, the pictures of the girls in their white gloves, upswept hairdos and fancy ball gowns shared space with news of the latest Lincoln High Tigerette basketball victory and pictures of us in our braids, sweatbands and basketball uniforms, jumping for rebounds and dribbling.

Lesbianism became more than an abstract idea the day a girl on our high school basketball team received a fan letter from a woman that was very explicit. My teammate was freaked out by it. She pulled me aside after practice one day and showed me the note. The letter was shocking. We'd

heard stories about women liking other women, instead of
men, but none of us had personal experience with it. My
shaken teammate asked me if the letter meant she was a lesbian. I told her no and urged her to give it to our coach.
We never heard any more about it and I never heard about
any other teammate being approached in that way.

I have never felt—I have a hard time even saying the
word—*unfeminine* while playing sports. Mr. Fennoy convinced us there was nothing unfeminine about it. "People
will try to tell you otherwise, but playing sports won't
change your sexual orientation," he said. "We're trying to
give you experiences that will broaden your horizons. You
should use sports as a springboard, the way whites do.
Through athletics, you can get a scholarship to college,
which will propel you into a career and allow you to be
whatever you want to be."

He told us stories about famous female athletes including Wilma Rudolph, a great lady and Olympian. Through
his stories, I discovered that Wilma and I had much in
common. Like me, Wilma came from a poor background.
She was one of twenty-two children. She had scarlet fever
and polio as a child and couldn't walk for many years.
When she was growing up, the other kids made fun of her
and didn't include her in activities because she wore braces
on her legs. But she used sports as motivation. She was determined to walk, and eventually Wilma not only walked,
she ran—very fast. She played basketball and ran track and
was a member of the champion Tigerbelles track team at
Tennessee State University. She also won three gold medals
in sprint events at the 1960 Olympics in Rome. Eventually,
Wilma married and had four children.

The day Mr. Fennoy told me about Wilma, I went directly to the library and found a book about her. At home
that night, I sat on my bed and devoured every word.
Wilma became my role model that night and has been ever

since. She was a superb athlete and a great lady who carried herself with dignity.

The community's reaction to our athletic activities confused and frustrated me. Initially, some parents told their daughters not to get involved in sports and a lot of girls with athletic talent dropped sports altogether in the face of such strong peer and parental pressure. But when our basketball and track teams became successful, those same parents showed up at every competition and cheered their lungs out. I initially thought it meant we were proving that we could run, jump and sweat, then go home, shower, dress up and be treated like the rest of the girls. But attitudes didn't change much.

Unfortunately, people aren't much more enlightened today than they were when I was coming of age in the 1970s in East St. Louis. Despite the advances female athletes have made and the growing popularity of women's tennis, golf, basketball, softball and soccer, the negative attitudes persist. It's true that there are gay women participating in sports. But I don't know whether they are more prevalent in athletics than they are in other professions. And I don't care. I would never criticize someone for the choices they make in their personal relationships. The most important thing to me is what's inside a person's heart.

I believe that many of the people who continue to label all female athletes as lesbians and shy away from women's sports for that reason are not only intolerant and prejudiced, they're also enemies of women's athletics. The labels and scare tactics are a way to justify their narrow-minded opinions and keep female athletics from succeeding.

It's really unfortunate. So many girls I knew back home got pregnant before graduating. Others got married soon after graduating and became housewives—not out of choice, but because they didn't consider the other options. Most of them never left East St. Louis. While I certainly don't look down on mothers or homemakers—I hope to be a mother and a homemaker myself someday—my point is that if those girls had developed other interests, they might have had more options. But either because of fear, intimidation or complacency, they didn't.

Some others in my neighborhood did see the bigger picture and their support kept me striving to prove the doubters and naysayers wrong. Squirrel, Doug and the other men in front of the liquor store were among my biggest fans. As I jogged by each afternoon, they cheered me on. The wife of the owner of Kaufman's, the big grocery store in our neighborhood, cut the pictures and articles about me out of the St. Louis daily papers and gave them to my mother. I taped them to the pages of my bulging scrapbook, beside the clippings I'd already collected from the East St. Louis weeklies, *The Monitor* and *The Crusader*. One of the sports columnists at *The Monitor*, Stanford Scott, heaped praise on me and my teammates. He called us the "proud and beautiful" Tigerettes. He referred to me as "little Miss Superwoman" and "a black pearl." After my picture appeared in *Sports Illustrated*, Mr. Scott wrote a column about what a great accomplishment it was. In it, he congratulated me on being "a great athlete and a beautiful young lady."

The route for my training runs intersected with the city bus route that ran near my house. Every afternoon, I encountered Skip, who drove the bus and who always waved as I jogged by. One day, as I approached 15th and Piggott, Skip stopped his bus, opened his window and shouted as I passed, "Just keep working hard, girl, you'll make something out of yourself." I flashed a big smile and waved as I bounded up the street, invigorated by his encouragement.

10

Painful Realities

When the letter arrived telling me I'd qualified to compete for a spot on the Olympic long-jump team and inviting me to the 1980 Olympic Trials in Eugene, Oregon, I couldn't stop staring at it and rereading it. I wanted to savor each word.

It was a time for fantastic dreaming. I couldn't get to sleep that night, I was so excited. I kept imagining myself on the medal stand. The next day at work, my mother started planning her trip to the Moscow Olympic Games. She was afraid to fly, so she and her friend Joyce Farmer tried to think of a way to get her from East St. Louis to Russia by train and boat.

The Olympic Trials were bigger than anything I'd ever experienced. After checking in at the bustling registration center, I received an identification tag and a big bag full of gear from Nike that included a pair of blue overalls with the word "Nike" across the bib, a jacket, lots of T-shirts and blue track shoes with a yellow swoosh. At Lincoln, we wore one pair of spikes until they wore out. That spare pair made me feel like Imelda Marcos. Mr. Fennoy had given me track shoes, but this was the first time I'd ever gotten so much free equipment. Because I'd already graduated from high school, I could accept it without breaking any rules.

But the grand prize was the blue and red sweat suit with the letters "USA" on the front, awarded to the athletes who qualified for the team. I looked longingly at a big stack of them folded and wrapped in clear plastic bags.

Whatever confidence I had vanished the moment I set foot on the track the first day. I walked over to the long-jump warmup area and there was Carl Lewis. He was a student at the University of Houston and the favorite in the men's division. I watched Carl warm up. His stride down the runway was breathtaking. He was so smooth and fast. Perfect tempo and such power! He sailed through the air forever before landing in the sand.

His sister, Carol, still in high school, was competing against me in the women's division. She and I had gone at it for years in AAU long-jump competition, trading first and second place. Another nemesis from junior competition, Gwen Loud, was also there. She was already in college, at UCLA. In 1979, Gwen's leap of 20' 9½" kept my 20' 7½" jump at the state championships off the books as the longest leap by a high school girl that year.

In high school, I was oblivious to my competitors. I just went out and jumped with confidence. But in Eugene, I was suddenly keenly aware of every potential threat. I knew both Gwen and Carol would be tough to beat. They were so at ease. The entire scene at the track overwhelmed me. My nerves got the best of me when it was time to compete, which only added to my timing problems down the runway. I finished eighth overall, managing only a pitiful jump of 20' 4". Carol's best jump, 21' 6¼", put her in third and on the Olympic team. Gwen jumped 20' 10¾" and placed fifth. I was in tears by the end of the meet. I had let a great opportunity slip away because I couldn't control my nerves. To top it off, not only didn't I get USA sweats, I didn't get any recognition at all. At the Olympic Trials, you were either one of the top three or you were nobody. It was a painful introduction to world-class competition.

My performance brought me back down to earth. Throughout high school I'd been the big fish in the pond. Now I was swimming with the biggest fish of all and I was back to feeling like a guppy. I was inconsolable. "It's a respectable performance," Mr. Fennoy said. "Build on it. Use it as motivation for 1984."

Brooks Johnson, the track coach at Stanford at the time, got into the elevator with me at the hotel after my event. He could see how blue I was. "You have a lot of potential," he said. "Even though you didn't succeed this time, just remember, the Lord works in mysterious ways."

I also met a young track coach from California named Bobby Kersee. I had read an article in *Track & Field News* about the program Bobby had built at Cal State-Northridge. The monthly magazine is the bible of the sport, and in high school I read it religiously. Mr. Fennoy passed me the latest issue as soon as he was done reading it. Bobby had just been hired by UCLA as an assistant track coach. I made a mental note of it, but otherwise I didn't think much about this fellow Bobby Kersee. He didn't say much, and seemed quiet.

College recruiters sent me information and came to our track meets and basketball games throughout my last two years at Lincoln High. It was both thrilling and nerve-racking. Mr. Fennoy was so worried that someone would try to take advantage of us or do something improper that he screened every phone call, read every letter and monitored every visit from coaches. He even ordered us to temper our enthusiasm when we saw recruiters and coaches in the bleachers before our games and meets. "You can smile;

but don't wave or yell 'Hello,'" he instructed Deborah Thurston and me before the games UCLA basketball coach Billie Moore attended. She and her assistant coach, Colleen Matsuhara, made several trips to East St. Louis to recruit the two of us for the Bruin squad.

My parents knew nothing about big-time college recruiting, but they understood human nature. They kept reminding me not to take anything from strangers. I didn't understand what all the fuss was about until late in my senior year. After the buzzer sounded at the end of the state championship basketball game, one of the city's wealthiest citizens congratulated me on our victory. As he shook my hand, he pressed something into my palm. I opened my hand and was startled to see a wad of bills. I don't know how much money it was because I didn't take the time to count it. As soon as I realized what it was, I handed the money back to him.

"Thanks, but I can't take this," I said, before running back to join my celebrating teammates.

I knew Mr. Fennoy had said there were rules against accepting money and gifts. But what really prompted me to give it back was my mother's voice inside my head saying: "Don't let anyone think you can be bought."

And it's a good thing, too. Later that evening I found out that several people had seen what the man tried to do. If I'd kept the money, they might have reported me. So, thanks to Momma's strict code of conduct and Mr. Fennoy's reinforcement of it, I avoided a lot of problems.

A few weeks after that, a coach from a top school showed up at our front door and offered me and Momma money to sign that university's letter of intent. I stood at the door with my mouth open as he made the offer. How did he find out where I lived, I wondered. Why was he offering us money?

Momma wasn't fazed by it. She was insulted by the assumption that because we were poor, we could be bribed. She dealt with him the same way she had the man from the Nation of Islam—politely but firmly. "We're not interested in your money," she told the coach. "Jackie will make a decision based on what's best for her, not money. Thank you." She shut the door.

I spent a day in Champaign-Urbana talking to coaches at Illinois, but quickly eliminated the school from my list. The place just didn't excite me. I also visited Madison, Wisconsin, and talked with Loren Seagrave, the very nice track coach there, whom I'd gotten to know over the years at AAU meets. Though I liked him a lot, Wisconsin was too cold for me. After suffering through all those bitter winters in St. Louis, I was anxious to go to someplace warm. I also eliminated schools that wouldn't let me continue to play two sports. UCLA met my criteria in all categories and was always my first choice.

My father didn't want to hear that I was considering going any place *but* UCLA. He'd been a fan of John Wooden and the UCLA men's basketball teams of the 1960s and 1970s.

I felt that way about the women's program. I'd followed coach Billie Moore since 1976. I was impressed that she'd coached the U.S. Women's Olympic basketball team and that UCLA won the women's national championship in 1978. I also knew she really wanted me on her team. Between them, she and Colleen made a total of four trips to East St. Louis to recruit me. After one of her trips, Colleen wrote a letter to our local paper, praising the girls' sports program at Lincoln.

Daddy scraped together the money to pay for a recruiting visit to UCLA. He and I flew out there on Friday morning for a weekend stay. We'd left St. Louis on a damp, chilly morning. But the sun shone brilliantly over L.A. when our plane landed. What a paradise.

On first sight, Los Angeles was an eyeful. The mountains in the background were magnificent. But I looked at the packed freeways in wonder and horror on the ride to campus from the airport. There were so many cars, so many lanes, so many exits and a confusing jangle of interlocking highways. I'd been itching to get out into the world. But now that it looked like such a big, busy place, I wasn't sure I was ready. It intimidated me. If I decided to go to UCLA, I told myself, I wouldn't venture far from the Westwood neighborhood surrounding the school.

We toured the campus with an athletic department official. When the tour was done, Daddy and I met briefly with the women's athletic director, Judith Holland. Then Daddy bid me farewell for the weekend. "Here's my number in case you need to reach me," he said. "You're on your own. That's how it will be when you get to college, so I'm not going to hang around and watch over you."

That trip was the best gift my father ever gave me. During that weekend on campus I got a different, less-threatening view of city life and freeway traffic from the passenger seat of Billie Moore's 300Z sports car. When we stopped for a Fatburger, I felt like I was having an authentic Los Angeles experience. I met the other coaches and stayed in the dorm with Susie Swenson, a point guard. She was friendly and very enthusiastic about the team and the school. Getting to know her and the rest of the team made me more comfortable with the idea of living so far away from home. I knew I'd have lots of friends. By the end of the weekend, UCLA and Los Angeles didn't seem so daunting. I knew I could succeed and be happy there.

To my surprise, the letter-of-intent signing back at school was a media event. Several newspaper photographers and reporters showed up for the occasion. Deborah Thurston committed to UCLA as well, so we both signed the same day. We had no idea anyone would make such a fuss. Neither of us bothered to dress up that day, showing up for school as usual in jeans and T-shirts. Mr. Fennoy sat us beside each other at a big table in the library and put a blue and yellow Nike track shoe and a basketball on the table in front of us, for set decoration. As we signed our names at the bottom of the letter, the flashbulbs popped.

Mr. Fennoy gave me a big hug when it was over. "You've done it all at this level," he said. "Now it's time for a new challenge. I know you're ready to meet it."

Momma was elated. Her dream for me had come true. "This is what I've always wanted for you," she said as she kissed me after school that evening. "A college education and a chance to make something out of yourself."

Some people in East St. Louis thought I was biting off more than I could chew by turning down schools close to home to venture far away. At school, some of my classmates were a Greek chorus of negativity. I overheard them talking about me when I walked by.

"Why she gotta go all the way out there?"

"That school's gonna be hard."

"She won't make it. Watch and see. She'll be back."

Some of it was jealousy. I'd gotten my first taste of that in tenth grade when I dislocated my elbow in a volleyball game against Eastside. I'd run summer track with some of the girls on that team and considered them friends, even though we played for rival senior high schools. But as I was being carried out in tears and severe pain, several of them laughed and cheered. One girl shouted, "That's what she gets for trying to do everything!"

I was voted "Most Popular" in the senior class poll, but when the teachers announced that I was also voted "Most Likely to Succeed," my popularity plummeted among some girls. I'd always felt that most people respected me for doing well in sports. But the reaction to the voting proved I was wrong. Usually the class valedictorian was voted "Most Likely to Succeed." The girls who objected to my selection said a female athlete wasn't likely to succeed at anything. I was highly insulted. Even though I'd already achieved a lot on the national level athletically, had a 3.5 grade point average, ranked thirteenth in the class, and had received several athletic scholarship offers, some people still considered me a dumb athlete. I think a lot of them were hoping I wouldn't succeed.

Many adults were just as bad. "There's no way you can go to California and be successful," one man said to me in the store after reading in the paper that I signed a letter of intent to UCLA.

I just smiled and continued my shopping. But the comments made me angry and they hurt my feelings. Here were black people implying that because I was a black girl from a small city I couldn't handle myself in a big place like Los Angeles. Why did people have to be so negative and small-minded? Why couldn't they be happy for me and wish me well? I wanted to ask them: When have *you* traveled anywhere outside of East St. Louis? When did *you* enroll in UCLA to find out what it was like?

Mr. Fennoy reminded me not to let anyone limit my ambitions. "Those people aren't your friends," he said. "Don't let them make you doubt yourself."

My mother let me vent about it for a long time one night while I sat in the kitchen. "Some people just hate to see anybody else get ahead," she said. "But when you're off at college doing well, they'll still be here."

My father was proud that both Al and I were going to college, felt it was a real tribute to him and my mother. Which it was. On the plane trip back from Los Angeles he'd told me, "I'm not worried about you. You'll make it out there because you can do anything you put your mind to."

As much as I appreciated the trip and his support, how-

ever, I didn't want or feel I needed Daddy's advice anymore. Part of it was teenage rebelliousness and arrogance.
But a bigger part of it was anger over things I'd witnessed
in our home. Daddy had changed. When he came home
drunk, he was verbally abusive to my mother. It upset me
to see him act like that and to hear the arguments and
angry words. His behavior got worse over the years. Initially the arguments only happened occasionally. Pretty
soon, every conversation between my parents was a full-
blown shouting match.

My feelings for Daddy were never the same after he flew
into a rage one night and knocked my trophies and medals
off two display shelves in the living room. He tried to apologize, but to me it was unforgivable. I started crying and
ran to the pile on the floor. Looking at them all shattered,
I felt like he'd shattered something inside me as well. I
gathered them up and ran into my room, not talking to
him for weeks afterward. I just couldn't understand how he
could be so mean.

Over time, resentment built up inside me. Why should I
listen to anything from him after the way he acted at home?
I never expressed any of this directly to him. Instead, my
feelings were manifested in my behavior and attitude. I
wouldn't take my father's advice about anything. I tuned
him out when he started talking. Sometimes, I left the
room when he came home.

My mother finally got fed up with his abuse and his
drinking. She decided to move out and file for divorce the
summer after I graduated from high school. I don't know
what specific thing prompted it, but one day, Momma just
decided she'd had enough. She walked into the family
room while my father wasn't home and said we were leaving. She called Della. Then, without packing a single piece
of clothing, she, Debra, Angie and I walked out the front
door, climbed into Della's car and drove away.

I understood how my mother felt. But I hated what was happening. My whole world was crumbling before my eyes. My family was tearing apart and the house that I'd grown up in was no longer my home. I didn't know what was going to happen to us.

11

A Motherless Child

As the UCLA basketball team bus drove onto the Westwood campus and turned into the parking lot at fabled Pauley Pavilion, the site of our home games and so many glorious moments in Bruin basketball history, I was feeling pretty glorious myself. No one was ready to hang my jersey from the Pavilion's rafters next to the ten championship banners; but I knew I was starting to come into my own. I'd just scored 19 points in our victory over Cal State–Long Beach.

"I really think I found my groove tonight," I told Necie Thompson, the backup center, as we hoisted our blue and maize Bruin duffel bags into her car trunk. Necie had scored 9 points and grabbed 11 rebounds.

"You sure played like it, girl," she said. She slammed the trunk shut and climbed behind the wheel.

We talked about the game all the way home. But by the time the car came to a stop in front of the Hedrick Hall dormitory, my euphoria had disappeared. After dropping me off, Necie was headed up the hill to Rieber Hall, where she and a bunch of other players would celebrate and relive every moment of the game. I wouldn't be there. I was the only team member living in Hedrick.

Each evening after basketball practice, the players who lived in the dormitories walked together from Pauley across campus to the high-rise housing units. We chatted about the day's events and laughed at each other's funny stories. When it was time for me to make that right turn into the Hedrick Hall entrance and watch my teammates continue up the sidewalk to Rieber, their laughter and excited voices echoing in the distance, I felt lonely and isolated.

And homesick. Even the weather made me nostalgic. It was frigid at home this time of year and the January night air in sunny California was chilly enough to remind me of those winter nights when our furnace broke and we had no heat in the house. I never thought I'd miss shivering and huddling around the kitchen stove with Al, Debra and Angie, but tonight I did.

Now, walking down the hall toward my dorm room, I remembered how different the aftermath of my big games at Lincoln High had been. I always floated home amid a thick mob of friends, singing, cheering and celebrating after a victory. I would burst through the front door ahead of Al, Debra and Angie, the details of the night's events already beginning to tumble out of my mouth like water from a falls. Inside, the lights were on, the television or the radio was playing and seated on the family room couch in her pajamas, robe and slippers awaiting the full report was Momma.

I opened the door to my dorm room. It was dark. My roommate was out. I turned on the light and was greeted by the framed picture of Momma that sat on my desk. One night before going out with Daddy, she'd posed in our living room in front of a gold-colored upholstered armchair. Her left hand was on her hip and her lips formed a pretty smile. She was wearing black flared pants and a gold sweater. Every teased strand of her short, black hair was in place.

Seeing Momma's picture always transported me back home to 1433 Piggott Avenue and to our conversations on the sofa. She didn't know a layup from a free throw, but after every basketball game and track meet, she listened intently and enthusiastically to my recap while Al and my sisters made sandwiches in the kitchen or watched television.

I hadn't seen Momma since that September morning when I bid her farewell at my aunt Della's house. We were living there and my parents were preparing to divorce. A few minutes before I was scheduled to leave for the St. Louis airport, she'd walked into the bedroom.

"You all packed?"

"Yep, ready to go," I said, beaming.

"Good," she said. "Well. I guess it's time to say goodbye then." My smile vanished.

"Aren't you going to the airport?"

"No. I'm afraid that your father will show up there and try to make a scene. I don't want to spoil everything for you by having a confrontation with A.J. So I'll just stay here."

The tears welled up in my eyes.

"But I wanted you to go with me and see me off," I said. "This is our big day, you know?"

"I know. I know," she said. She took my hand and led me to the side of the bed, where we sat and embraced. "I've been dreaming about this day since you were born. I really want to be there. But I think it's for the best."

I didn't think it was. I hated the idea. Tears streamed down my cheeks as she continued to explain.

She hugged me for a long time and said, "I'll be at the airport with you in spirit, just like I'll be with you at UCLA."

As I wiped away my tears, I quietly said, "Okay."

"I'm going to miss you a lot," she said. "But we'll still have our talks. I want you to call me every night. That way, it will seem like we're still together. I know you can take care of yourself out there. I love you, Jackie." Then she kissed me.

Life for my mother in the months since that conversation hadn't been easy. My father was contesting their divorce after initially agreeing to it. Momma was supporting herself, Debra and Angie on her meager salary as a nurse's assistant. At the same time, she was always having to send money to Al, who was having financial problems at college. Just a few days before, she'd written to me complaining that Debra made her angry by not doing her household chores and going out without permission. In the note, she apologized for not including any money. Al had phoned her, saying he needed money for books. She said she knew I'd understand. And I did.

My first quarter at UCLA had been trying, too. My homesickness was almost unbearable. During one of our nightly calls in November, Momma had asked me if I wanted to come home for Christmas. I put up a brave front.

"No. We have practice the day after Christmas. I'd only get to spend a week at home and I'd have to leave on Christmas Day to get back for practice. It doesn't seem worth it."

There was a long silence. Then she asked, "Aren't you homesick?" Her voice cracked. "Don't you want to come home for Christmas?"

I cried silently and had to clear my throat to keep my voice from quavering. After a pause, I said, "Uh, no. I'm not that homesick. I can wait until June to come home."

"Okay, if you're sure that's what you want to do. But if you change your mind, just let me know and I'll send money for the plane ticket. I'd love to have you home for the holidays."

I would have loved to go home. I was heartsick about not being with my family. I wanted so badly to say, "Momma, I want to come home." But I knew what a strain it would be for her to come up with $700 for a ticket. That was just about a whole month's salary.

At the instant the digits on my alarm clock switched from 8:59 to 9:00, I picked up the telephone receiver. Finally, it was time to call home. I couldn't wait to tell Momma all about the game against Cal State–Long Beach.

To avoid expensive long-distance charges, I didn't dial direct. It was after 11:00 P.M. in the Central Time Zone where my mother was; and direct-dial rates there were lower than in California. So she and I practiced an elaborate ritual every night.

"Hello, operator, this is Jackie Joyner and I'd like to make a collect call to this number and I'd like to speak to Mary Joyner," I said.

The call was merely a signal to Momma that I was in my room awaiting her call. She refused to accept the collect call, then hung up and immediately called me back. I grabbed the phone before the end of the first ring. "Hello? Momma?"

"Hi, Jackie. Everything okay?" her voice sounded nasal, as if she had a stuffy nose.

"Yeah, we had a game tonight and I played really well. It was against Cal State–Long Beach. You sound like you have a cold."

"I don't feel too good. I think it's the flu. I have a really bad headache and I'm running a temperature. I'm going to the doctor tomorrow. Do you mind if we talk tomorrow night?"

"No, that's fine. I can tell you about the game tomorrow."

"I'm so tired. I just want to go to bed now."

"Okay. Hope you feel better. I love you."

"I love you, too. Bye."

The phone rang early the next morning. It startled me and my roommate, who'd returned and was asleep in the twin bed across the room. The voice on the other end was instantly familiar. It was my aunt Della, my mother's younger sister. She sounded upset and started sniffling when I answered.

"Della? What's wrong?"

She continued to sniffle.

"It's Mary," Della said. She spoke in a whisper. I could barely hear her.

"You need to come home right away. Mary's dead."

The words hit me like a two-by-four across the face. I dropped down into the chair at my desk. My eyes went directly to Momma's picture. I couldn't believe my ears. Did Della really say Momma was dead? Surely I misunderstood her.

"What?" I asked her.

There was a long pause. Della was sobbing into the receiver. They were the moans of someone in the midst of unbearable grief. I knew then that I'd heard right. I shut my eyes.

"Oh my God! Oh my God, no!" I stared at Momma's picture as I cried.

My mother was just thirty-seven. How could she be dead? She was too young to die. She was healthy. She'd never been seriously ill while I was growing up.

"It can't be, Della. It just can't be. She *can't* be dead! I just talked to her a little while ago."

"She had a bad fever and we had to rush her to the hospital," Della explained. The words, mixed with moans and whimpers, slowly seeped out of her mouth. "The doctors think she might have had meningitis, but they don't know for sure. It just happened so fast. She started internal bleeding . . ."

I have no idea what Della said after that. All I kept hearing in my ears were the words, internal bleeding, internal bleeding, internal bleeding.

That condition was usually fatal. Ironically, it was Momma who'd told me so. She was terrified of it. When I was in high school, she never let me go to track or basketball practice after having a tooth extracted because she worried that if I started running, internal bleeding might set in. She would come home from work and tell me about patients who started bleeding internally and then died. Now the condition had claimed *her*.

Della put my mother's best friend, Joyce, on the phone. Joyce was head nurse in one of the surgical units at St. Mary's Hospital. Momma was a nurse's assistant in the same section on the fourth floor.

I asked her how Momma died. She explained that Momma wasn't quite dead. *Huh . . . what?* She was on life support, Joyce said—a respirator.

Joyce's voice was sad, but calm. "We're going to get you home right away. Don't worry about the money. Just make a reservation and call me back with the flight information and I'll pay for the ticket."

I thanked her and hung up. My roommate had heard enough to figure out something was tragically wrong. She walked across the room and put her arm around me. As I cried, I clutched Momma's picture to my chest.

The plane ride was pure torture. It seemed to take forever to get to St. Louis. I couldn't eat or drink anything. Awful thoughts and questions tumbled around inside my

Named after Jacqueline Kennedy, I was the first baby girl of the Joyner family. But my grandmother had grander aspirations for me, predicting that someday I would be "the first lady of something."
COURTESY OF DELLA GRAY

Initially, my parents didn't want me to play basketball because they considered it unfeminine. They changed their minds when they realized how much I enjoyed it and everyone told them how good I was. PHOTO BY JAMES A. FINLEY/FROM THE AUTHOR'S COLLECTION

My mother, Mary, gave birth to me when she was only eighteen. That's the age I was when this photo of us was taken at a reception honoring me and my Lincoln High teammates for winning the 1980 girls' state basketball championship. People often said she and I looked like sisters.
FROM THE AUTHOR'S COLLECTION

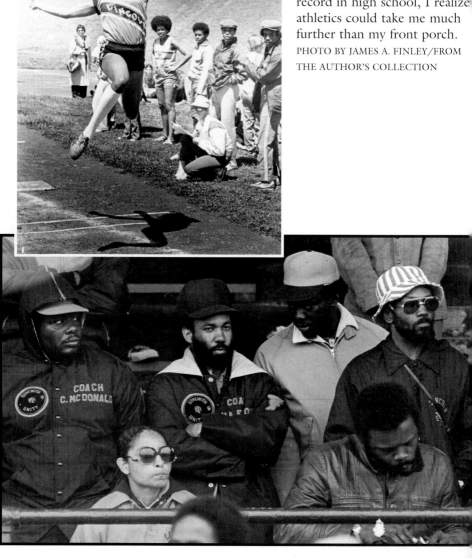

I started leaping off my front porch for fun when I was in grammar school. But when I broke the state girls' long jump record in high school, I realize athletics could take me much further than my front porch. PHOTO BY JAMES A. FINLEY/FROM THE AUTHOR'S COLLECTION

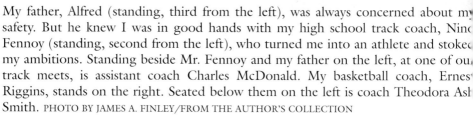

My father, Alfred (standing, third from the left), was always concerned about my safety. But he knew I was in good hands with my high school track coach, Ninc Fennoy (standing, second from the left), who turned me into an athlete and stoked my ambitions. Standing beside Mr. Fennoy and my father on the left, at one of our track meets, is assistant coach Charles McDonald. My basketball coach, Ernes Riggins, stands on the right. Seated below them on the left is coach Theodora Ash Smith. PHOTO BY JAMES A. FINLEY/FROM THE AUTHOR'S COLLECTION

My mother did exercises every night to maintain her hourglass figure and was always the picture of health. But she died suddenly during my freshman year in college. When I got the news, I clutched the frame holding this photograph of her as I cried in my dorm room.
FROM THE AUTHOR'S COLLECTION

In addition to refining my basketball skills, UCLA women's basketball coach Billie Moore (pointing) gave me plenty of emotional support after my mother's death.
COURTESY OF THE UCLA ATHLETIC DEPARTMENT

My brother, Al, has always loved the spotlight. When he won the gold medal in the triple jump and I won the silver in the heptathlon at the 1984 Olympics, he basked in the attention. PHOTO BY JAMES A. FINLEY/FROM THE AUTHOR'S COLLECTION

Over time, Bobby Kersee became my confidant as well as my coach. During a trip to Japan for a track meet in 1982, as a joke I told a woman who was flirting with him that Bobby was my husband. Four years later, it was no joke. DUOMO PHOTOGRAPHY/FROM THE AUTHOR'S COLLECTION

My parents' marriage was rocky, and for several years after my mother died,
I was angry with my father. But we eventually reconciled.
PHOTO BY TONY DUFFY/COURTESY OF ALLSPORT

My joy over winning the heptathlon
gold medal and setting a world record
at the 1988 Olympics was quickly
shattered by speculation that I used
performance-enhancing drugs.
PHOTO BY TONY DUFFY/COURTESY OF
ALLSPORT

I got off to a flying start during the long jump at the 1991 World Championships . . .

. . . But I was nagged by ailments. Al and Bob Forster, my physical therapist, had to help me walk off the field because I twisted my ankle en route to winning.

Eventually, an injury did me in at the 1991 Worlds. I was forced to withdraw from the heptathlon after pulling my hamstring during the 200 meters. PHOTO BY TONY DUFFY/COURTESY OF ALLSPORT

For too many years, I didn't take my asthma condition seriously. But by 1995 I'd learned my lesson. As much as I hated wearing this breathing mask during the 800 meters at the U.S. Championships, I also knew the pollen in the air that day could trigger a fatal attack if I didn't.

PHOTO BY KIRBY LEE/THE SPORTING IMAGE

Monica Seles and I have been through a lot together since she hired Bobby to improve her strength and conditioning in 1993. I consoled her while she recovered from being stabbed, and she was with me and Bobby the night I almost died during an asthma attack. Here we are, healthy and happy, in 1995 with Sheryl Swoopes at a Women's Sports Foundation dinner. COURTESY OF VALARIE FOSTER head as I stared out the window and wiped away the tears. After hearing my mother was dead, and then being jolted with the information she was still technically alive, I didn't know what to think. Was there any hope of her regaining consciousness? Part of me knew I'd never speak to my mother again. But another part, the little girl who now felt all alone in the world, prayed desperately for it.

What was meningitis? It sounded so gruesome. How could it have overtaken her so fast? Had someone made a mistake? Had she suffered? Had she said anything? I kept imagining her in the ambulance and then in the hospital bed. The picture wouldn't leave my mind. It tormented me.

My racing thoughts turned to the rest of my family. Della sounded awful. How was Al taking the news? I should have called him, but I didn't think of it. How were Angie and Debra coping? Were they with Momma when it happened? Where was Daddy? What was going to happen to us now?

Mostly, I wondered why this had happened to my mother, after all she'd been through in her life. Was God punishing me by taking her away? I replayed in my head that conversation with her about not coming home for Christmas. She was so sad about my not coming home. If I could just go back in time . . . make a different choice. I should have followed my heart and gone home. But no, I had to act like I was so strong, pretending not to be home-sick.

Endlessly, I berated myself for making the decision I had. I'd missed out on Christmas and forfeited the opportunity to be with my mother one last time, all because I'd been too proud. Now, she was unconscious, hanging to life by the thinnest of threads. An overpowering sense of regret washed over me. I'd never been so sad and so sorry about anything.

The sun was setting as the plane touched down at Lambert Field, the St. Louis airport. It was about 5:30 in the afternoon when my aunt Marcella greeted me at the gate. She was dabbing away her tears with a tissue.

As we drove to East St. Louis, I stared blankly out the window into the distance. Cars, buildings and road signs whizzed past, but I noticed none of it. I was lost in my sorrow.

The temperature outside was right around freezing when we stepped out of the car at the hospital parking lot. An ache burned inside my stomach. As we rushed through the sliding glass door and entered the hospital, my throat and eyes started burning as well. I wanted to go straight to Momma's side. But Joyce wanted to talk to me first.

The despair was palpable as the elevator doors opened to the fourth floor. Most of the nurses and orderlies who worked with my mother had gathered on the floor after their shifts ended at 3:00 that afternoon to hold a vigil. Marcella walked beside me and put her arm around my shoulder as we greeted Eva Wren, Helen Sandkuhl, Eula McKinley and Eula Royer and the rest of Momma's friends on our way to a small room at the end of the hall. Although there were dozens of people standing around the nurses' stations and milling around the hallways, it was strangely quiet on the floor. Everyone was still dressed in their white, green and blue hospital uniforms. They all wore name badges and sad expressions. Most of them looked just like I felt: grief-stricken and dazed.

It was the same way in the crowded room at the end of the hallway where the rest of the family was waiting. As I walked in, I forced a smile to my lips. I don't know why I thought it was necessary to smile. I couldn't keep it up for long. The first face I saw was Al's. He'd been at a track meet when he got the news. Della, Al, Debra and Angie ran to me. We hugged and cried. I also hugged my mother's uncles, Albert and Joseph Rainey. Everyone had bloodshot eyes from crying all day. Daddy was there, too. Rev. Owens was consoling us when Momma's doctor, Dr. Rene Julien, and Joyce came into the room. Joyce walked over to the couch and stood beside us. Her eyes were red but she was completely composed.

"What happened? When can I see Momma?" I said.

"Your mother developed a really bad bacterial infection," Dr. Julien said. "We think it was meningitis, but we're not positive."

Dr. Julien said she started running a very high fever as the bacteria infected her and quickly spread throughout her body. She'd experienced a lot of bleeding internally and externally and it had caused swelling all over her body. He told us she was on a respirator, which was keeping her body alive. "She's suffered irreversible brain damage," Dr. Julien said. "Her body is still functioning, but essentially, she's dead. I'm really sorry. There was nothing we could do."

Joyce looked at all of us. "When you go in to see her you'll see that she has a pulse. But the machines she's connected to are the things keeping her body going. Mary can't do it for herself because her brain is dead."

I'd been nurturing the irrational hope that my mother had a chance to recover. But Joyce's and Dr. Julien's words foreclosed any possibility that we'd all wake up from this nightmare and Momma would be alive again. For everyone standing there, Joyce's words were like the irrevocable locking of a door. The Mary Joyner we all knew—my mother, and my life's greatest inspiration—was gone.

Angie and Debra, sitting on opposite sides of Al, burst into tears and collapsed into his arms. They were completely consumed with grief. I just wanted to see my mother's face one last time.

"Can I see her?" I asked.

"Yes, but first I need to prepare you for what you're going to see when you go in the room," Joyce said.

I couldn't take much more of it. The bad news just wouldn't end.

"Your mother doesn't look the way you remember her. The bleeding caused her skin color to change and made her body swell. It also made her skin very fragile. You'll have to be careful if you touch her because in her condition, the skin ruptures easily. This is a horrible, horrible disease."

Dr. Julien explained that her disease, whatever it was, was probably highly contagious. Momma was isolated from other patients. Anyone who came in contact with her had to wear protective clothing and had to take an antibiotic pill.

Al and I went in together. The protective gear made us look like we were ready to assist in surgery. A white shower cap covered my head. I pulled on the baggy white pants over my jeans and tied on a long white gown over my sweater. I covered my shoes with white footies and my hands with white plastic gloves. After swallowing the pill, I closed my eyes, took a long, deep breath and walked with Joyce and Al to Momma's room.

Though she'd tried, Joyce could never have prepared me for what I saw when I walked into my mother's room. When I saw Momma, I was devastated. My knees buckled. Joyce and Al caught me as I collapsed into a heap of tears and sobs.

The person lying in that hospital bed looked nothing like the beautiful smiling woman in the picture on my desk. The disease had ravaged her. She looked as if she'd gained 100 pounds. Her now-swollen head was the size of a big honeydew melon. Her lovely face was stretched out of proportion and the caramel-colored skin on her face, neck and hands had turned as black as licorice. Her nose was packed with white gauze. Her eyes were shut. She looked as if she was in a deep, deep sleep.

Momma's lips were taped around the respirator tube. She was also attached to a jangle of intravenous tubes. They pumped in the nutrients, antibiotics and other drugs that staved off the final vestiges of death. Half the room was taken up by assorted machines monitoring her vital signs.

Looking at her lying there, I ached all over. She was so helpless. I wondered if she was in pain. I wanted so badly to do something to comfort her but there was nothing to do now. She couldn't feel my kiss or hear me say I loved her. I couldn't even caress her because I was afraid I might tear her skin. It broke my heart. I was crying hysterically. Someone carried me out of the room.

I couldn't imagine the agony my mother had endured from the time the paramedics wheeled her into the emergency room at 5:00 A.M. With the infection racing through her and her temperature soaring, the ER staff had wrapped her in a green plastic cooling blanket that looked like a sleeping bag. She was conscious and alert but the internal bleeding had already begun. Within an hour, her eyes had a vacant, glassy look. She was losing consciousness. They moved her to intensive care, but her condition rapidly worsened.

Every doctor in the hospital came by the room to consult with Dr. Julien about a diagnosis and treatment. No one had ever encountered anything like it. The fever and flulike symptoms suggested meningitis, but others didn't match. Not until several days later did they discover the cause of death. Momma had contracted a deadly bacterial infection that led to a rare condition known as Waterhouse-Friderichsen syndrome.

In ICU—hours before I would arrive—Momma's skin began to darken. Then, shortly before 8:00 A.M., one of the monitors blurted out a loud, long beep. The nurse in the room screamed "Code Blue!" Momma was dying.

Joyce and a half-dozen others rushed to ICU, but it was too late. A technician wheeled in the electroencephalograph to check for brain activity. The only mark on Momma's EEG was an unwaveringly straight horizontal line, indicating total brain death. The doctors immediately put her on the respirator. But over the next twelve hours, her condition never improved. The EEG readings were always the same—a long, flat line.

Back in the family room, Al and I finally managed to compose ourselves. But Debra and Angela continued to cry and cry. They couldn't stop. I really felt sorry for them. They were awfully young to have to deal with something like this.

Actually, none of us was exactly grown up. Al had just turned twenty-one, I was eighteen and Angie and Debra were seventeen and sixteen, respectively. Despite the bad relations between him and my mother, my father was at the hospital with us. But Al and I felt responsible for our little sisters. And seeing how upset they were made us realize how important it was for us to be strong. As we hugged our sisters, my brother and I looked into each other's eyes for emotional support.

The question now was: What to do? Joyce came over to the sofa where we were sitting and pulled up a chair. She said it was time to make a decision. Della was seated nearby and Rev. Owens stood next to her. He led us in a prayer for strength. Then he advised us to turn the respirator off.

"Children, it's time to let your mother go," the minister said. "Her spirit's already gone. What you see in there is just her body. Mary is already in heaven."

Angie and Debra just lost it. They were hysterical. Al and I held them. Tears were streaming down Della's cheeks.

Through it all, Joyce remained stoic. "Mary's never suffered a day in her life," she said. "By keeping her connected to the respirator all you're doing is prolonging her agony and yours. Being hooked up to machines is no way to live, and Mary wouldn't want it."

But who would make the decision? Who would tell the doctors to turn off the respirator and let what was left of my mother die? Given the deterioration of his relationship with her, Daddy had no say in the matter. Della bowed out, saying the decision was up to the children. Poor Al had his hands full consoling my sisters. He looked at me.

I didn't know what to do. Even though she was only alive because of the machine, I told myself, at least some part of Momma is still with us. But the more I thought about it, the more I realized she wasn't really living anymore. That was the point Joyce was making.

After a long, tense silence, I looked at Al, Debra and Angie. We all held hands. Tears started to well up in my eyes, my lips were quivering and my voice cracked.

"This is the hardest thing in the world to say. But, I think we should take her off the machine," I said. "I don't want to do it. But we have to do what's best for her. We'll never be able to talk to her again. We can't even touch her. Leaving her like this would be torture. If we disconnect it and it's meant for her to breathe on her own and live, she will. If not, she'll go to heaven and find peace."

Al agreed, "That's what she'd want."

Debbie and Angie nodded slowly. We embraced each other. One at a time, everyone went in to say good-bye to Momma. The process took a long time. Everyone had to put on white clothes again. People cried and consoled each other. More of my mother's colleagues and friends came into the family room and told us how sorry they were.

Finally, it was my turn to bid my mother farewell. I dreaded this moment. Slowly, I walked in the room and approached her bed. I looked at her for a long time, gently stroking her arm. I still couldn't believe this was happening. The lump in my throat burned. The tears stung my eyes. I could barely talk. I bent over and whispered in her ear: "Momma, I'll never forget you. I love you and I'll miss you. Rest in peace."

We were all in the family room and most of the crowd was still scattered along the corridor when Joyce walked down the hall and into Momma's room to supervise the respirator shutdown. All of a sudden, a woman's anguished voice echoed down the hall, piercing the silence. It was the head ICU nurse whose job it was to turn off the respirator. She ran out of my mother's room wailing, "I can't do it! I just can't do it to my friend! They're not going to make me do it, Mary!" When we heard her, all of us started crying.

Joyce stepped over to the respirator. She glanced upward. "Lord, this isn't what I planned for this lady. This must be your plan."

Then she looked down at Momma. "Old friend, you know I love you. This is the last thing I get to do for you."

She flipped the switch to the off position. It was 10:00 P.M. After several minutes, the pulse monitor flatlined. The doctor pronounced Momma dead at 10:30.

Della and Marcella led us out of the hospital an hour later, after we signed the pile of medical papers Joyce shoved in front of us. It was a clear, crisp frigid night. But everything looked foggy to me. I felt lost and helpless. Like an explorer who's lost her compass, I had nothing to steer by.

My mother meant everything to me. She was my confidante, my teammate and my best friend. Whose words would pump me up when I was deflated? Whose shoulder would I cry on? And who on earth would listen so patiently while I yammered on and on about my athletic feats?

Irrationally, I blamed my father for her death. If he hadn't

been so mean to her and caused her so much pain and tor-
ment, she might have been strong enough to fight off the
infection. And now that she was gone, I didn't know if I'd
ever be able to forget what he'd put us all through.

Immediately after Momma's funeral, an avalanche of
problems, responsibilities and decisions fell on my family.
The top priority was providing for Debra and Angie. Al
wasn't sure he wanted to return to Arkansas State; and I
was considering taking the semester off and getting a job.

"Oh, no. Mary would have a fit if you and Alfrederick
didn't go back to college," Della said when I told her what
we were thinking. She sat us down on the sofa in her living
room and looked us straight in the eyes. "I know it will be
hard. But you just have to get through it. The last thing
Mary would want is for you all to quit school."

Della invited Angie and Debra to live with her while they
finished high school. We learned that Momma had taken
out a life insurance policy on herself and named me bene-
ficiary. I don't know for sure, but I suspect she purchased
the policy with the money she made me give her from my
earnings that summer I worked at the movie theater. The
policy proceeds only added up to about $12,000. But the
sum was enough to support my sisters through graduation,
with some left over for Al and me. It was just like Momma
to make sure we were protected in case something happened to her. Our welfare was always her first concern.
Knowing that she left the money to me made me realize
how much confidence she had in me.

She saw in me the possibility to have the things she
missed because she got pregnant as a teenager and had to
drop out of school to raise her family. I always felt I was living not only my dreams for success, but hers as well.
Dreams that she wasn't able to realize. Dreams of going to
college and finding a better life in the world beyond East
St. Louis. I considered that money a message from

Momma that she was relying on *me* to make sure those dreams didn't die with her.

As I packed my bags to return to UCLA, I was a jumble of emotions. I wanted to be strong and self-reliant. But I wasn't. Though I had the love and support of Della, Marcella, Joyce and my brother and sisters, and though I carried Momma's spirit and energy around in my heart, I felt terribly insecure. I felt like a motherless child.

12

Mourning

I bravely tried to pick up where I'd left off at UCLA. I rejoined the basketball team and threw myself into classes, practice and our games.

I'd missed only one game, a loss to Louisiana Tech, while I was at home. Coach Moore was sympathetic and supportive throughout the ordeal. At one point during my mother's funeral, I looked around the church and to my surprise, there was Coach sitting in one of the pews. She'd flown all the way from California. I never guessed a college coach would take the time to do that for an athlete, especially in the middle of the season. I hugged her and thanked her when she came over to express her sympathy.

Later, I called her to discuss my plans. Although I was a starter on the team, she advised me to withdraw from school and take the semester off to grieve and heal. "The team needs you and will miss your contribution," she said. "But I think the best thing for you would be to take some time off. We'll keep a spot open for you next season."

Although I decided to return to UCLA and finish my freshman year, it meant a lot to know that she was willing to put my welfare ahead of her own needs. It took a week or two for me to get back in the groove. I didn't start the first game back, against Delta State. It was just as well. During the short time I was on the court I wasn't very effective. I didn't score a single point, though I managed to get three rebounds. The team performed just fine without me and we won easily, 90–65.

Necie Thompson, who played center and power forward and was a freshman like me, tried to bolster my spirits. She dragged me along on shopping trips and to the movies. Necie was from Cerritos, a community just south of Los Angeles. On weekends, we drove to her house and spent time with her family. The house was always filled with laughter and the aroma of food cooking. The Thompsons made me feel welcome, like a part of the family. It was nice to experience that kinship so far from my own home and family, especially after Momma died. I went to church and ate dinner with the Thompsons before going back to the dorm on Sunday evenings. When it was time to leave, Mrs. Thompson wouldn't let me out of the house unless I accepted a loaf of banana bread, warm from her oven, wrapped in aluminum foil. She didn't have to twist my arm.

I couldn't eat too much of it on Sunday night, because Coach Moore conducted a team weigh-in every Monday. Except for one time in high school when I had to lose a few pounds to get ready for track season, I've always been able to control my weight.

But Coach Moore's hard-nosed philosophy kept even me on my toes. A disciplinarian and a fanatic about conditioning, she said weight control had to be a team effort because basketball is a team sport. So, even though I didn't have a weight problem, I was treated like someone who did because some of my teammates were overweight.

Every Monday afternoon before practice, we stood in line in our practice uniforms, barefoot and anxious. The heaviest girls stripped down to their underwear to be as light as possible. One by one, we stepped up to the scale. It was so tense in that room during weigh-ins, you'd have thought the scale was a guillotine. The weekly ritual never failed to be foreboding. While an assistant adjusted the scale, Coach Moore stood in the background, expressionless. She peered over our shoulders at the numbers and recorded them on the sheet attached to her clipboard. After the last girl stepped off the scale, we stood around, fidgeting while she silently added up the total and compared it to her targets. It was like being on trial for murder and waiting to hear the jury's verdict. For each pound we were overweight as a team, we had to run a minute after practice.

Our worst nightmare came true one day during freshman year. Coach Moore finished her calculations and looked around the room. "This is terrible! You're thirty pounds over. After practice, it's suicides for thirty minutes," she said, pointing to the door. "Everybody out on the court!"

Coach was furious. We were miserable. We knew practice would be a back-breaker and the running would kill us. Just as we feared, she treated us with disgust during practice. It turned out to be more of a scrimmage than a practice. She drilled us on offense and defense from one end to the other, back and forth. First we played offense, then hustled back on defense. By the end of the session, I felt as spent as if I'd played the first half of a competitive game. I looked it, too. My jersey was drenched. But the fun had just begun. Now we had thirty minutes of suicide drills.

They're called suicides for a reason. Half the team lined up shoulder-to-shoulder on one end of the court under the basket, while the other half did the same on the other end. In the drill, we ran from the end of the court to the center line, then back to the end, then up to the three-quarter line, then back to the end. Next time, we ran the full length before returning to the end. We had only thirty seconds to complete a cycle and we had to repeat them continuously, without a break, for thirty minutes.

It was a miserable experience, even when you were in top condition. That day, my lungs and stomach started burning after about ten minutes. I couldn't get enough oxygen, no matter how much I panted. My legs felt like lead and began to sting at the joints. My sides ached. My whole body became as hot as if I were running inside a 100-degree oven. Sweat dripped from every pore, into my eyes and ears and down my neck, back, arms and legs. I felt as if I were ready to collapse. And at that point I wasn't even halfway done.

Coach Moore's words were muffled by the sound of my own labored breathing and the groaning all around me. One girl threw up. After cleaning herself up, she got back in line, knowing she'd have to make up the drills she missed at the end. The rest of us kept going despite the pain and waves of nausea. Each time we slowed down and exceeded the time limit, Coach Moore added on more time.

When it was finally over, we instinctively stooped over and grabbed our knees. Then we dropped to the gym floor, our bodies heaving furiously. Once our breathing returned to normal, we picked ourselves up and dragged our bodies off to the locker room showers.

Coach Moore wasn't always the implacable drill sergeant, though. She checked in with me periodically after practice, offering a heartfelt "How's it going?" or "Everything okay?" and a comforting smile. One day, after I'd been back for several weeks, she called me into her office and I saw her wearing a look of concern. "I'm glad to have you back, don't get me wrong," she said. "But I'm worried about you. I didn't see you cry at the funeral and I haven't seen you cry since you've been back. When something like this happens, a shocking, traumatic event, you have to unload the grief in order to put it behind you. That's why I thought you needed to take some time off."

"I'm fine. Everything's okay," I said quickly, hoping to bring a fast end to the conversation. Coach Moore didn't look convinced. But thankfully, she didn't press the issue.

"Okay, fine, if you say so. But if you ever need to talk about anything, I'm here."

I thanked her and left. Della, Joyce and Marcella had said much the same thing to me about letting everything out. They called once a week, as did my mother's brother, Uncle John, who also sent me money a couple of times during the semester. Everyone wanted to know how I was feeling, whether I needed anything, whether I wanted to talk about anything. They tried and tried to get me to open up. But I wouldn't do it. I *couldn't*.

Shortly after my mother's death, while I was still at home, I had horrifying nightmares about her. Every night for about a week, I woke up in the middle of the night and saw her walking toward me. The visions terrified me so much I couldn't get back to sleep. It got to the point where I was afraid to go to bed. I stayed up late one night and talked to Marcella about it.

"You probably are seeing Mary," she said. "But you shouldn't be afraid of her. She loved you; she wouldn't hurt you. She probably just wants to say good-bye."

After that conversation, I stopped having nightmares. But my lonely agony didn't end. I'd never allowed myself to express my profound sadness over my mother's death. From the moment I said good-bye to her that day at the hospital and walked out of her room, through her funeral and burial, I shut down emotionally. I blocked out as much of that awful day at the hospital as I could. For years I didn't know the exact date she died. I never cared to know, because I didn't want to focus on her death. Even now, I carry some of the sorrow with me. The mere thought of her death still brings tears to my eyes.

With so many people falling apart around me, I had to be strong for everyone else and to lend them my shoulder. My sisters especially needed me for that. At one point during the funeral, Angie got up and ran screaming out of the church. She ran all the way to our house on Piggott Avenue and refused to leave.

The wound Momma's death left was still raw when I returned to UCLA. But no matter how much it ached, I just couldn't let myself dwell on it. The thought of letting my guard down and confronting those emotions scared me. Yet I could feel an ocean of sorrow welling up inside me. It weighed on me more and more, day after day. I was still in deep mourning.

I tried to keep the feelings dammed. If I let even one drop seep out, I knew the gates would burst and I wouldn't be able to stop the flood of tears and pain. I was afraid it would drown me. I kept my feelings pent up for the entire spring semester and during the summer back at home. But I couldn't block out the pain forever.

Back at school for my sophomore year, toward the end of the quarter in December, I was sitting at the pregame meal in a restaurant with my teammates. We were playing a game on the road, our last one before Christmas. The conversation turned to what everyone was getting and giving as presents. One girl started talking about the presents she was giving her parents. She was laughing and smiling. Everyone was happy. But a wave of sorrow surged through me. I realized I didn't have a mother to buy presents for anymore and that there would be no more Christmases with her.

Before I could catch myself, tears filled my eyes. My throat tightened. My heart actually hurt. The sadness just overwhelmed me. I began to sob and moan out loud.

There was no use trying to fight back the tears, they were pouring out of me. My whole body was shaking. I couldn't get myself to stop crying. My teammates all jumped up and rushed to comfort me. I continued to sob for several minutes, my face buried in my hands.

I was finally crying over Momma. All of the talk about the holidays and parents had been the trigger. I remembered how just a year ago I'd wanted to be with her for the holidays but money and geography kept us apart. Now, a year later, I couldn't be with her because she was gone. The longing and sense of loss finally became unbearable.

Coach Moore and Necie led me into the bathroom. Coach Moore said she was relieved. She'd been waiting for me to break down for almost a year. Now that I had faced my grief and given in to it, I felt like my burden had been lifted. I was finally ready to move on.

13

College Life

Although I excelled in two sports at UCLA, I didn't have any trouble juggling academics and athletics. I took my classwork seriously and achieved my goal of completing my education, graduating with a degree in history in 1986, after taking the 1983–84 academic year off to train for the Olympics.

I went to class until about 2:30 every day. Then I headed to study hall, where I received tutoring at a room inside the athletic complex. I preferred individual tutoring to the group sessions. As far as I was concerned, the group meetings were a waste of time. The other athletes who participated talked and made wisecracks. I got much more accomplished in one-on-one sessions.

The basketball team practiced every afternoon from 4:00 to 6:30. Following practice and dinner, I returned to mandatory study hall from 7:30 to 9:30. I also spent Saturday mornings in the library studying, even on mornings before our games.

Attending lecture classes at UCLA was like going to the movies or a play. They were conducted in auditoriums that

held 300 people. The first time I went to one as a freshman—it was either a history or political science class—and
saw so many people, I thought I'd taken a wrong turn. Lincoln High had over 1,000 students, but there weren't
more than forty people in any one class at a time. And I
knew all my classmates and teachers. At UCLA that was
impossible. It was completely anonymous and impersonal.
Not that it really mattered. No one took attendance in
those big lectures, or called on us in classes. The professors
talked. We took notes. That was the drill. On exam sheets
we printed our names, but the most significant item, besides our answers, was our student identification numbers.
The ID number was the only way to find my test score
when the pages full of numbers were posted outside the
professor's door.

I didn't mind being just another number. I really didn't
want the teachers to know too much about me. My older
teammates warned me not to advertise the fact that I was
an athlete. Don't wear your sweats to class, they told me.
And whatever you do, they said, don't tell the teaching assistants—who met with small groups of students twice a
week to review in detail the topics covered in lectures—that
you're a basketball player. My teammates said some teachers resented athletes and gave them a harder time in class
because they expected us to be lazy dummies looking for
special treatment and passing grades.

Their warnings scared me so much, I was jittery in my
classes the first couple of weeks. I sat there in my jeans and
logo-less shirts and sweaters, trying to be inconspicuous,
furiously taking down every word the professor said. My
teammates had also scared me into studying hard. That's
one reason I spent so much time in the library and with the
tutors. Coach Moore scheduled most of the games requiring extended travel on holidays and quarter breaks so that
we didn't miss much class. Still, with daily practices and

games twice a week, I wanted to stay on top of my studies and not get behind. Above all, I didn't want to flunk out of school and have to go back home and face those people who told me I couldn't make it at UCLA.

As time went on during freshman year, it was harder to maintain my anonymity. Even though I was a first-year player, I was a starter and I played very well. After the Delta State game, I got back into the groove. I played my best games of the season over the next month. Against San Diego State, I scored 15 points and had 8 rebounds; I piled up 14 points and 7 rebounds in the game with Arizona, and collected 18 points and 7 rebounds when we played Arizona State. Increasingly, my name was mentioned and my picture appeared in stories about the women's team in the campus paper, the *Daily Bruin*. Also, six of our games during the season were doubleheaders with the men's team. We played first, and their games followed. Attendance for our games was higher than usual on those occasions, and more students saw me. I was a Freshman All-America in basketball and received the All-University Athlete Award, given to UCLA's top all-around athlete, as a sophomore in 1982 and as a junior in 1983. Upon returning to campus for the 1984–85 school term to finish my degree requirements after the Olympics, I was voted All-University Athlete for a third time and won the Broderick Cup as the nation's best female collegiate athlete. With all of that publicity, more and more people recognized me. But I didn't suffer because of it. Quite the contrary. During those years, as I walked from one building to another or when I entered a classroom, a few students said, "Nice game," "Congratulations," or "Hi, Jackie."

Despite what my teammates told me, I didn't think being recognized was so bad. No one said a negative word to me—at least not to my face. And I didn't feel that teachers singled me out or treated me any differently in class. I had great relationships with many of my history and speech professors. I earned As, Bs and a few Cs and graduated with a B average.

It was shaping up as an exciting time to be a basketball player at UCLA. The women's team was young and strong and we expected to be one of the best teams in the country for the next four years. We ended my freshman year with a 29–7 record that put us second in the Western Collegiate Athletic Conference, just one game behind Cal State–Long Beach. In the post-season national women's collegiate tournament, we surprised everyone by coming within a game of making the Final Four.

The men's team had gone to the Final Four the season before I got there and lost in the final game to Louisville. People were expecting great things from the team and coach Larry Brown in the coming years. (The team's name was subsequently deleted from the official tournament record for that year because several players were involved in NCAA rules violations.)

The guys on the team were great players and great fun to be around. When we played doubleheaders against the University of Southern California and the two Arizona schools, the men's and women's squads traveled together. We got to know each other pretty well. I felt like I was a part of one big team.

We were regarded as equals by the athletic department. We weren't treated like stepchildren, the way some women's teams at other schools were during that time. The women's team had the same privileges and used the same facilities the men's team did. We lifted weights in the same room. Our locker rooms were the same size and just as nicely appointed. We stayed in the same first-rate hotels the men did. On the road, we ate in the same restaurants, rather than in diners and fast-food joints. And, like the men, we could order anything we wanted. There were no spending limits. Money was not an issue for the basketball program. It was a far cry from my junior high school days with the Railers when I had to scrounge for nickels and dimes to afford a McDonald's hamburger. And it was light years away from the political battles at Lincoln High over practice time in the gym.

I later found out, when I joined the track team in the spring, how different being on the basketball team was from being on other UCLA teams. Basketball was a big, big deal in Westwood. Because of the winning tradition established during John Wooden's coaching tenure, a period during which the Bruins won ten NCAA Championships over twelve years, including seven consecutive titles between 1967 and 1973, the basketball teams received generous alumni and athletic department support. At most big universities, football is king. But at UCLA, football and basketball shared the throne. And because of Title IX, which required university athletic departments to give women's teams the same things they gave the men, my teammates and I shared in the riches equally.

I believe our high self-esteem contributed to our success. We had winning seasons each year I played with the Bruins. We never duplicated the success we had during my freshman year, but I believe that was mostly because both Long Beach and USC, our conference rivals, had some of the finest players in the country. LaTaunya Pollard of Long Beach set a single-season scoring record in 1983, an amazing 907 points. Cheryl Miller, the most heavily recruited female high school basketball player in the nation, joined the USC squad in 1983 and dominated on both ends of the court.

At 6' 3", she was a revelation for women's basketball and took the game to a new level. Cheryl set new standards for the big women that followed her, players such as Carla

McGhee and Lisa Leslie. What Cheryl did with a basketball was remarkable and exciting. She had Shawn Kemp's strength inside and Magic Johnson's flashy skill outside. She blocked shots and ruled the territory under the basket. She moved well without the basketball and could wear you down roaming around the court getting into position for a pass. And she had a deadly outside shot. Almost always, she was the tallest person on the court, making it nearly impossible to post up against her. You couldn't push her around. The only hope was to vex her.

Few people did it with any success. She swiped 474 rebounds in 1985 and scored 3,018 points during her college career, the third highest total in women's hoops history. Helping her were Paula and Pam McGee, known as the Twin Towers, and Cynthia Cooper.

I'm not making excuses for the Bruins, but that's what we were up against. Sophomore year, 1981–82, our record was 16–14 and we finished fourth in the conference. The next year we improved to 18–11. We finished my final season 20–10.

The USC and UCLA campuses are across the city from each other and the rivalry between the two schools is as bitter as that between Lincoln and Eastside back home. In 1985, as USC tried to win a third consecutive national title, we were the only team in the nation to beat them twice during the regular season. Those games were the Bruins' proudest moments that season. In the first game, I nagged Cheryl like a gnat. She shot just 32 percent from the floor and we narrowly beat them, 77–73. The second USC game was my best as a Bruin. I couldn't stop Cheryl, who shot 52 percent and scored 26 points. But I ruled the backboard. That night I had a double-double, 11 points and 12 rebounds. Cheryl pulled down only 7 rebounds and we escaped with a 57–56 win. The Trojans didn't three-peat;

but they were such an awesome team that when you beat them, you knew you'd beaten the very best.

My battles under the basket with Cheryl were intense. She was as tough a competitor as I was. Unlike me, she loved to talk trash on the court. In that regard, she's just like her brother Reggie, who plays for the Indiana Pacers. She was quite impressed with her talents. But she had a right to be. People often confused her flamboyance and self-confidence with arrogance. I think that was a misimpression. I got to know Cheryl off the court, when a bunch of us got together after games. We shared lots of laughs. When she took off her basketball shoes and dropped the game face, Cheryl was very funny, very friendly and she always praised the performances of other players.

The Bruin men didn't fare as well over the same span. During my sophomore year, Larry Brown left to coach the New Jersey Nets and the men's team was placed on probation by the NCAA for two years. The violations cast a pall over the program for several years afterward. It was a real shame because there was so much talent on that team. I respected the athletic prowess of Rod Foster, Mark Eaton, Michael Holton, Cliff Pruitt, Kenny Fields and Michael Sanders.

Of all the players, I was closest to Rod. He was a little sweetie-pie. I had a crush on him before ever meeting him. Sitting on the floor at Della's house one night after graduation, while watching a UCLA men's game, I blurted out to Della and my sisters, "Oooh, I'd like to date him!" Once I got to UCLA and got to know him I admired him even more. But there was never anything romantic between us. He was just a really nice guy. I knew he had a girlfriend he seemed to care for and he talked about her all the time.

Despite what I'd said in that unguarded moment at Della's house, I probably wouldn't have dated Rod if he'd been available. He and other athletes faced temptations from other girls all the time. Most of the male athletes were extremely popular on campus. Wherever they walked, a crowd gathered. Girls fawned over them at school and waited for them outside the locker room after games, trying to get their attention. It was clear to everyone who saw them standing around wide-eyed, with enough makeup on for two people, sporting spiffy hairdos, and wearing tight pants, that they would do anything to spend time with the guys.

I saw how inconsiderate a lot of the male athletes were toward their girlfriends, making them wait or standing them up for dates, and talking disparagingly about them. I saw them go out with other girls, particularly when they were on road trips. A lot of those guys went off with girls who were waiting around after the game. They knew they could have anybody they wanted. I expressed shock at a story one football player told about his secret escapades. I knew his girlfriend and felt terrible for her. He just shrugged and said, "It's no big thing."

I vowed to keep my relationships with my male colleagues strictly platonic. There was no way I would put up with a boyfriend who took me for granted or had two or three other girls on the side. My experience in high school had made me gun-shy about relationships. It had been so emotionally draining, I decided that getting head over heels over some guy would distract me from what I wanted to do. So, if I really liked a guy, I never let him know. I just admired him from afar.

Eventually I let my guard down and started dating a guy on the track team. He was a 400-meter runner. I met him through Andre Phillips, a 400-meter hurdler who went on to win the gold medal in that event at the 1988 Olympics. He teased me about being a country girl because of the way I talked and dressed. He and Andre called me Ala, as in Alabama.

He came to my basketball games and said I was the first girl he'd ever seen who played like a guy. He seemed like a sweet guy—at first.

I moved into a dormitory next door to Rieber Hall in my sophomore year, which put me closer to the other athletes. The following year, I moved into an apartment in Culver City with my boyfriend and another female track athlete, LaShon Nedd.

Things quickly turned rocky in the relationship. Living with him night and day, I saw a different side of his personality. We were completely incompatible. He was selfish and possessive, while I was stubborn and independent. He was also insecure. He was a speedy quarter miler who garnered his share of victories and awards. Yet, the more successful I became, the more he resented me. He could deal with me as a girlfriend, but not as his athletic equal. Every time I achieved something in basketball or track, he tried to make me feel like I shouldn't be proud of it. He belittled my accomplishments and criticized me in front of our friends. He didn't like the fact that I spent so much time at practice and ordered me to stop. I just laughed, which infuriated him.

We argued a lot. Several times, the arguments turned into fights. He would hit me or shove me and I'd punch him back. The first time he did it, I was startled. But I quickly retaliated. There was no way I was going to let a man hit me. I wasn't a battered woman or anything close to it. But I didn't like where the relationship was headed.

I would have broken up with him, but he became seriously ill in the fall of 1982 and had to leave school for a semester. I visited him for a weekend at his parents' home during his recuperation. He looked awful and frail. When he came back to UCLA in the spring of 1983, although I no longer had romantic feelings for him, I let him move back in because he didn't have a place to stay. But I felt uncomfortable about it.

He tried to resume his track career, but his illness had wiped out the bulk and strength he once had. He couldn't run the 400 in less than 47 seconds, which was nearly 3 seconds slower than most world-class competitors at the time. It was sad. His athletic career was finished.

In the meantime, Al, who had continued to do well as a triple jumper in college, was thinking of coming to L.A. to train for the Olympics. I strongly encouraged him. I knew Bobby Kersee, the UCLA assistant coach, could help him improve technically, and would instill the discipline Al still lacked. I had an ulterior motive. I knew Al would be a buffer between me and my boyfriend in the apartment. I wanted to make sure he didn't get the idea that we were becoming a couple again just because we were roommates. The three of us lived together from 1983 through the Olympics. I ended the relationship and moved out right after the Games were over.

Growing up, I'd told my mother everything. After she died, I didn't feel comfortable discussing my personal problems with anyone else. So, as much as the deterioration of my relationship with my college beau weighed on me, I didn't confide in my friends. Even when we started fighting, I didn't tell my closest girlfriends about it. I didn't even tell Al the details when he came to live with me. All I said was, "He's living in the apartment, too, but our relationship is over. I'm about to break up with him."

I didn't think I'd ever find someone in whom I could confide the way I had with Momma. When I got back to school after her funeral, I got a message that Coach Bobby Kersee wanted to see me. The note puzzled me. As I walked across campus to the track after my last class of the day, I wondered why he wanted to see me. The basketball season hadn't ended. Furthermore, he wasn't my track coach. He worked with the sprinters and hurdlers. I was a multi-eventer and a long jumper. My first thought was: I must be in trouble.

Since our first meeting at the Olympic Trials in Eugene a year earlier, I hadn't thought much about Bobby. And because I played basketball during the fall and winter quarters, I hadn't had any contact with him since arriving at UCLA. But I'd heard from the girls who trained with him that he was a terror. He's mean, they said. He yells and screams until you want to strangle him, they said. He works you to death.

As soon as I entered the stadium I heard a man shouting, "Let's go!" I looked across the field, letting my eyes follow the sound. They stopped at a thin, dark-skinned, bearded man wearing a T-shirt, shorts and a baseball cap. It was Bobby. He didn't have a bullhorn, but his voice carried across the field as if he did. He clutched a clipboard in one hand and a stopwatch in the other. He was putting Alice Brown through hurdle drills. She was still at Cal State–Northridge, the school Bobby had left in August to come to UCLA that year; but Bobby continued to help her train.

The dark sunglasses he wore made him look even more dictatorial. I walked over to him, anticipating bad news or a furious tirade. Instead, his countenance softened when he saw me. A small gold cross dangling on the chain around his neck glistened in the sunlight. In a low voice, he said, "I just wanted to tell you how sorry I was to hear about your mother passing."

I was relieved, and taken aback. "Thanks, I appreciate that," I said.

"Have you decided what you're going to do about school?" he asked.

"I'm not sure yet. I'll see how it goes."

"Well, I know what you're going through. I lost my mom, too—when I was fourteen. So, if you ever want to talk about anything . . ."

"Oh, sorry to hear that," I said.

". . . Before you make any decisions about your future, please come and talk to me. Will you do that?"

"Okay, thanks."

How thoughtful. It opened my eyes. Here was the man everyone had described as a monster being very considerate to me. He wasn't my coach. He didn't have to concern himself with my problems. Yet he did. He was offering to help me, just like he was helping Alice Brown. That told me a lot about the kind of man Bobby Kersee was. I saw a sensitive and considerate side to a man everyone told me was mean and brutal.

14

Frustration

Going from basketball season to track season was like going from the penthouse to the outhouse, in terms of privileges. When the basketball team traveled, we stayed at Marriotts and Hyatt Regencys. The track team checked into Days Inns and Motel 6s. On basketball road trips, we ate in restaurants and ordered whatever we wanted. When I was with the track team, I got $3 for breakfast—including tip! We ate most of our meals at Denny's or a fast-food outlet.

But for all my complaints about the lowly status of track athletes, our facilities were cushier and grander than anything Lincoln Park or Parsons Field could offer. The university had a separate track and field facility, Drake Stadium, that was on par with some college football arenas. The seats were sturdy aluminum, and the steps were wide concrete. Quite a contrast with the Parsons stadium, which creaked as people moved up and down its stairs. A dozen female runners assaulting the flights all at once didn't disturb Drake at all.

As I jogged around the spongy Tartan track, the only

obstacles in my path were the overachieving joggers who pooh-poohed the outside lanes reserved for novices. No need to use landmarks and bits of debris as starting and finishing points at UCLA. Distances and lanes—there were eight wide ones, rather than one narrow path—were clearly marked. The long-jump runway, high-jump setup, and shot-put and javelin areas were fine enough to host a world-class event. Shoes were available, free of charge, in unlimited supply, as were shirts, shorts and sweats.

I also had to adjust to changes in the multi-event. That spring 1981 season, two events, the 200 meters and the javelin, were added to the pentathlon, making it a heptathlon. I had to learn to throw the javelin and to brush up on my sprinting.

I wasn't the only one settling into new environs. It was a transition year for the entire track program. Bobby was starting his first year as an assistant and brought along a group of girls who transferred with him from Cal State–Northridge including Florence Griffith and Jeanette Bolden. We all had to adjust to each other.

I showed up at the track after classes in the early afternoon, squinting from the glare of the relentless sunlight. All my multi-event coach would say was, "Work on whatever you feel like."

One day, as I trudged off alone to the long-jump pit, I looked across the track and saw that Bobby was already at work with his athletes. He had an agenda every day and his athletes had to get to work right away. The more I watched Bobby, the more I wished I had a coach like him. He reminded me so much of Mr. Fennoy. He wanted his athletes to succeed and was willing to go out of his way to help them.

The calendar said spring, but the temperature felt more like summer and my motivation was as low as the mercury was high. I was competing sporadically in the long jump and heptathlon that first season and the results weren't inspiring.

My long-jump performances were dismal. I wasn't even a contender. As a senior in high school, I'd been jumping 20 and 21 feet. Now, a year later, I couldn't even reach 19 feet. It was crushing. I'd always felt like the long jump was my bread-and-butter event, something I could do in my sleep and do well. And I loved the event so much, I always looked forward to it. But my timing was off on the runway, which threw my whole jump out of synch. To have this kind of trouble at this critical stage of my career shook my confidence. What was worse, my coach was no help at all.

Things were just as bad with the heptathlon. I typically finished third, but I knew I should be winning. Among other things, I wasn't in shape because I hadn't been pushed to work hard in practice, the way I'd been in high school. I felt like I was going backward rather than progressing. As I looked around the track that afternoon, I had a sinking feeling. This experience wasn't going as I'd expected. I was miserable.

I'd gotten a bad feeling about my coaches as soon as I turned my attention to track after basketball season was over in March. During spring break week the team traveled to Austin for the Texas Relays, a big meet that drew the best women's squads from all over the country. My coach wanted me to travel with the team to the meet to get a feel for what collegiate track competition was like. That was fine with me because I was anxious to get going. The Texas Relays was a premier event. I felt the excitement as soon as I walked into the stadium and looked out on the track. Standing at the railing, surveying the scene, made me long to be out there. My competitive juices were flowing and I could hardly sit still during the meet.

I seethed all weekend about the fact that I wasn't competing. What kind of coaches were these? Why have an athlete on the team if you don't enter her in one of the biggest competitions of the year? I could barely stand it, I was so frustrated. Jeanette Bolden was my roommate in Austin and she listened to me complain about it without saying a word. It was pretty funny when I think about it now. We roomed together regularly on the road and became great friends. But that week in Texas we were still strangers. Anyone listening to me carry on, unloading my feelings that way, would have thought I'd known her all my life. I can just imagine what she was saying about me to herself: "Boy, this girl sure can talk. I don't know how good she is, but she certainly thinks she's the best."

After losing a heptathlon competition early in the season to Patsy Walker, who'd been at UCLA but had transferred to the University of Houston, I asked my coach for help. He looked at me and said, matter-of-factly, "It doesn't matter what you do, there's no way you're going to beat Patsy Walker."

I was dumbstruck. And livid. He'd hit a raw nerve. First of all, I couldn't believe a coach would tell his own athlete something like that. He wanted me to give up before I'd even tried to fight back, which was completely contrary to my approach to athletics. I took the attitude that no matter who I faced in competition—world's best or world's worst—I was going to go out and give it everything I had. Every time I competed, I put my heart and soul into it. I was prepared to work as hard as necessary, to endure whatever it took, to win. Just as I couldn't stand those people back home telling me I wouldn't survive at UCLA, I wouldn't tolerate someone deciding that I couldn't measure up to another athlete.

How did my coach know I couldn't beat her now with a little coaching help?

"*Because he doesn't have any faith in you*," said a little voice in my head. The realization infuriated me.

I was so upset, I marched straight back to my dorm room and called Mr. Fennoy. I was ready to transfer right then and there. When I told him what my coach had said and how I'd been treated, I just knew he'd sympathize with me and help me find another program.

"I know this is UCLA and these are supposed to be the best coaches in the country," I told him. "But I don't think they know what they're doing. They're ignoring me. I'm not doing anything here. I'm not making any progress."

After a brief silence, he said, "Jackie, I think you need to calm down and remember why you went to UCLA. You went there for an education."

That was not what I wanted to hear. Now I was mad at Mr. Fennoy as well.

"Yeah, but they don't have any faith in me and . . ." I tried to make him see my point of view. But he wasn't interested.

"I told you that athletics is a means to an end, not the end itself. You've been given a scholarship to attend a fine university. Your top priority should be excelling in the classroom. Whatever happens with athletics is secondary to that."

I felt like I was hitting my head against a brick wall. No one understood how I felt. But I respected Mr. Fennoy so much, I told him I'd think about what he said. I decided to be patient and give it more time.

For the rest of the season, I tried to think of track as secondary. But it was hard to swallow because that's not how I wanted to treat it. Basketball was fun. But competing and excelling at track and field was what I truly loved to do. I was considering making athletics my career. But even if I ultimately decided I couldn't make a living competing, I wanted to be the best I could be. I couldn't bear the thought of having the talent and not fully using it. That seemed like a sin to me. If God had given it to me, I should use it.

As spring went on, I became more miserable. I didn't win a single long-jump or heptathlon competition. My attitude was sour. No one tried to find out what was bothering me. There were days when my coach asked, "What do you feel like working on?" and I would say "Nothing." His reaction: "Okay, see you tomorrow."

I wasn't prepared for competitions or in shape. At the National Collegiate Championships, I didn't even qualify for the long-jump finals, and I finished third in the heptathlon, behind Patsy Walker and Nancy Kindig. It was dreadful. It may sound strange to nonathletes, my complaining about only being the third best collegian in the country, but I knew I was better than third. The trouble was, I couldn't improve without help.

By the end of the season, I could see that things were never going to get better. Accepting third place when I knew I was capable of winning was killing me. It was demoralizing. I'd rather not compete at all if I couldn't give it my best effort.

Being shunted aside by my own coaches was humiliating. It was bad enough that as a heptathlete I didn't get any respect from the rest of the track and field community. Our competitions were usually conducted outside the main track, off in some distant corner away from the other events. At some major national meets, like the U.S. Championships, they weren't even held at the same site as the other competitions. As a result, no one knew what our event was about or who we were.

There was a definite hierarchy at track meets as far as spectators and the media were concerned: Sprints were considered most significant, distance races second, the male decathlon, then field events, and finally, the female multi-eventers. It made me feel like an alien. We didn't attract many spectators. There was never any hoopla surrounding the heptathlon competition. Our results, if they were mentioned at all in the stories about the meet, were confined to the last paragraphs.

Most people knew that the men competed in the decathlon and that it was ten events. They could even tick off the names of several past winners: Rafer Johnson, Bob Mathias and Bill Toomey. Of course, everyone knew Bruce Jenner, probably the most famous decathlete of all. Typically, people's awareness of male decathletes derived from the media's declaration that the Olympic decathlon winner was "the world's greatest athlete." That there was a female multi-eventer worthy of an equivalent title rarely occurred to anyone.

The treatment I was getting now from the UCLA coaches added to those feelings of inferiority. But my irritation about being undercoached in the heptathlon was minor when compared to the disgust I felt over my dismal performance in the long jump. Back when I was twelve, I expected to be jumping 23 feet by the time I was in college. Here I was age nineteen, at the end of my freshman year, unable to get past 19 feet.

I just couldn't understand how things had deteriorated to this point. I'd taken the long jump to heart. From the moment I took that first leap off my porch railing, I loved the event. Seeing the look of excitement in Mr. Ward's eye when I took that furtive leap after practice, I knew I had a knack for it. The long jump was a part of my identity. I cared about my long jumping the way Maya Angelou cares about her poetry and Whitney Houston cares about her voice.

The U.S. Championships were the last event of the season. For most track athletes, the competition was held in Sacramento over a weekend. But the heptathlon competition was in Spokane, Washington, earlier in the week, which meant I had to go to the heptathlon and then join the rest of the team on the weekend in Sacramento for the long-jump competition. I assumed someone would go with me to Spokane since it was so far away. But my coach said he was traveling to Sacramento with the rest of the team. "You can meet us there when you're done in Spokane," he said.

That was the final straw. They didn't care enough about me to accompany me to a major national meet. It was clear to me now that they didn't consider me, my development or my competitions important. I told Jeanette I wouldn't be on the team next year.

As I pulled out my trunk in the dorm room and stuffed my belongings inside, I decided to give up track altogether. When I returned in the fall I would play basketball and focus on my studies. But the thought of quitting track broke my heart. It was like having to cut off part of my body.

15

Bobby

A week before the U.S. Championships, Bobby walked over to me on the track and asked me about the meet. "Who's going with you?" he asked.

"No one," I answered.

Bobby went into a tirade. "You mean to tell me your coach isn't going with you? That's outrageous!" he said. I hadn't expected that reaction.

"If a UCLA athlete is competing anywhere for the school, one of the coaches should be there," Bobby said. "I'm going to the athletic director right now and telling her that since your coach has decided he isn't going, I'm going. And if she won't pay my way, I'll pay for it out of my own pocket. But I won't have you competing up there by yourself. It's just not acceptable."

He stalked off. I wanted to shout. At last, someone was in my corner.

Bobby was so passionate about coaching and so proud to be in a prestigious program. As a child, he wanted to be a football coach, like his idol, Vince Lombardi. Later, when his interest turned to track, he wanted to coach an Olympic team. But he first had to pay his dues at a big-name school and build his reputation by coaching individual Olympic athletes. His father, Manch, was a chief petty officer in the U.S. Navy who met his mother, Daphne, a citizen of Panama, while stationed in that country. Bobby was born there, but later his family moved to San Pedro, next door to Long Beach. Bobby went to college at Cal State–Long Beach and earned a degree in physical education and studied physiology at Cal State–Northridge.

He'd been a hurdler of impeccable technique in high school and college. Unfortunately, his technical brilliance wasn't enough to compensate for his lack of talent, and he was never a standout.

When I was on the track, I couldn't help but notice Bobby's overpowering desire to win and his respect for and pride in the Bruin tradition. All day long under the blazing heat on the track, his intensity never wilted. He was a tyrannical, whirling dervish. "Look, if you just want to perform halfway and act like it doesn't matter, get off the track now!" he shouted at Florence and Jeanette each time they started to slack off or balked about the repetitions. They were doubled over at the waist, gasping for air, dragging themselves back to the starting line, looking at Bobby as if he were a lunatic. But Bobby didn't let up with the drills or the dogma. "You're UCLA!" he said. "You better have some pride because believe me everyone is going to be coming after you. They want to be able to brag that they beat UCLA. They can lose to everyone else in the race, but as long as they beat you, they'll feel like world champions!"

Jeanette and Florence's eyes would roll, their jaws would clinch and their muttering would start. Bobby was oblivious. He went on and on: "Do this, do that. No! Not like that! Do it again and do it right this time! Don't roll your eyes at me, just do it! Since you have enough energy to talk back, you can do two more laps!"

Bobby was working as hard away from the track as they were on it. His office was cluttered with books on physiology and conditioning he'd read or was reading in search of ways to help his athletes improve. Armed with that knowledge, he stood on the grassy infield, his index finger pressed to his lips, his clipboard tucked under his armpit, studying the athletes as they sprinted down the track and completed hurdle drills every day, searching for flaws in technique. Bobby believes the key to perfect performance is perfect execution. He says flawless technique can compensate for less than superior athleticism. According to him, a misplaced hind leg while clearing a hurdle or improper arm movement through the turn adds the fractions of a second that mean the difference between gold and silver and turn a world-record performance into just a very nice run.

When Bobby detected a flaw, he was like a bulldog with a raw steak. He wouldn't let go until he'd obliterated it. While the others continued to go through their paces, he'd call the athlete over, get right in her face and explain what was wrong. If she didn't get it, he'd drop his clipboard and mimic the wrong movement, then mimic the right movement. He looked like Marcel Marceau, the famous French mime, out there. Or he'd treat the athlete like a mannequin, grabbing a leg or arm and placing it in the wrong position, then repositioning it the way he wanted it to be. Then it was back to the track to apply the lesson just learned. He wanted the motions repeated over and over and over.

His perfectionist tendencies became a real sore spot for some of the girls. Mr. Fennoy had warned me before I left East St. Louis, "Leave your ego at the door and submit to the criticism. It will be constructive."

But some of my teammates didn't feel that way. All of us had been superstars in high school and some of the others thought they didn't need to be told how to run a race anymore, even if the advice was from a coach. To prove his point to headstrong athletes, Bobby started videotaping practices, just like the football coaches were doing. After an exhausting afternoon of drills, his athletes had to come to the office to review the film with him. That meant listening to more preaching and more tirades. His voice reverberated through the hallway outside his office.

Along with discipline and proper technique, Bobby stressed mental preparation. One of his favorite expressions is, "Those who know *why* will always beat those who know *how*." Here's how he explained it: "I can be on the track with you all day. But when it's time for the competition, all I can do is sit in the stadium. That's why I want you to know not only how to run this way, but why you're running this way. You have to be able to cope with any situation that occurs during a race. If you listen and internalize what I'm teaching you, the other guys will have to beat you to win—because I'm giving you the tools to make sure you won't beat yourselves."

Bobby ended up paying his own way to Spokane. The experience changed my life. After the first day of competition at the U.S. Championships, I was in fourth place and I was starting to regain confidence. I'd never been a great hurdler because my technique was ragged. Hurdlers should step smoothly over the obstacles, not hop over them, the way I did. I also didn't high-jump well. I kept my head up and my legs pulled up near my chest as I fell over the bar, instead of lying back and allowing my body to flop over. But my shot put was okay and I had run a good 200 meters. Bobby and I went back to the hotel. The long jump would be the first event of the second day of the competition.

As I put my track shoes away in my hotel room and started to unwind, there was a knock at the door. It was Bobby. He was still wearing the clothes he'd worn all day at the track. "Come out into the hall with me for a minute and bring your spikes and your tennis shoes," he said.

I didn't know what he had in mind as I followed him out into the corridor. We walked all the way to the end of the hall, to the foyer near the elevators.

"I want to work on your approach in the long jump out here," he said as he pointed up the hallway. "I want to see if we can make you more consistent on the runway."

That was music to my ears. All season long I lacked consistency. Confidence on the runway was the problem, just as it had been in high school when Mr. Fennoy asked Mr. Ward to work with me before the state meet in my sophomore year.

The long jump is a three-step process. First, you need a strong run down the path. Then you need to hit the board—a strip of wood at the end of the runway—with your plant foot. It results in good trajectory in the air. Finally, you need proper form and good body control in the air, extending your legs and arms fully, to stay in the air as long as possible.

The key to a good run for me is rhythm. Runways vary in length but they average about 160 feet. After I pick the right starting point, I like to start off at moderate speed and at about 30 feet away from the board, accelerate as fast as I can, while generating as much power as possible by bringing my knees up as I run. Then I want to plant my foot as close to the board as I can without going past it and fouling. If any part of my foot is over the board when I take off, the jump is declared a foul and doesn't count.

If I know I'm running the right speed, I can settle into

a rhythm down the runway and concentrate on my launch and my form in the air. If I'm insecure coming down the runway, I start slowing down at the end to look for the board, and that spells disaster. That had been my problem all year. At the end of the collegiate season one track and field writer had analyzed my jumping and the reasons why I struggled during the long-jump competition at the collegiate national championships. The writer said: "If she ever finds the board, she'll win."

Bobby put a strip of tape on one end of the hallway, then pulled out his metal measuring tape, extended it to 127 feet, and put another tape strip at that spot, placing my shoes on each side of it, to mark where the eight-inch board would be. I put on my spikes and ran down the hallway just as fast as I would during competition, while Bobby timed me with his stopwatch. "Do it again," he said after the first try. "This time move up a foot."

Eventually, we figured out that I needed to run 127 feet in 4.64 seconds or better, or about 19 miles an hour. That speed and that time would give me a jump of 23 feet, if I could hold myself in the air for one second.

It was a good thing the hotel room doors opened toward the inside. Otherwise, I could have gotten seriously hurt if a door opened in front of me as I was flying down the hallway. We kept our ears opened to hear doors unlocking so that we could stop when someone came out of their rooms or got off the elevator. When they did, they shot puzzled looks at us. Several people heard the footsteps and stuck their heads out of the doors to see what was going on.

What was going on was the development of a drill that I would use for the rest of my career to train for the long jump. In practice, we work on getting the timing and speed right. Then, just before the competition begins, I place some kind of mark on the side of the runway—a track shoe, a piece of colored tape or a shiny metal stake—at the precise spot from which I want to start and another where I want to speed up. That way, I don't have to worry about hitting the board at the end, because I do it automatically. Bobby continues to time every run during competition and helps me adjust. Holding his thumb and index finger apart and pointing either left or right, he signals how far forward or back I need to move at the start to jump farther next time.

We worked for forty-five minutes in the hotel hallway that night. "You'll do fine tomorrow," he assured me as we walked back down the corridor to my room after finishing. "Just try not to think so much during the run and stop putting pressure on yourself."

"Okay," I said, smiling. "Thanks for the help."

"You have to stop thinking that you have to be the best long jumper in the heptathlon," he said. "Remember, it's just one of the seven events. You can't take it so personally. It's making you tighten up and that's just adding to your problems."

After just one day with me, Bobby had put his finger on both my technical and mental problem with the long jump. No one had ever picked up on how I felt about the event, or considered whether those feelings might be hampering my performance. I'm not even sure I had realized it myself. But as soon as Bobby said it, I knew he was absolutely right. I felt so much more secure with him than I had with my assigned coach. He'd locked into my mind-set. For the first time all season someone from the coaching staff was on the same wavelength with me.

Bobby also encouraged me, trying to boost my flagging confidence. "You have a lot of talent," he said.

My face lit up. "You think so?"

"I've never seen an athlete as gifted as you," Bobby said. "You just have to be patient. I'm willing to work with you if you're willing to work with me."

"Sure! That would be great!" I said. His words gave me new life.

The one thing every athlete wants and needs is somebody who's as motivated and committed as she is. Someone who's willing to work hard along with her.

That was the wonderful thing about Mr. Fennoy. He recognized my talent and honed it. He could see how eager I was to improve and he helped me to do it by pushing me in practice. That's why I was so successful in high school. I had come to UCLA hoping to have the same kind of relationship with my coach, but instead, Bobby was taking on the role Mr. Fennoy had played. Like me, Bobby was always striving to be the best. He was as excited as I was by the challenge of helping me improve. I walked into my hotel room that night feeling like I'd finally found a kindred spirit.

I finished second at the U.S. Championships in the heptathlon, my best performance all season. The 5,827 points I scored in the seven events were more points than any UCLA athlete had ever amassed in the event, and would have been high enough to beat Patsy Walker at the college championships that year.

When he returned to UCLA, Bobby asked for and received permission to coach me full-time. Beginning in the fall of 1981, we spent a lot of time together. He was the first person I saw every morning and one of the last people I saw every night. During basketball season, I couldn't work out with the track team. But Bobby asked me to come out to the track at 6:00 A.M. to work on technique before my first class at 8:00. I'd bring him breakfast and we'd work out. After basketball season was over, I'd finish classes and tutoring, pick up lunch for us and spend most of the afternoon at the track, then go back to my room or to study hall at night.

Spending so much time with Bobby made me increasingly comfortable with him. Each evening after practice he drove me from Westwood to my apartment in Culver City. During the twenty-minute drive, I found myself talking to him about things I wouldn't dare tell other people. All sorts of thoughts and emotions, from the goals I had set for myself in track and field, to my ups and downs with my boyfriend.

He opened up to me, too, telling me about his girlfriend problems. He was dating a woman at the time who didn't think track was important and was jealous of the fact that he spent so much time with other women—namely Florence, Jeanette, Alice and me. He said she hated it when girls from the team came home with him to have dinner or watch videotapes of practice. He was constantly arguing with her about it. It seemed we had similar problems. And, it seemed, the reasons were the same. Like me, his devotion to athletics superseded everything else in his life. Whenever he talked about ambition, he repeated the same line. "A person shouldn't let personal setbacks destroy his dreams," he said.

I agreed with him.

Bobby said he knew I would become successful, but hoped I wouldn't be spoiled by it. "Your status is going to change," he said. "Everyone will become your friend, you'll be showered with compliments. The key to remaining on top will be not letting any of the hoopla change you or your basic values." I told him he didn't have to worry about that. If I was lucky enough to find success, my attitude wouldn't change.

The more time we spent together and talked about our professional and personal goals, the more it seemed that we were soul mates. Still, as far as I was concerned, the relationship was nothing more than that of athlete and coach. I considered Bobby compassionate and committed. But it was all business. It was the same kind of dedication and support Mr. Fennoy had given me in junior high and high school. If Bobby was sizing me up as a potential mate, he didn't send any overt signals.

I thought of him as an authority figure, just as I had Mr. Fennoy. The fact that he was eight years older than me also kept me from thinking of him as a potential boyfriend. He seemed too old for me. Even when we had those talks in the car or on the track, I called him "Mr. Kersee" and said "Yessir" when I answered him. It drove him crazy. He said it made him feel old.

Even after my feelings started to change toward him I wouldn't allow myself to think of him as a possible boyfriend while I was at UCLA. For one thing, I didn't know how he felt about me and I wanted to protect myself from rejection. Also, I didn't want to damage our on-track relationship. The last thing I wanted was for him to feel uncomfortable about coaching me because I had feelings for him that he didn't share. Most important, dating a coach was taboo in my book. It was like dating a professor. I also didn't want to start a scandal or engender bad feelings among team members by dating the coach. I knew it would cause trouble if the other athletes thought Bobby was favoring me because we were involved romantically. I also knew that relationships between coaches and athletes were considered unethical and that getting involved with Bobby could jeopardize his job. Therefore, I never brought up the subject with him or gave him the impression that I felt more for him than professional respect and admiration.

16

Back on Track

With Bobby coaching me, I was happy to be competing in track and field again. I looked forward to practice each day. I felt like my old self.

I won the 1982 NCAA heptathlon competition as a sophomore, scoring 6,099 points and setting an NCAA record. I repeated as champion in 1983, with a total of 6,365 points, another NCAA record.

Having put my athletic career back on track and confronted my grief over my mother's death, I was ready to tackle my anger toward my father. Blaming him for Momma's death was wrong. Disrespecting him was wrong, too. He wasn't perfect in my eyes; but he was the only father I had. I'd already lost one parent. I didn't want to shut the other one out of my life permanently. So, while I was home for the summer after my sophomore year, I spent time with Daddy, talking about what we'd been through. We sat on the living room sofa at the house. He didn't apologize for anything he'd done. And I didn't excuse his behavior. Like two peace negotiators, we decided to focus on the things we agreed on. "What's past is over," I said.

"The bottom line is, we're family and we need to stick together."

He agreed. "I support everything you're doing at UCLA and I'm proud of you. But I'm the parent and you can't tell me how to live my life," he said.

Gradually, the gulf between us narrowed and we were able to peacefully coexist.

By 1983, by junior year, I was focused on the upcoming Olympics. My leg muscles were rock hard, thanks to Bobby's running drills. But my overall health was only fair. For about a year, I'd endured chronic respiratory problems. I had one cold and bronchial infection after another. The condition flared up whenever I trained hard. First came the shortness of breath—a couple of times, my chest tightened up and I started wheezing as I strained to catch my breath. But after resting for a few minutes, the trouble subsided and I was fine.

I'd experienced similar problems during basketball practice. But I hid it from Coach Moore by running to the back of the line or crouching down behind my teammates until I caught my breath. Knowing what a stickler she was for conditioning, I didn't want her to think I was out of shape.

Bobby had to drive me to the student health center several times when my chest tightened up and the breathing problems became serious. The doctors there told me it was bronchitis and walking pneumonia. Bobby said there was no such thing as walking pneumonia. He kept nagging me to see a specialist.

"These aren't ordinary colds or pneumonia or bronchitis attacks, Jackie," he said one day on the track as I struggled to catch my breath. "I don't care what the doctors at student health say. You've got a serious respiratory problem. The same thing happens to Jeanette Bolden and she's a severe asthmatic. You need to go to a specialist and have it checked out."

I ignored him. I'd hated hospitals ever since my mother died. Also, I thought he was overreacting. I was an athlete in peak physical condition. How could I possibly have a severe health problem? I'd never had breathing problems or asthma attacks in high school. I ran for miles at a time with ease. Besides, I had other things to think about, like the 1984 Olympics.

To get a taste of intense international competition, I competed in the 1983 World Championships in Helsinki, Finland. I was at a distinct advantage going in because there was no pressure on me. I was an unknown. All eyes were on the East Germans and Jane Frederick, the veteran American heptathlete.

The crumbling of the Iron Curtain was still years away. Germany was still a divided country and American athletes viewed their counterparts from the Communist state of East Germany with suspicion and frustration. The East Germans dominated swimming and many track and field events, including the women's long jump and heptathlon.

"Just go out there, learn as much as you can and enjoy the competition," Bobby told me on the flight to Europe. He didn't want me to get wrapped up in the pressure and mind games. "Above all, don't be intimidated by the East Germans. They do their best to psych people out and American athletes fall for that stuff all the time. Don't look at them like you're in awe of them."

It was good advice. I wasn't thinking about the East Germans. I was just doing my own thing, taking care of my own business. They say ignorance is bliss and for me at those World Championships, it was. I was going up against the world record holder, Ramona Neubert of East Germany, but thanks to my own naïveté and Bobby's coaching, I was treating it as just another meet. It was only my second trip abroad and my eyes were as big as saucers, taking in all the foreign sights.

In each of the first-day events I set personal records, which means I turned in my best performance ever. After four events I was in fourth place and on pace to break the American record. Andre Phillips, Florence Griffith and Jeanette Bolden made the trip, along with Al, who was training with us. Valerie Brisco and Alice Brown, two athletes Bobby had coached at Cal State–Northridge but who hadn't transferred with him to UCLA, were also part of our group. Back at the hotel after the competition, we were all ecstatic about the way things were going for me. The hotel served the most delicious ice cream and we celebrated my success over bowls of vanilla ice cream.

But I could feel that something was wrong the following morning. "My legs feel funny," I told Bobby at the track during warmups. I was lying on my back with my right leg extended straight in the air. He was standing in front of me, pushing the leg back toward my head to stretch out my hamstring muscle. Al and the other athletes in our group were out, warming up and practicing.

"Look how flexible this leg is," he said as he continued pushing the leg back, against my resistance. "It's okay."

I was still worried. "No, something just feels strange."

As the minutes passed, the leg continued to tighten, as if someone had wrapped the area between my knee and my hip with an Ace bandage and then kept rewrapping it tighter and tighter.

My leg just wouldn't relax, even after I warmed up and stretched some more. By the time I was ready to jump, the stiffness was bothering me. There was no pain. Just tightness. It tightened to the point that I couldn't move it freely. Jogging was difficult and I wasn't able to stretch it very much.

I tried to forget about the leg and focus on just going full blast down the runway as I stood at the line for my first attempt. I ran down the runway as hard as I could, but before I got to the board, I felt a jolt of pain in the back of that same leg. Then it gave way. The sensation made me scream.

I grabbed the back of my leg and stopped running. My hamstring was throbbing now and I couldn't put any pressure on my leg without feeling excruciating pain. Bobby and Al ran toward me. They slipped their shoulders under my armpits and supported me as I limped over to the first aid tent. I was crying and moaning, "Oh, it hurts . . . it hurts."

Through tears, Bobby kept saying, "I'm so sorry. I didn't know. I didn't know."

Al was crying because he thought I'd seriously injured myself and because he was disappointed that I had to withdraw when things were going so well.

The three of us were quite a sight. Brooks Johnson, the Stanford track coach, came over to us to make sure everything was okay. No one who's involved in sports likes to see an athlete go down during competition, because they always fear the worst—that the injury will be career-ending.

Aside from bad shin splints in high school, I'd never been seriously injured. So I had no idea what was wrong. A physical therapist massaging the log-sized legs of decathlete Mark Anderson, who was laid out on a stretcher, came over and looked at my leg. He gingerly poked around the tender area and diagnosed it as a pulled hamstring. He introduced himself and said his name was Bob Forster. He started kneading the back of my leg to get the hamstring to relax and soften. It hurt each time he touched it. The pain from his poking and prodding was almost as bad as the pain shooting up and down my leg.

Afterward, he said it wasn't a serious pull and that if I strengthened the muscle I would be okay in a few months. Eventually, Bob became my full-time physical therapist and accompanied me to every competition. Unfortunately, we'd replay that scene too many times in the years to come at major competitions.

My withdrawal from the heptathlon marked the end of my first World Championships. It was a sad ending, but it taught us some valuable lessons about preparation. Just a few weeks before the Worlds, I'd competed in six events at the NCAA Championships to help the team rack up points and win the national championship for a second straight year. Looking back on it, Bobby said my leg was probably fatigued from that, as well as from the strain of the first day's competition.

After my experience at the Worlds, he paced all of us better during the year. He didn't push any of his athletes too hard during the collegiate season if it might jeopardize their chances of competing at an upcoming World Championship or Olympic Games.

Just as the Junior Olympics in Yakima had, the World Championships proved to me that I could hold my own against the best athletes. Bobby was even more optimistic, though. He estimated what he thought I could score in each event at the Olympics if I maintained my pace of workouts and steered clear of injuries. One morning before practice, he handed me a sheet of paper from his clipboard showing the calculations.

The big number circled at the bottom was 7,000! My eyes practically jumped out of my head when I saw it. No woman had ever scored 7,000 points in a heptathlon. It was unheard of. The world record at the time was 6,836. I was scoring in the 6,200- to 6,400-point range on a good day. I wasn't sure I could add another 700 points to that in a year's time.

Strategizing for the heptathlon is a complicated process. The judges set performance standards in each event and assign points to those standards. I earn points by meeting the standard, and extra points by exceeding it. The better I perform, the more points I earn.

The first phase of strategy involves accurately estimating how I'll do against the standard in each event and calculating the points I'll earn, taking into account my strengths and weaknesses in each event, as well as fatigue and weather conditions.

Second, I have to at least consider what my competitors' point totals will be to assess how the rest of the field will stack up. I have to set targets in each event that will allow me to get more total points than all the others. From there, I go to the track and try to make it all come together.

The way Bobby figured it, I had the ability to run the hurdles in less than 13 seconds. "I don't see how that's possible, considering that I'm running 14.6 now," I said, pointing to the number at the top of the column of figures.

My best high jump was 5' 8" but Bobby saw me going 6' 0", 6' 1" or even as high as 6' 6". I pointed to that number and shook my head in disbelief.

"You haven't gotten close to your potential in that event because your technique is so bad," Bobby said confidently. "When we correct it, you'll be jumping 6 feet easily."

Before I could question the rest of his figures, he said, "The same is true for the hurdles, javelin and shot put."

Then he launched into a detailed description of what I was doing wrong in each event and how much minor corrections would improve my results and how that translated into points. By the time he finished breaking it down for me, my head was spinning. It was difficult to imagine. Yet, I was starting to believe I could do it. I wanted to go for it.

I took the 1983–84 school year off to concentrate on the Olympics. My day began at 8:00 A.M., when I left my apartment in Culver City and hopped on the Venice Boulevard bus and took it to Sepulveda Boulevard, a long thoroughfare running north and south alongside the 405/San Diego Freeway. Bobby wanted me to jog to UCLA each morning to our sessions. From the bus stop on Sepulveda, I had to run the four to five miles to the UCLA campus in less than thirty minutes. For a while it took thirty-five minutes. After a couple of weeks, I shaved it down to thirty-two. The morning I ran it in twenty-eight minutes I felt like celebrating. It was a tough route; I dodged traffic, waited at stoplights and inhaled exhaust fumes while I ran uphill and down. Getting the time down was significant. It was a signal to me that I would be stronger and faster in the 800 meters, the event that might determine whether I got a spot on the team.

From 8:00 A.M. to 8:00 P.M., I worked six days a week. I sprinted up and down and around one half of the track stadium, trying to climb every step before the hand on Bobby's stopwatch reached the five-minute mark. Then I lifted weights, working each body part. In the afternoon, I worked on the heptathlon skills.

I had never worked harder at athletic training. My palms were decorated with calluses from weightlifting. As I limped off the darkening track at the end of each day, my calves ached, my buttocks were tight and my feet screamed for a pail of warm water. But I saw the rewards every time I looked in the mirror. My arms and legs were lean and sinewy. My body fat count was in the low single digits. My stomach was as stiff as a washboard. The results showed on Bobby's clipboard. I was throwing the javelin and putting the shot farther. The seconds were disappearing from my 800, 200 and hurdle times. I was jumping farther down the sand and the high-jump bar was moving up.

17

The Carnival

There's always a carnival atmosphere at track and field events. Athletes in the multi-events suffer more than others because our competition goes on for such a long time. Just as you're about to start your approach to the high jump, the crowd starts to roar about something that's happening on the track. Or they start playing the music for an awards ceremony and throw your concentration off when you're in the middle of crouching for the shot put.

During the Olympic Trials, however, the carnival takes place inside a pressure cooker. The media and the people involved in the event make it hard to stay calm and focused. Journalists love to play up the fact that the Trials are an athlete's one and only shot every four years to make the Olympic team. Athletes get spooked by such talk and start thinking, "Oh my God, I gotta be ready, this is it." Some put too much pressure on themselves, overtrain and get injured before the meet. Or their nerves just get the best of them.

And then there are all the requests for interviews and photographs. Here you are, trying to prepare for the biggest event in your life, and suddenly you're bombarded with attention. Of course, the exposure, interest and publicity are exciting and flattering. They're what you've worked for and it's hard to turn down a chance to savor some of the benefits. But I always remember what Mr. Fennoy told me when I went away to big meets in high school—take care of business first and reap the rewards afterward.

I think track and field athletes are more easily seduced by the limelight than, say, football or basketball players, because, normally, we attract little publicity or fan interest. Some of us act like the reporters are on the last train leaving the station and if we don't get on board, we'll miss our one and only chance at celebrity. I wish our sport was covered more consistently and that officials who govern track and field would do a better job of promoting the sport so that people would be interested in covering us year round rather than just every four years. Unfortunately, that's not the case.

Some say the solution is to change the system for selecting the Olympic track team. They think U.S. athletes who hold world records should get automatic spots on the Olympic team. Others say the team should be made up of athletes who win the most competitions during the previous four years.

I believe that the system in place now, which uses results from the Olympic Trials to determine the makeup of the track team, is the fairest, most objective way of doing it. Every athlete knows the rules—that the Trials are where the decision is made. All of us should have to get out there and perform when the time comes. That's the only way to level the playing field for veterans and newcomers. Doing it any other way is just asking for trouble. It would be an invitation for mischief by unscrupulous agents, promoters and sponsors who could help certain athletes build up their records while avoiding tough competition.

In 1984, I wasn't distracted by interview requests or photos for sponsor ads. As relaxed as I was about the competition, though, I was only cautiously optimistic about my chances of making the team. The four women who were favored were hungry. Jodi Anderson won the 1980 Trials but the American team's boycott of the Moscow Games dashed her hopes of winning a medal. Jane Frederick held most of the American heptathlon records but had been plagued by injuries for most of her career during major international competitions. Patsy Walker hadn't competed in 1980 because of a broken bone in her foot. Cindy Greiner was trying to emerge from the shadows of the others.

The first day of the competition, I won my heat of the 100-meter hurdles in 13.61, a personal record. But Jodi ran 13.52 in the next heat. In the high jump, I started at 5' 4" and, along with a group of others, cleared it. Jane conserved her energy and passed at that height. Her strategy didn't seem unreasonable considering she'd cleared 6' 2" just a month earlier. The bar went to 5' 6". Several of us cleared it, but Jane was still passing. Finally, she set it at 5' 7¼", but when she rose into the air the bar toppled. Then she missed again. Suddenly, there was just one chance left for her. Several girls cleared the height. But Jane missed again on her third try. She'd no-heighted, which means she wouldn't get any points for that event and couldn't possibly make the team. We were all stunned. Jane was devastated. She just sat on the mat, holding her forehead in her palm, looking dazed. I felt so bad for her. What can you say to someone in that situation? I walked over, gave her a hug and patted her on the shoulder. The Trials were over for her before they really began. She had high hopes of winning her first Olympic medal after decades of working toward the goal. Now she'd fallen short again.

Jane was one of those athletes who always seemed to have trouble handling the pressure leading up to the Trials. In 1980 she came in with a hamstring injury, which she blamed on overexertion. She told *Sports Illustrated* she couldn't help it. "I get worried. I'm not good at keeping myself from over training." This time, after jumping 6' 2" at the Pepsi Invitational meet, she said her legs were tight. But she just felt she had to keep working out. It was similar to what I'd experienced in 1983, going to the Worlds just a few weeks after exerting myself in the NCAAs. Bobby and I learned our lesson from that experience. But even when you know better, the temptation to continue training is almost too much to resist. You don't feel pain, so you think you can do it. But contrary to what we athletes like to believe, the body can only take so much pounding. A muscle might not hurt but it can still be fatigued, and when it is, you have to lay off it and allow it to rest. If you don't, you're flirting with serious injury. The words are easy to say, but they're hard to follow, especially when a spot on the Olympic team is at stake. Jane kept training after that Pepsi meet and ended up tearing her right Achilles tendon. Then she was forced to stop working out at a crucial time. She hadn't put on a pair of spikes for a month before the Trials. So she was rusty and out of synch on the high jump.

The high-jump competition continued without Jane. I cleared 6' 0", another personal best, which gave me a 15-point lead on Jodi Anderson, whose best jump was 5' 10¾".

Patsy Walker won the shot put. In the 200 meters, she ran a really good 24.68. But I ran it in a personal best of 23.77.

We began the second day at the long-jump pit. Patsy hit 20' 4¼", a personal best. I reached 22' 4¼". The judge who sits at the end of the runway watching to see whether jumps are foul hadn't given a signal. There was a pause. He stared at the line for what must have been an eternity. I kept my eyes on him while he kept his on the board. There were no instant replays in track and field in those days. Finally, he raised the white flag indicating a fair jump. I threw my head back in the air and let out a big sigh. It was a new American heptathlon record for the long jump.

There are two sets of records that apply to heptathlon competitions. One is the record for the event *within* the heptathlon competition. The other is the overall record for the event itself, whether contested within a heptathlon competition or outside it. In the long jump, the overall American record was still Jodi Anderson's 22' 11¾".

The heptathlon record for an event can only be broken or tied in a heptathlon competition. But an individual event record can be broken at any time. So, if I'd broken Jodi's record on that leap, it would have stood as both the new American record in the individual long jump and as the new American heptathlon long-jump record.

Setting that long-jump record meant a lot to me. I'd struggled so long to regain my form from high school. The jump also put me back on pace to break the American heptathlon record for total points.

Jane came over to me during the lunch break and encouraged me to go for the record. I really appreciated her support and told her so. It showed real sportsmanship for her to cheer me on when she was obviously hurting so badly. I realized, though, that this wasn't the time to worry about records. The goal here was to make the team. I wanted to avoid straining so hard for the record that I wound up injured and watching the Olympic heptathlon competition on television. I could worry about the record another time.

After lunch, we walked to the javelin area. The event, always a question mark for me, went unbelievably well. The first time I had tried to throw the implement in 1981 I hit myself in the head. I didn't win the competition at the Trials, but I threw 148' 11", another personal best.

Things were clicking for me. I was in a cocoon of confidence and calm. I focused clearly on each event and on what I had to do. My mind was unpoisoned by pressure and self-doubt. It's a state athletes refer to as "the zone." I was still on pace to set a record, but most important for me, I was in first place heading to the 800 meters, with a comfortable cushion.

Patsy, Cindy and Jodi were in a dogfight for the other two spots and the 800-meter race reflected it. Jodi, running beside me on the outside, interfered with me as I tried to pass her. There were only 300 meters left and she had lost the lead to Patsy, who was on the inside lane and had started her kick to the finish. I was ready to charge to the front with Patsy and tried to move closer to the inside. But Jodi threw her elbow out in my direction and pushed me away. I had to run the rest of the race outside in the third lane. I was furious. But unlike now, the tactic wasn't considered grounds for disqualification. In the end it didn't matter. Patsy won the 800, but I won the competition. I ran 2:13.41 on the outside lane, which gave me 6,520 points, a new American record. Jodi finished 107 points behind me in second. Cindy edged Patsy for the third team spot.

I crossed the finish line filled with a wonderful sense of accomplishment. From the despair that almost drove me out of the sport three years earlier, I'd rebounded to fulfill my great expectations. I savored the moment and the emotion, not realizing that even more happiness was in store. Several days later, I finished second in the long-jump competition and earned a spot on the Olympic team in that event as well.

Meanwhile, Al was having fun in the triple-jump pit. He opened with 54' 8" and took the lead. The crowd was stunned. No one expected Al to figure in the competition. But he was holding his own in a struggle with Mike Conley and Willie Banks, the two favorites. Banks jumped 56' 2¾". Then Conley went 56' 10" and everyone's jaw dropped. Al would have to really give it all he had to stay with them. He walked to the line and showed a determination I'd never seen before. He just flew on that jump, landing 56' 4¾" down the pit, ensuring himself of a spot on the team behind Mike and Willie. We embraced on the infield. I was so happy and proud.

What a great day for the Joyners. We'd survived that grueling test of heart, tenacity and nerve and emerged victorious. We were going to the Olympics together! It was a dream come true for the two kids who'd once raced each other to the mailbox on Piggott Avenue.

Back at the apartment that night, Al and I phoned my father. He'd watched the whole thing on television, cheering us on from his chair in the family room. The trip to Los Angeles for the Olympics was already on his itinerary. He said everyone in the neighborhood was sky high about what we'd done that day. Al and I smiled at each other. It was Sunday, June 17. We wished Daddy Happy Father's Day.

18

A Silver Lining

The Trials were a triumph not only for Al and me, but also for Bobby. Besides my brother and me, he coached five of the athletes who made the 1984 Olympic track and field team: Alice Brown, Jeanette Bolden, Florence Griffith, Valerie Brisco and Greg Foster. But there were no wild celebrations afterward. That wasn't Bobby's style. "It's too early to celebrate," he said. "We haven't done anything yet. The objective is to win gold medals."

Immediately after the Trials, Bobby packed up the seven of us and moved his training operation to the University of California at Santa Barbara, two hours north of Los Angeles. We spent the next three weeks there, preparing for the late July Games with our friend Brooks Johnson, who, as the head Olympic track team coach, was holding tryouts for the various relay teams. Alice and Jeanette were both candidates for the 4 x 100 relay team. Valerie Brisco, one of the three best female 400-meter runners in the nation, was a shoo-in for the 4 x 400 team. While they worked out with Brooks, the rest of us trained for our events with Bobby looking on.

That training camp was a bustling operation. Every day, all day long, sprinters who'd arrived to try out for the relay teams circled the track, some jogging leisurely, others running as if they were in an actual race. Brooks divided his time between the two track straightaways, working with the relay runners. On the days he wasn't sweating through running drills, Greg set up his hurdles on an outside lane. Meanwhile Al worked in the infield jumping pit or did his running drills on the track.

I was all over the place. First, on the track for a warmup jog, followed by quarter-mile and sprint drills. Then to the long-jump pit with Al or to the hurdles with Greg or in the throwing area with the shot and the javelin. Brooks also saved a chunk of time periodically to help me with the 800 meters.

Brooks helped me unravel the mystery of that event. It's a race that is neither sprint nor distance, requiring physical strength, precise strategy and mental discipline. My work with Brooks on the 800 began that summer and continued, off and on, for the next four years. We worked first on my endurance and speed. He put me through a series of sprints in rapid succession, first 300 meters, then 500 meters, then 500 meters again, and finally, 300 meters. He timed each of them and insisted that I hit precise time targets. The last 300 had to be completed in 45 seconds, no faster, no slower. The point, he explained, was learning to divide the race into those two segments, 500 and 300, and to discipline yourself to hit those target times. The reason: Running the race efficiently and successfully required proper pacing and careful strategy. Going out too fast too early or waiting too long to move to the lead would spell defeat.

He took me for a walk around the track, pointing to target areas on the track and explaining the objectives. "Here's the point where you accelerate," he said as we rounded the first turn. A little farther along, he said, "Through here, you just sit back and look pretty." Into the second lap, he explained, "When you get here, you're gathering your strength and preparing for the final kick." Rounding the final turn, he smiled and said, "And here is where you punch it and come on home."

After hearing that explanation, I realized it was another example of Bobby's adage about those knowing why beating those who know how. Brooks had just given me the why and how of the 800 meters.

My training was intense and rigorous, but it was proceeding extremely well. I was in great shape, with plenty of stamina. And I was brimming with confidence from the Trials. Each day I felt more and more comfortable with the long jump, and was consistently hitting 22 feet. My hurdling, javelin and shot-putting skills were improving as well. For instance, from a high of 14.88 seconds in 1980, my time in the 100-meter hurdles was down to 13.5 seconds. At 23.8 seconds, I was two seconds faster in the 200 than I had been just three years earlier. I was finally putting it all together.

Bobby crunched the numbers and matched them against the results from the European Trials and the East Germans' performance. He believed I had a very good chance of winning a bronze medal.

Then, the unthinkable happened. Bobby lined up all the women for sprint drills. I was running alongside Florence, Val, Jeanette and Alice. I got out of the blocks well, and started my charge, full-blast, down the straightaway. Suddenly, I felt a twinge creep up my left leg. Immediately, I knew what had happened. It was the same sensation I had a year earlier in Helsinki. As I slowed up, the pain increased. It was all too familiar. I'd pulled my hamstring again.

"Oh no! Oh my God!" I cried as I grabbed the back of

my leg and slowed to a stop. I was trapped in an excruciating vise, between physical pain and emotional devastation.

"It's my leg again," I cried out to Bobby. Al ran over from the jumping area.

The other girls, who'd been in fourth gear running down the track, slowed abruptly and raced back to see what was wrong. They all circled around me. I stood on my right leg and shifted all of my weight to that leg. I couldn't bear to put any weight on the left leg, couldn't even allow my foot to touch the ground. Around the track, everyone else was frozen in place, looking in our direction.

"This can't be happening! Why does this have to happen to me now?" I said as Bobby and Al helped me hobble off the track.

It was two weeks before the Olympics. Looking down at my swollen leg, I just knew my chances for a medal were doomed. It looked awful. I felt as if someone had just ripped our game plan into a hundred little pieces.

Bobby and Bob Forster worked on my leg, massaging the muscle to get it to relax. After a few hours, it calmed down and the pain subsided. But it remained very tender. I couldn't put any weight on it. They wrapped it tight with an Ace bandage and told me to stay off it for a week.

When the leg was stronger, I resumed my training, but I had lost my enthusiasm and determination. I sulked around the track feeling sorry for myself. Even the news that the Eastern Bloc countries were boycotting the Los Angeles Games—in retaliation for President Carter's decision to keep the American team out of the 1980 Moscow Olympics—depressed me. With the East Germans out of the competition, I knew the heptathlon gold medal would be up for grabs. Everyone else on the track was ecstatic because it meant their chances for winning were even better. No one viewed the Games as being tainted or insignificant because of the Communist Bloc boycott. Let the pundits have fun with their asterisks and their debate about the significance of the performances. To us, an Olympic gold medal would still be a gold medal. Because I wasn't healthy, I figured I'd miss my golden opportunity. Nothing seemed to be going my way.

I just wasn't myself. Usually I'm Jackie the Joker, the lighthearted, upbeat person who keeps smiling no matter what, giving pep talks and trying to cheer everyone up. Now, everyone was trying to raise my confidence and encourage me. Day after day, every time they massaged the leg, Bob Forster, the physical therapist, and Bobby kept telling me that the leg was getting stronger. But I couldn't climb out of my funk.

Compounding my worries were the performances being turned in by an Australian heptathlete I'd read about in the months and weeks leading up to the Games. Her name was Glynis Nunn.

I wasn't sure if she was a heptathlete, but the fact that she was competing in the sprint hurdles and jumping events aroused my suspicions. And the fact that her times, heights and distances were improving got my attention. Nunn and several Australian athletes had moved to the U.S. to get acclimated to conditions here in preparation for the Games. I knew from the numbers she was posting that she could be a threat. She was high jumping in the 5' 6" to 5' 8" range, only four to five inches less than my personal best of 6 feet.

In those days I read the magazines and newspapers closely each month to keep track of how other multi-eventers were performing. I wanted to know who was out there who might be a potential threat. It helped my preparation, gave me targets to shoot for. After reading about Glynis, I knew if I wanted to win the high jump, I'd have to clear 5' 9" or better because there was a girl out there who was capable of jumping 5' 8".

It drove Bobby crazy every time I brought up her name. He was worried I was psyching myself out. "Bobby, she's jumping 5' 6", 5' 7" and 5' 8"," I'd say. "I think she's really good."

"Why are you so preoccupied with this woman?" he asked, agitated. "The key to your success is you, not Glynis Nunn or whatever her name is."

His worry, it turned out, was well founded. I couldn't get her out of my mind. I was constantly talking about her and thinking about her, worrying she'd exploit the advantage my injury presented. And Bobby was thoroughly frustrated with me. He tried to brainwash me into thinking positively, constantly telling me the leg was healed and that there was nothing wrong with it. And he begged me to stop reading the sports pages. But I can be pretty stubborn when I want to and for some inexplicable reason, I just wouldn't budge from my defeatist attitude.

The truth is, I was physically ready. But not mentally. And because of that, I kept telling myself that I wasn't ready physically. I was a limping self-fulfilling prophecy. It was really a case of mind over matter. The leg was getting healthy, based on the way I was running. But because I was so afraid of reinjuring it and so consumed by negative thoughts, I wouldn't let myself believe it.

Everybody, from Bobby to Al to Valerie Brisco, kept telling me I could do it. But when I looked at the leg in the mirror—I stared at it all the time—it didn't look normal. It looked swollen, which to me meant it wasn't okay. The little voice inside my head kept telling me I shouldn't strain it and I started to believe it. Never once in the days leading up to the Games, or during the Games, did I ever consider just going out and trying to win. All I kept thinking to myself was, "I'm not going to make it. I just can't do it."

I had no faith in myself. It was an awful feeling.

• • •

We didn't participate in the opening ceremonies, nor did we stay in the Olympic Village. The ceremonies look beautiful on TV and I regret that I've never participated. But they're also very tiring. There's so much walking and standing. In 1984, we decided it wasn't a good idea, particularly with my ailing leg.

As for the Olympic Village, it's too crowded and it's too hard getting around. We needed to be able to communicate with Bobby whenever we needed him and that was impossible if we were in the Village and he was somewhere miles away in another part of the city with no credentials to get inside. To make our lives easier during the Games, Bobby reserved a block of rooms for all eight of us at a TraveLodge.

The first event of the heptathlon is the 100-meter hurdles. I walked to the starting blocks at the Los Angeles Coliseum with my left leg wrapped in a tight, twelve-inch Ace bandage. I wasn't nervous. But I was apprehensive, afraid to go all out. After I cleared the first two hurdles with ease, I realized my leg was okay and I tried to run faster. Yet the voice in my head told me to hold back. "Don't really attack, be careful about pushing off too hard on the lead leg, you might do more damage."

At the high-jump pit, during the shot put and the 200, I had the same fear. I used my left leg to push off on the high jump and I ran tentatively up to the bar. Maybe I thought I was giving it my all, but I wasn't. Prompted by that voice in my head, my first instinct was to protect myself. I was acting as if there was a tomorrow. But this was my one and only shot at a gold medal in 1984. There was no tomorrow.

All day long, Bobby kept bringing me bagels and water, begging me to eat something to build up my strength and to drink something to keep myself hydrated. I wouldn't take a sip or a bite. Also, during the breaks, he told me to put ice packs on my leg to keep it from tightening up. I knew I should do it. Failure to ice my leg overnight after the first day in Helsinki at the 1983 World Championships had contributed to the tightness and the pull I suffered the next day. But I ignored the advice and sat pouting in the tent.

Mr. Fennoy was in the stands, along with my father and my youngest sister, Debra. During the first day of the competition, Mr. Fennoy walked to the front row of the virtually empty Coliseum and got my attention. He bent over the wall a few feet above the track and motioned for me to come over. Because of my mood and his own preaching over the years that we should leave spectators alone and keep our focus on the track, I tried to brush him off with a wave and a half-smile. But he kept gesturing. Reluctantly, I walked toward the wall.

He read the dejection and apprehension on my face and tried to reassure me. I knew what he was trying to do. In high school, I would have hung on his every word, absorbing it like oxygen and feeding off it for the rest of the day. Not now. Leaning against the wall below him as his pep talk continued, I was only half-listening, half-lost in self-pity. "Don't shut me out," he said. "Draw strength from me and the others here who are supporting you."

"Okay," I said, offering a wan smile. I walked back to the tent.

By the next day and the start of the long-jump competition, I was inconsolable. I'd lost my concentration and my form. My first two jumps were fouls. My third was fair, but I'd taken off from three inches behind the board, on my left leg—too far back and on the wrong leg. I jumped just 20' ½", two feet off my best.

I started crying. Bobby sat me down inside the tent and tried to calm me down. "You can't give up," he begged me. "You've still got two more events. You have to pull yourself together." Finally, I got the message. But there was no way to know whether it had reached me in time.

Al's triple-jump competition was starting as we walked to the javelin field. He jumped 56' 7½", a lifetime best, and took the early lead. I threw the javelin 146 feet and pulled closer to Glynis, who had been steady all day.

Going into the 800, we were virtually tied. I had to stay within two seconds of her to win. The problem was that because I hadn't eaten all day or consumed enough liquids, I didn't have any reserve energy at the end of the race and Glynis was charging ahead. Al, who'd passed on his fourth jump to watch the finish of the 800, ran over to the final curve and hollered, "Come on, Jackie, use your arms." He was on the grass, running beside me down the home stretch. "Keep pumping your arms, come on, you can do it!" he screamed.

My face was a tight ball of anguish and strain. My legs were cramping and I was spent. I didn't have anything left. Nothing. I wanted to tell him, "I'm trying, Al, I'm trying to go as fast as I can."

Glynis crossed 2.98 seconds ahead of me. It took about ten minutes for the officials to figure out what I knew as soon as I crossed the line. I'd lost the gold medal by five points.

I was completely sapped of energy. As I stood on the track several yards past the finish line, getting my breath back, the realization slowly sunk in. Bobby walked up to me, handed me a bottle of water and gave me a hug. He asked if I was okay and told me I'd done a good job, which I knew wasn't true.

Al hugged me, too, then ran back to the jumping area for his final jumps. Turning my thoughts to his competition was a relief. It diverted my attention from the bitter disappointment I felt.

Al was the decided underdog and the journalists covering track and field had ignored him since the Trials. That morning before the competition, he'd been all wound up about it on the warmup track at USC. When I asked what was wrong he went into a tirade about a report he'd seen on television. "They were talking about America's hopes in the triple jump and they said they had to rely on Mike Conley and Willie Banks and flashed their pictures on the screen," he said. "Jackie, they didn't even mention my name!"

He was so hurt that he'd been overlooked. Ever since his starring role at our high school dances, Al has loved the spotlight. I told him to ignore it. "You just get out there and jump," I said. "Then they'll be scrambling around trying to find out who you are. You'll have the last laugh."

Al couldn't improve on his first effort; but neither could his competitors. He was still leading. Mike Conley came to the line for a last try. He landed 58 feet from the board, far enough to beat Al. But the line judge raised a red flag after he landed. He'd fouled. Al was the gold medalist! After the medal ceremony, we ran to each other and embraced on the field. I was in tears.

"Don't cry, Jackie," he said. "You did great."

"I'm not crying because I lost," I said. "I'm crying because you won. I'm so happy. You fooled them all."

We looked around the gigantic Coliseum, packed with people. Not even my father's voice could carry far enough to prevail in that place. So, if he uttered his familiar chants, we didn't hear them. But we knew wherever he was up there in the seats, he was overjoyed. We also knew that wherever she was up there, Momma was, too.

People crammed the streets of East St. Louis to attend the parade in our honor when we returned home. The sun was shining on the city that cloudless August day and it was reflected in the dispositions of everyone along the parade route. From our perches on the back seats of matching white convertible Mustangs, Al and I saw the thrilled faces of all of our school chums and old teammates. The motorcade crept along the streets of our neighborhood past our old haunts: Lincoln Park, the schools, our house and the place it all began for me, the Mary Brown Community Center.

Whatever doubts anyone had about my leaving town and striking out on my own in the big city had been erased. The love I felt from everyone that day was overwhelming. People waved posters and signs that read "Welcome Home Al and Jackie," "East St. Louis Is Proud of You!" I couldn't stop smiling and laughing. It was a great day as well for East St. Louis, which hadn't celebrated anything in such a long time.

The parade wound up at City Hall, where we received the keys to the city. We also got the keys to the two Mustangs. Because I still had a year of eligibility remaining at UCLA, I had to leave the car at Joyce's and promise not to use it until after graduation. But I was staggered by the generosity. The city also pledged to build a brick house for our family about three blocks from Piggott Avenue, across the street from a park to be named after Al and me.

19

Baseball, Hot Dogs and a Proposal

At home that summer, I spent a long time staring at my silver medal dangling on the end of that red, white and blue ribbon and reflecting on my Olympic experience. My fifth-place finish in the long jump didn't bother me because I performed well and was simply beaten by the four best jumpers in the world. I wasn't even ranked internationally in the event at the time.

Pondering the heptathlon was much more upsetting. Although I had tried hard, I knew my sour attitude had doomed my chances at the Olympics. Physically, I could have won the gold medal. But my defeatist attitude kept me from believing that and going after it in the javelin, the hurdles and the long jump. An ounce more of courage could have given me the extra inch or second necessary to change the final outcome. To me, that was a tragedy larger than the five points that separated my silver medal from Glynis's gold.

I replayed in my mind that state track meet when I was a high school sophomore, where I competed despite aching shins and helped Lincoln win its first championship.

I'd shown so much fearlessness and so much faith in myself, running and jumping as the pains shot up my bandaged legs. I had to find that courage again.

I held the shiny silver medal in the palm of my hand and promised myself I would work harder and use everything I'd learned from the 1984 experience to prepare for 1988. I was ready to begin the mission anew. I had made it to the Olympics and performed respectably; but I had come up short. Now, I had to prove I could meet the mental and physical challenges standing between me and the gold medal.

Bobby and I discussed it when I returned to campus in the fall. I was worried that I didn't have what it took to be a champion. He reassured me.

"This will make you stronger mentally," he said. "You will be a champion precisely because you've confronted the mental obstacle and you're ready to get over it. The athletes who aren't are the ones who fail."

Our relationship had grown so much over the past three years that I now considered him much more than a coach. He was my good friend, someone I increasingly relied on for emotional support as well as professional advice.

I realized my feelings for Bobby had changed when I started going to the movies with him. He always invited all the girls from the team, and occasionally Valerie, Jeanette and Alice went. I wasn't a movie buff. My tastes ran more to bowling and video games. But I so enjoyed his company, I accepted every invitation.

I don't remember many of the films we saw because I usually dozed off halfway through. I do remember the great music and dancing in *Flashdance*. I didn't nod off once during that film. I also remember laughing and screaming through the scene where Anthony Perkins hits the woman over the head with a shovel in *Psycho II*.

I was living with Valerie Brisco and her family in Inglewood, in a house with a front-door view of the Forum, where the Lakers play. Val was married and had a toddler. At the 1984 Games, she'd set Olympic records in the 200 meters and the 400, running the latter in 48.83 seconds en route to winning her second of three gold medals. During her victory lap around the Coliseum after the 400, she spotted Bobby standing on the first step of the victory platform. She ran to him and leaped into his outstretched arms. Her momentum knocked them both to the ground and they rolled around, laughing, crying and rejoicing. Besides Al and Val, Alice and Jeanette had won gold medals as part of the 4 x 100 relay team. In all, athletes Bobby coached won ten medals.

When I first met her, I thought Val was loud and inconsiderate. She could be so gruff with people. But as I got to know her, I saw how truly sweet and considerate she could be. I also came to appreciate her directness. I liked the fact that Val wasn't a phony.

By my sophomore year, Val was my closest friend at UCLA and one of my role models. She grew up in the Watts section of Los Angeles, where her brother, Robert, a budding track star, was killed by a stray bullet to the back. Although I grew up in a rough neighborhood, I wasn't nearly as streetwise as she was. Val knew exactly what she wanted and how to get it. After giving birth, she immediately went back to the track, training diligently to make the Olympic team. Watching her out there, anyone could see Val's hunger.

Like Andre Phillips and my old boyfriend, she thought I was pitifully unsophisticated. She called me "the old lady," because she said my way of thinking, acting and dressing was old-fashioned. She always teased me about the kinds of purses I carried and the fact that I took them everywhere I went.

In an act of unbelievable generosity, she had opened her

doors to me after the Olympics so that I could finish up at college and save money. During that year, I traveled with Val as a kind of assistant. She was a celebrity in Los Angeles after the Olympics, the hometown girl who made good, and she handled her fame with consistent class. Even as people at filling stations, shopping malls and airports were asking for her autograph, she took the time to introduce me. And each time she did, I said to myself, "I want to be like that one day."

I always joked with Val about Bobby. "I think he likes me," I announced one night after a workout. "He's cute, huh?"

That got her attention. "Bobby? Our coach? You must be kidding."

"He's coming to pick me up. We're going to the movies."

"Yeah, right, Jackie. We'll see."

When the bell rang and she opened the door to find Bobby standing there, she looked back at me in shock. "You were for real, weren't you?"

I just laughed. I joked and teased so often, Val and Jeanette didn't know when to take me seriously, especially when I talked about Bobby. I was always careful to cloak comments such as "He's nice" or "I kinda like him" in a laugh or a sarcastic tone of voice.

I was expressing my true feelings, but I wanted to protect myself in case the feelings weren't returned. So my affection for him remained a secret, even to my closest friends. After my two experiences with the opposite sex, in high school and college, I felt like a real loser when it came to relationships. I had told myself, "Oh well, it's not meant to be. You just can't win in that arena."

During a track team trip to Taiwan in 1982, I watched Bobby flirting with the Chinese woman serving as our interpreter. She was flirting back, giggling and calling him pet names in Chinese. Perhaps, subconsciously, I was jealous. But I was dating my boyfriend at the time. I just wanted to have some fun at Bobby's expense. During an afternoon shopping trip through one of the outdoor markets, I sidled up to the interpreter and told her to watch her step because Bobby was my husband. The woman was so angry and humiliated, she walked over to him, chewed him out and stormed off. Bobby stood there flabbergasted, in the middle of the street, surrounded by screaming peddlers and grasping tourists. Jeanette and I were over in the corner, watching the scene and cracking up. The next day, Jeanette told him what I'd done. He was so mad at me, I thought he'd strangle me. Stunts like that were the reason no one took me seriously when it came to Bobby.

I really did think he was cute. When I looked at him I saw a man who possessed the ideal qualities. I respected his judgment and his advice. He brought out the best in me as an athlete and as a person. I knew I could rely on him and confide in him about anything. All of those attributes made him really attractive to me.

I sensed that Bobby's feelings might be changing toward me, too. In addition to the trips to the movies, he started buying me presents. He bought me clothes because he said I wore too much polyester. One spring night in 1985, he picked me up in his car and drove to the beach. He wanted to sit on the sand and watch the water. He said it relaxed him. I had no idea what was coming next. I wondered if he wanted to talk about starting a romantic relationship. He seemed tense. He said he had a lot on his mind.

I always knew instinctively when Bobby wanted me to talk or to just be an ear for him. So I sat silently and listened. He'd become head track coach earlier that season, after returning from a year's sabbatical to help us all train for the Olympic Games. He wanted to do well in the job. He talked about the women's track team and its chances at the NCAA Championships. He wanted me to play a game with him and predict the final team scores at the Championships. I couldn't believe it. We had the beach, moonlight and stars and he wanted to talk about track!

Finally, he asked me if I felt like he'd become more than a coach to me. This was what I'd been waiting and hoping for. But, I hesitated before answering. Still guarded, I hedged and said something evasive like, "Yes, kind of."

I told him I didn't know if that was off-limits or not, because he was still my coach. "I don't know how to explain what I'm feeling," I said.

He looked at me and smiled. "That's okay. I have deeper feelings for you, too."

We left it at that until the end of the spring term. In the meantime, we continued to work together and go to movies alone and in groups. It was all very casual, though. Nothing romantic.

Bobby and I were so guarded and cagey about our feelings, it's a wonder we ever got together. But when we finally let down our guard with each other, it was like the Berlin Wall being demolished. The chain reactions occurred with dizzying speed. The turning point came later that summer. I was preparing to fly home to finally take possession of my Mustang and drive it back to Los Angeles, where I'd decided to live and train for the next Olympics. Bobby offered to meet me in St. Louis and drive back with me.

During the drive we got to know each other on an even deeper level. We talked about a thousand things. Our families, the future, our values. Bobby told me about how his mother had helped to shape his personality and his values. She'd raised him to be an independent person. That's why he didn't open up to a lot of people. But he was very relaxed and happy during that long trip. I could tell he was enjoying himself. He also talked about what he was looking for in a wife. It was eye-opening. But I didn't hear anything that troubled me. I was having a ball. We drove past the horse farms in Kentucky and stopped in Knoxville to take in the UCLA-Tennessee football game and spend the night.

We also stopped in Houston, where he made a recruiting call on Carlette Guidry, one of the country's best high school sprinters who wound up going to the University of Texas. Bobby is fascinated with sports arenas. So, before taking off for L.A., he wanted to see a game in the Astrodome. It just so happened that the Dodgers were in town and the night's pitching matchup was Fernando Valenzuela against Nolan Ryan. Bobby was in seventh heaven.

Midway through the game, in between Nolan Ryan fastballs and bites of his hot dog, he announced that he'd found someone he wanted to marry. My heart sank. He wanted to know what I thought about the idea. I forced a smile to hide my disappointment and said, "Oh, I think you'll be a good husband for someone."

He laughed and looked at me with astonishment. "You don't understand, Jackie. I want to marry you."

I was so relieved and thrilled! Not until I heard the words from his mouth did I know for sure how he felt. Bobby wasn't one to pour out his heart. So when he did open up, I knew he meant every word. Although he hadn't romanced me, or conducted anything resembling a normal courtship, we'd known each other for four years. We'd seen each other at our best and at our worst. I knew I loved him. When he proposed to me in that awkward, roundabout way and told me he loved me, I knew he was serious about making a commitment.

"Oh! Okay, yeah!" I said, the words stumbling out of my mouth just as awkwardly. "I'd like to marry you, too!"

And so we were engaged. I was ecstatic. I ran to the concourse to find a pay phone to call my aunt Della with the news.

20

Mr. and Mrs.

The morning we were to be married, Bobby was in the bathtub when his cell phone rang. He picked it up and heard Bill Cosby's voice.

"Hey, Bob, you gonna do this thing? This is your last chance to back out!"

"Yeah, Bill, I'm gonna go through with it."

"Do you need any advice? Where's Jackie?"

"She's at her place getting ready."

"Oh, yeah, I guess it would be bad luck to see her. Well, what are you doing? It's almost time."

"I'm in the tub, Bill."

"Well, get your naked self out of the tub and get over to the church. Put on your clothes first, though!"

"Okay, Bill."

"Camille and I will send something. We wish you and Jackie all the best, Bob."

"Thanks, Bill."

After one trip to a department store with Jeanette and seeing the paperwork involved in joining the bridal registry, and the $900-plus price tags on the wedding gowns, I abandoned plans for a big wedding.

Our ceremony was a simple, sweet affair at the church Bobby and I attended, St. Luke's Baptist in Long Beach. January 11, 1986, was a sun-drenched, picture-postcard-pretty Southern California day. I wore a white lace dress and the veil from my Easter hat. Al gave me away, then picked up his camera and served as wedding photographer. Val was my matron of honor. Bobby's best friend, Dave Harris, was his best man. Bobby's family and all of our friends from track and field and basketball attended. Al was the only member of my family who attended. I told my family back in East St. Louis not to worry about coming. It would have been an expensive trip.

Instead of a honeymoon, Bobby and I flew to New Orleans, where I received the 1985 Broderick Cup, which is awarded to the nation's best female collegiate athlete. It was one of my favorite wedding gifts. At the dinner, I was so sure Cheryl Miller would win that I actually thought I heard her name when mine was called. I felt so honored to have been selected. Elizabeth Dole, the U.S. Secretary of Transportation at the time, was the dinner speaker and presented the award to me. We had a nice chat afterward. I thought then, as I do now, that she's a very classy lady. So smart and so accomplished.

Being Bobby's wife as well as his athlete was a difficult role adjustment for me. In my private life, I wasn't accustomed to somebody telling me what to do. After my mother died, I'd been on my own, in control, taking orders from no one. Now suddenly, Bobby was carrying over our relationship from the track and telling me what to do all the time. I resisted it. And my rebelliousness even spilled back into the athletic arena. I mouthed off about every tersely worded order he gave. Before we were married, they didn't bother me. But now that I was his wife, I didn't think he should talk to me that way.

Meanwhile, Bobby was having similar problems adapting to the dual role of coach and husband. It took him a long time to realize that I wasn't still the nineteen-year-old he'd grown used to ordering around on the track. When I was young I accepted whatever he said without question. But as I matured, I became more opinionated. While I accepted the fact that on the track he was the boss, I nevertheless wanted to discuss the reasoning behind those decisions so that I understood why I was doing things a certain way and to make sure we'd considered all options. Before our marriage, he'd voluntarily explained why. Now, every time I asked why, he called me hardheaded and viewed it as a challenge to his authority. "Don't ask me why," he'd snap. "Just do it."

I reminded him that we both were adults and that he didn't have to yell at me to get the point across, that it was humiliating when he did it in public. He's come a long way in that department. But occasionally, in the heat of the moment, he forgets.

He's taken a lot of flak for some of the things he's said to me while television cameras were rolling and reporters were taking notes. People have accused him of everything from exploitation to wife abuse. A woman approached us in the airport after the 1991 World Championships, where I'd twisted my ankle during the long jump and Bobby told Bob Forster, "If it's not broken, tape it. She's taking her last jump."

She and many other people saw that and were outraged. Bobby received dozens of angry letters. Anyway, this woman who approached us congratulated me. Then she looked at Bobby and said, "I know what those initials B.K. stand for: Bobby Knight. You're the Bobby Knight of track and field. I don't like him and I don't like you."

I was stunned. Bobby took it in stride. He said to me afterward, "When Phil Jackson sends Michael Jordan back into an NBA Finals game with a sprained ankle it's a gutsy move by the coach and a display of Jordan's heart. When I do that with you, because you're a woman and my wife, I'm an abusive husband and you're a victim."

I agree with Bobby. That woman and the others who say such things aren't giving me much credit. They assume that I'm some kind of doormat who would let a man exploit me without standing up for myself. Believe me, that's not my personality.

In Tokyo in 1991, once Bobby determined that the ankle wasn't broken or seriously sprained, he didn't want me to start doubting myself or become tentative, the way I did after the hamstring injury during the 1984 Olympics. Suffering an injury is like falling off a horse. You have to get right back on or you'll be afraid for the rest of your life.

Also, not all the yelling is negative. When I'm in competition, I want to hear Bobby's voice shouting out technical instructions, split times and firing me up. Usually, he's saying things like, "You're not going home with me unless you give me a 7 [-meter-long jump]!" Or, "You're not on target, pick it up!" during the 800. Or, "It's about time you woke your ass up!" if he thinks I'm not performing my best.

One of our worst days together occurred after we'd been married for about a year and a half. We were working at the high-jump area at Drake Stadium at UCLA. Bobby was talking to Daley Thompson, the 1980 and 1984 Olympic decathlon gold medalist, and a couple of other athletes while I tried to master the flop technique and break my habit of crossing the high bar in the sitting position. I've had a phobia about laying my head and arms back and allowing myself to fall backward since high school. Early on, I tried it that way, missed the mat and fell on the ground on my tailbone. Bobby wanted me to practice flopping off a trampoline and I refused to do it because I was afraid.

"Damn it, I'm the coach out here," he screamed in front of Daley and the others. "Do it my way or leave the track." I marched off. I was never so embarrassed and angry in my life.

After a few minutes Daley came over and consoled me in that beautiful British accent of his. "Jackie, you're going to have good days and you're going to have bad days," he said. "It's okay to leave, but remember that Bobby wouldn't do anything to hurt you. He's trying to help you. He's in your corner."

I appreciated Daley's comments. Bobby and I had to find a way to peacefully resolve our differences and maintain both our marriage and our on-track partnership. Later, we both agreed we loved each other and we couldn't allow track and field to interfere with the personal side of our relationship.

We designated the office next to our garage as the mad room. It's the place where we aired our feelings about the day's events on the track and where we left the coach-athlete relationship. Once we stepped out of the mad room into the house, everything about track was forgotten and we were husband and wife again. The arrangement worked.

Bobby loves to tell people he's the boss at home, that if we are deadlocked over an issue he has the tie-breaking vote. I always laugh when I hear that or read it in an article, because that's not the way it is at all. We each have equal input, 50-50, and that's the basis upon which decisions are made, not 49-49, with Bobby holding the last 2 percent like some kind of trump card, the way he's always saying. I know it makes him feel good to think that. If he wants to say it, he'll have to put it in his book, because that isn't how it is in my book. Or in our house.

People have also accused him of sponging off my success to advance his career. The fact is, he was already gainfully employed as a coach at UCLA and was developing a group of potential world-class athletes when I got there. I joined *his* group.

The other thing people don't know about Bobby is that he's never collected a coaching fee from any of the athletes who've worked with him, no matter how long he's coached them or how successful they've become. Neither Al, nor Florence, nor Gail Devers, nor Jeanette Bolden, nor Val Brisco, nor Greg Foster has ever paid Bobby a dime for coaching help. After the 1984 Olympics, while he was head track coach at UCLA, he formed the World Class Track Club, with sponsorship money from Adidas. The club's pool of money covered training and traveling expenses for the team members who were out of school. They included Al, Florence, Jeanette, Val, Greg and me.

In 1986, Imperial Chemical Industries, ICI, came on board as a track club sponsor. The two companies continued to sponsor the club for several years. During that time, we all wore Adidas warmup suits and uniforms and T-shirts and baseball caps emblazoned with the ICI logo. Bobby also started a management firm, World Class Management, and negotiated sponsorships and endorsement deals for members of the track club. After I graduated, he negotiated my shoe and apparel deal with Adidas, which also paid me a monthly stipend for living expenses. He acted as Gail Devers's agent in negotiations for her sponsorship contract with Nike when she finished at UCLA. As a coach, he did not allow any of his athletes to be charged more than a 10 percent commission fee, which I think was reasonable. He continues to have the same arrangement with Gail, who's a client of JJK & Associates, the sports marketing and management firm we formed after folding World Class Management several years ago.

Bobby's interests extend far beyond the weight room and the track. He resigned as head coach at UCLA in 1993, not only to work full-time with track athletes such as Gail and me, but to train competitors in several sports besides track, including professional tennis players Zina Garrison and Monica Seles, and hockey goalie Grant Fuhr. Impressed by his results with Grant, then–St. Louis Blues coach Mike Keenan hired Bobby to be the team's strength and conditioning coach in 1996.

Sometimes, I think that deep down Bobby's a good ol' boy. His favorite pastimes, other than attending hockey games and listening to George Strait and Reba McEntire songs, are going line dancing with his cowboy boots on, watching stock car races and hanging out with Jeff Gordon, Bill Elliott and the other drivers he knows on the NASCAR circuit.

Despite what others may think, I know that Bobby always has my best interests at heart. I think I'm the most important person in the world to him. He wants me to be happy and will do whatever it takes to ensure it.

21

World's Best

One of the reasons I love competing in track and field is that the results are determined by objective standards. No points added or deducted for style. Run the fastest, throw the farthest, leap the highest and you win.

But track and field does have its subjective moments. They come at the end of the season when *Track & Field News* hands out its rankings and awards. By the end of 1985, I was ranked third in the world in the heptathlon by the magazine, even though I posted the top score among all competitors worldwide, 6,718 points. That performance came at the National Sports Festival. The reason offered by the editors for my placement: I hadn't compiled those scores during a major international competition. In their eyes, I couldn't claim the number one spot until I did it against the world's best, namely the East Europeans.

It perturbed me. In the heptathlon, unlike other track and field events, points and results are awarded based on how an athlete fares in comparison to an objective standard, rather than on the athlete's performance relative to the rest of the field. I don't see why it should matter who else was at the meets I entered. The way I saw it, my 6,718 should be compared to the best scores of the other top heptathletes: Sabine Paetz, Sibylle Thiele and Ines Schulz of East Germany, and Natalya Shubenkova, Marianna Maslennikova and Larisa Nikitina of the Soviet Union. The athlete with the highest score in a given year is the best that year. Simple, straightforward and objective. But that's not the way it goes.

As time went on and I gained more experience, I became increasingly cynical about the media's assessments of my performances. But in 1985, I was new to international competition and accepted the magazine's decision. The following year, 1986, I tried to play by their rules and give them what they wanted. I headed to Europe to face those women and other foreign competitors in the heptathlon. At the time, the world record stood at 6,946 points, scored by Sabine Paetz in 1984. My goal was to be the first woman to score 7,000 points in the event.

It was impossible not to notice the stark differences between track in the U.S. and Europe. The crowds abroad were routinely larger, more enthusiastic and more knowledgeable. At the Mount San Antonio College Relays earlier in the spring, the first major track competition of the year in the U.S., the crowd watching our event had shrunk to a dozen coaches by the time we started the 800 meters. In contrast, at the Gotzis Invitational in Austria, the promoters delivered enormous and enthusiastic standing-room-only crowds, even for the heptathlon. Despite blustery winds, cold temperatures and rain, the stands were filled to capacity, around 20,000 people, during both days of our competition. And they understood the competition. Everyone had been given a program listing our personal bests and the standards in each event. I remember the thrilled faces of the children as I competed. It was such a revelation to see them celebrate and wave their programs wildly when

I broke Jane Frederick's American record and won the meet with 6,841 points. It was gratifying and exciting to be appreciated that way.

Next stop was the inaugural Goodwill Games in Moscow. I was excited about the trip to Russia. I couldn't wait to observe life behind the Iron Curtain. As a child, like other American kids, I'd heard so many horror stories about what it was like in Communist countries, I wanted to see for myself. I expected to see men in trench coats, fedoras and sunglasses in alleys and on park benches, as well as frowning, uniformed Russian policemen stalking the streets. I had no idea how they treated American citizens over there.

The reality, surprisingly, wasn't far off from those caricatures. Security was as tight as an Ace bandage. We were escorted to a car at the airport, and as we drove along the highway into downtown Moscow, we saw security guards along the side of the road, for miles and miles. Not until the car passed Red Square and the Kremlin did I start feeling somewhat at ease.

I was immediately struck by how seriously the Russians took everything. There was an attendant on every floor, checking keys each time we got off the elevator to go to our rooms. Our hotel was clean and nicely furnished, but the room was about the size of a closet. When more than two of us wanted to hang around and talk, we sat outside in the hallway because we couldn't all fit comfortably inside. Creepiest of all, I felt like the walls had ears. I kept hearing strange noises as I walked around. When I talked on the phone, there was an almost constant clicking sound in the receiver. I was sure the line was bugged.

We all were afraid of getting sick. The threat of diarrhea was ever present, U.S. track officials had warned us. After experiencing a day of dining Russian-style, I stopped eating the food and started subsisting on bagels and bottled water.

Everyone ate the same dish at mealtime in the hotel restaurant. No choices. No substitutions. On the first morning there, we were served a tasty breakfast of chicken and rice. When the waiter walked in with the same chicken and rice dish at lunch and again at dinner, I knew something was wrong. The food had been hot at breakfast. By lunch, it was warm. At dinner, it was cold. Sure enough, the second day of the heptathlon, I developed diarrhea and a queasy stomach.

Bobby arrived the day after I did, without the credentials or hotel room American track officials had promised to provide. A liaison to the event organizers who met him at the airport helped him get to the hotel. There, one of the American chaperones gave him a pass for the stadium and put him on the shuttle bus.

Meanwhile, we endured a steady stream of logistical snafus at Lenin Stadium during the meet. They changed the starting time for our event after we'd left the warmup track and were waiting to go onto the competition track. There were nearly a dozen of us crammed in the tiny waiting space.

There was a real Cold War atmosphere in the room. The Russian competitors mostly kept to themselves. They were very cliquey, not at all friendly. We knew they were under strict orders from their coaches not to mingle with athletes from the West. Every move they made was monitored and they could be severely reprimanded if they showed any friendliness. After learning about the strict system under which they lived and competed, I didn't criticize them for their attitudes and actions. I actually felt sorry for them that they had to suppress so much of their personalities. I couldn't imagine living and competing under such restrictions.

I chatted with my teammate Cindy Greiner, whom I'd known for years from the collegiate circuit. As we waited in the cramped area, our muscles started to get cold. We all jumped around and bent over, doing anything to keep our legs and arms loose.

Once the competition began, everything went smoothly. But I was apprehensive. I was still battling the demons of self-doubt that had undone me in Eugene in 1980 and four years later at the Los Angeles Games. A week earlier in Oslo, Norway, I'd been sitting in my hotel room with Val, discussing whether I was being unrealistic in expecting to run the 100-meter hurdles in 13 seconds. Bobby overheard me and started chastising me for the lack of faith in myself and his coaching. I knew he was right, but I couldn't help myself.

I didn't see Bobby or hear his voice when it was time for the first event. That was unusual. He always let me know where he was at the start of a competition. No matter how loud the cacophony on the track, I could always pick up his voice and hear him shout, "Okay, Jackie, let's do it!"

At the starting line, I stared down the track, past the precisely arrayed hurdles to the finish line, wondering how long it would take me to get there. As I stepped into the blocks, I remembered what Bobby had said to me that night, "Stop doubting yourself! You're ready to run this in under 13 seconds."

The gun fired and we were off. I crossed the finish line 12.85 seconds later, well ahead of everyone else. It was a new American heptathlon record and .59 seconds off the overall world record. I was thrilled. In the time it took me to clear the ten hurdles, my doubts had vanished. My eyes searched the stadium for Bobby. No sign of him. I listened for the familiar scream of triumph. Nothing.

Inside the stadium concourse, he was running up the steps as the announcer was reading the results in Russian.

He found an American journalist and asked how I'd done. When the reporter told him 12.85 seconds, Bobby broke into a big grin. He knew I'd scored 1,147 points. A very good start. He was still beaming when he emerged from the stadium entrance, wearing a suit and tie. He hollered and waved to me at the high-jump area.

I jumped 6' 2" that day, which was truly remarkable considering all the trouble I had with the technique. The world record stood at 6' 9¾" and Bobby had set our goal at around 6' 4". But looking up at his smiling face in the stands, I knew I'd done just fine: 2,227 points. Inside, I knew it, too. I savored the feeling of accomplishment. It was another personal record. The minimum we expected was 6 feet. Those extra two inches bought me nearly 100 bonus points.

I felt so confident and so relaxed. No rushing. No getting ahead of myself and thinking about the world record. Just moving serenely from one event to the next. I was entering that trancelike state I hadn't visited since the 1984 Olympic Trials.

I was way ahead on points as I took the shot in my hand and tucked it between my jaw and shoulder. I put it 48' 5¼", another personal best and well within our target range. My total jumped 845 points to 3,072. No bonus points this time. I was disappointed that I hadn't thrown 50 feet, but I reminded myself that anything between 48 and 50 was fine because the high jump had given me a comfortable cushion. I wasn't in any danger of breaking any shot-put records. The overall world record was 73' 11" and the heptathlon world best was 68' 8½". But as far as my personal goals were concerned, I was right on target.

The final event of the day, the 200 meters, lasted just 23 seconds for me. I'd shaved nearly a second off my previous best time! I was overjoyed with the performance. The time was 1.3 seconds off the world record. I'd racked up a stag-

gering 4,151 points the first day, 216 points ahead of Anke
Behmer, who was in second place, and 277 points more
than Paetz, who was fourth.

In the stadium, Bobby was beside himself, cheering and
applauding wildly. He was standing beside Ted Turner, the
president of Turner Broadcasting, who'd organized the
quadrennial international competition. Turner envisioned
the meet as a way to restore goodwill after the dueling
Olympic boycotts in 1980 and 1984. His assistant had introduced him to Bobby.

Ted was wearing a blue blazer, a blue button-down shirt
and slacks. He was about to go down to the track to present an award and needed a tie. He turned to Bobby. "Can
I borrow your tie?" he asked. "I'll give it back to you. They
want me to give this award and I didn't wear a tie. I mean,
nothing personal, but who the hell wears a tie to a track
meet?"

Bobby's blue and red striped tie matched Ted's outfit
perfectly. While Ted was down on the track, Bobby told
Turner's assistant he needed a favor. He had no place to
stay. When Ted returned and heard about Bobby's predicament, he got all riled up. "This is a disgrace!" he said. "Call
the people at my hotel and get Bobby a room."

Bobby ended up at my hotel, though. The U.S. track
people found a room for him. He wanted to be close by to
counsel me that night, to work on my legs and to get ready
for the second day of the heptathlon. But the hotel staff
wouldn't let us stay in the same room, even though we
were husband and wife. Only women were allowed on my
floor, they told us. Bobby's room was on another floor. I
couldn't believe what a weird place it was.

Reporters and spectators were buzzing about the possibility of my breaking the world record, but Bobby and I
stayed away from the subject. We focused on protecting my

legs, icing and rubbing them down. That night, we discussed only our approach to the next day's events.

If the strategy for winning the heptathlon is seven times more complicated than that for any single event, the calculus for breaking a heptathlon world record is forty-nine times more complex. To have any hope of reaching 7,000 points, I either had to score at least 1,000 points in each event, or get pretty close to it and find several hundred bonus points in selected events along the way. That was our plan; and so far, it was working. The throwing events were, as they had always been, my weak spots. It was hard for me to get 1,000 points in either the javelin or shot put. The best I could hope for was 850 points in both, and to pick up 1,200 or 1,100 in the long jump, the 200 and the hurdles to make up the difference. I'd done as well as I could in the 200 and the hurdles and come away with several hundred bonus points. The final piece of the puzzle was the long jump, the first event of the second day. If I did extremely well, the possibility of a new world record would be real.

Anything past 22' 10" in the long jump would give me the 1,100-plus points I needed to stay on world record pace. And as it turned out, my first leap was textbook-perfect. It wasn't 21', or 22' or 22' 10". It was 23 feet, a mere 1' 5½" off Heike Drechsler's world record; 1,176 more points. Total: 5,327.

If I could hold my own in the javelin and keep my wits about me through the trying 800 meters, my name would enter the record book. Up in the stadium, Bobby couldn't sit still. He paced. He ran up and down the stadium stairs, rubbing his hands together. As with the shot put, the world record in the javelin is out of my range. A British woman, Fatima Whitbread, had thrown it 254' 1" to establish the best mark. Still, on my first throw, I heaved it nearly 16 feet farther than I ever had before, 163' 7": 6,184 points. I forfeited the other two throws and awaited the 800.

I was just 816 points away from 7,000, a little more than one point for every meter I had to run. That was my thought as I headed to the starting line. Cindy Greiner, who was out of the running for one of the top three spots, walked beside me and said, "Go for it. You can do it. The 800's not going to be that bad."

Cindy, like Jane Frederick, was a great friend to me through the years and competitions. She wasn't blessed with extraordinary athletic gifts; but she had desire, heart and discipline, which made her an extraordinarily tough competitor. She was also among the most generous people I knew in track and field, a sport that is rife with envy and mean-spiritedness. No matter how she was faring, whenever we were in competition together, she always offered encouragement.

My goal in the 800 was 2:10. I knew it would be a challenge. That time was 16.7 seconds off the world record, which meant I would have to really haul it the entire way. But if ever there was a moment to push myself, this was it. I felt comfortable with the pace through the first lap and Bobby shouted that I was on target as I started the second. As I finished the backstretch and hit the curve before the final straightaway, the announcer was telling the crowd of 25,000 that I was on pace to break the record. Alternating in Russian and English, he shouted "Go, Go! Go!" The crowd stood and cheered. There may have been only 25,000 people there, but they sounded like 250,000 to me. Being greeted by such enthusiasm coming off the curve gave me chills. I was an American athlete, competing in their country, beating their best athletes, and yet they really wanted to see me break the record. I finished in 2:10.02, good for 964 points. Total: 7,148. I waved to the crowd to express my appreciation. The announcer in the press box shouted, "It's marvelous! It's magnificent!" The ovation lasted several more minutes. Photographers, television cameras and reporters with microphones surrounded me. Bobby came flying onto the field carrying a water bottle. He made his way through the media throng and emptied it down my back. I was the first American woman since Babe Didriksen to hold a multi-event world record.

Despite all the mishaps during the trip, the feeling I got hearing that roar as I ran down the stretch during the 800 meters made it a wonderful experience. Ted Turner was criticized and made the butt of jokes for creating the Games, but I thought it was a wonderful concept. The reception I received from the Russian fans exemplified the spirit of goodwill he wanted to achieve. I was proud to have been a part of the first meet, and I've participated in the Goodwill Games ever since.

Bobby and I left for London first thing the next day, hoping to finally get a good meal. When we arrived at the hotel room, bouquets and vases full of roses and other flowers were waiting for me, along with a greeting card reading, "SO, YOU DID IT!" that Florence Griffith had gotten everyone from our World Class Track Club to sign. We were in London to meet officials of ICI, one of our sponsors, and to meet Nigel Mansell, the Formula One race car driver also sponsored by ICI.

Three weeks later, Bobby and I found ourselves in Houston for the Olympic Festival. I was tired and sore and eager to go home for a rest. But Bobby insisted that I was ready to break another record and told me not to squander the opportunity. The Houston newspapers were filled with stories about the world record. Everyone in the press corps wanted to know whether it was wise for me to compete so soon after exerting myself.

It wasn't difficult getting motivated to compete, despite my initial reluctance. I wanted to keep competing against the best to prove that I was the best. Also, the fact that the event was on American soil made it important to me. I'm patriotic that way. I think it's more gratifying to win on American soil, in front of American fans. Plus, I had another reason for competing. My father and Coach Fennoy had come to the meet.

I also viewed Olympic-type events like the Olympic Festival, Goodwill Games and Pan Am Games as great ways, in non-Olympic years, to expose more Americans to track and field in general and the heptathlon in particular. Whenever I try to explain the event to youngsters or non–sports fans, they're surprised to hear what's involved. I always urge them to come out to the track and watch the event. It's the only way to develop an appreciation for the skill involved, to realize that we don't just wander out, run the hurdles, have lunch and then come back and throw the shot and do the long jump. I believed then, as I do now, that because track and field competes against so many other more popular sports for fans' attention, greater exposure is the only way American audiences will ever become as enthusiastic about the sport as the Europeans.

My flight from London to Houston had been delayed by several hours so I didn't arrive until 11:00 A.M. the morning of the first day of heptathlon competition. By the time I got to the track that afternoon to warm up, the temperature was reported at 102 degrees and the humidity was oppressive. On the track it was 118 degrees. It was so hot, my hands blistered while holding the 8-pound, solid metal shot and again, while gripping the javelin.

The Mondo track surface, which is even softer than Tartan, seemed to melt in the heat, turning from rubber into a gluelike sponge. It stuck to my fingers and burned my knees when I assumed the starting position in the blocks. It gripped my spikes as I ran. To counter the blast-furnace conditions, officials handed us a steady supply of cold, wet towels and bottles of icy, cold water.

I was happy that the fans didn't desert us. In fact, 100 of them followed us around the corner to the back of the stadium to watch the shot-put competition on the first day. It was a tiny group, but their support cheered all of us. Cindy turned to me with a big smile on her face and said, "Isn't it nice to have all these people watching us?" Her comment said a lot about our low expectations.

My score after the first day was just six points less than my first-day total in Moscow. Cindy was 392 points behind. On the second day, the heat had sapped my energy by the time we gathered for the 800. I needed to run 2:10 to improve on my record. But in that heat, I wasn't keen on pushing it. I took it easy on the first lap and was starting to labor on the second. But the announcer revved up the crowd of 17,000 as I started the final 200 meters. Hearing them, I got a burst of energy. "Okay, I'll run," I decided. I crossed the line in 2.09 seconds. I was exhausted. But I'd added 10 points to the world record, raising the bar to 7,158.

Track & Field News named me female athlete of the year. After feeling overlooked by the publication the year before, the recognition pleased me. But I was positively overwhelmed by my selection as Sullivan Award winner. The trophy goes to the nation's top amateur athlete. When I heard my name at the awards dinner in February 1987, I burst into tears. I was deeply honored and genuinely shocked. The other nominees included Vinny Testaverde, the University of Miami quarterback, and David Robinson, the basketball star from Navy. I just knew one of them would win because they were so well known, their accomplishments so well publicized. Vinny was the Heisman Trophy winner and David had set a slew of college basketball records on his way to being named Collegiate Player of the Year by *The Sporting News.* ·

My selection indicated that the voters had taken the time to find out who I was and what the heptathlon was about. It was gratifying. I hoped it signaled the beginning of a higher profile for my little sport. That night, I recalled the reaction of a young boy who asked me for an autograph after the Olympic Festival. As I signed his program, he asked what I did. I told him and he asked me to explain the heptathlon. I was in the middle of the list when he said, "Wow! You do all those?" I hoped my award would prompt other people to get similarly excited about the event in coming years.

22

Super Woman

The heptathlon is such a rigorous competition, it completely drains me. Even in reasonably good weather—no humidity, moderate temperatures—I lose about five pounds over the course of the two-day competition. In conditions like those in Houston I've sometimes lost almost ten pounds during the forty-eight-hour period. I'm also on the brink of dehydration by the end of the 800 meters, which is why Bobby rushes to me with water as soon as I'm finished. Add to that strain a long-jump competition a few days later and it's almost too much for one human body. But my love for the long jump blinds me to the perils.

Bobby has a completely different attitude. Because the risk of injury is so great in the long jump, for many years he resisted the notion of my competing in the event while I'm competing in the heptathlon. But in 1987, after much begging from me, he relented.

Even I knew I was flirting with disaster by trying to long-jump at the Pan Am Games in Indianapolis in August, just two weeks before the World Championships. I would surely have to withdraw from the Worlds and miss the chance to defend my number one ranking if I pulled a hamstring, twisted an ankle or worse in the long jump. So I promised Bobby that at the first indication of injury or pain, I would withdraw. I adored the conditions on the track in Indianapolis. They were ideal for long jumping. The weather was mild. The sand was soft. The runway was Mondo.

I couldn't wait to jump. Because Bobby was so reluctant to let me do it, I felt like a ten-year-old girl again, sneaking a jump while the coach wasn't looking. I guess I was overanxious. On my third run, I charged down the runway so fast I had to slow up to find the board. I jumped 23' 9½" and won the competition. The photographers, seated on a bench inside a trackside pit that resembled a baseball dugout, began packing up their gear for the night and shuffling off the field. But I still had a jump left. Bobby held his thumb and index finger about an inch apart and pointed away from the starting line—a signal to move the start of the run back a smidgen. As I walked back to the start line, Tony Duffy, a photographer who lingered in the pit, asked if I was taking the last jump. I said yes. He set up, and so did I. Running as hard as I could, I attacked the runway, pumping my arms and trying to lift my knees to my throat. I planted my right leg without looking and came down some 24 feet later. The officials huddled around my landing spot in the sand. Someone put a yellow mark in the spot where my heels sunk in the sand. Another pointed a telescope-like object containing an optical laser at the yellow mark and peered through the eyehole. More huddling. Another official-looking man arrived and pulled out a steel tape. The rules required a steel tape measure to confirm all world records. My heart leaped. I watched the ten men study the area for several agonizing minutes more. One of them finally came over to me and said, "Jackie, you tied the world record. I couldn't stretch it." I had jumped 24' 5½", which equaled the record held by Heike Drechsler of East Germany.

I was elated. And so glad I had been selfish, just this once, and insisted on competing in the long jump. This one was for me. I raised my arms and cheered for myself. On that calm August night, I'd leaped all the way from my porch railing to the top of the world, and the feeling was fine.

I get such satisfaction from competing in individual events. Not only does it alleviate the boredom of just doing the heptathlon, it puts a new set of challenges on my plate. I have to hold my own against the very best specialists in the world, which means my performance must reach a higher level than that demanded in the heptathlon. From time to time, I've also competed in the 100-meter hurdles and the 400 hurdles. I like testing myself that way. It's fun.

But with the 1988 Olympic Games in my sights, I turned away from such diversions after 1987 to concentrate on the serious business of trying to win gold medals in the heptathlon and the long jump. We arrived a few days early in Rome, the site of the 1987 World Championships. Our first day there, Bobby and I spent a harrowing morning driving through the city streets on our way to tour the Vatican. The traffic is crazier than anything I've ever seen. Cars got tied up and drivers would jump out and start shouting at one another, in the middle of an intersection. I was relieved when we arrived at the Vatican in one piece. While Bobby read the panels and brochures describing the history, I studied the artwork and the sculpture, imagining the patience and dedication it took to craft something so perfect and beautiful. It was inspiring. It reminded me of the process I went through to break the 7,000-point barrier in the heptathlon.

The competition was held in Olympic Stadium, site of

Wilma Rudolph's triumph during the 1960 Games. But it was the upcoming 1988 Games that were on everyone's mind.

The biggest challenges for me in Rome were the conditions. First, 75-degree temperatures and 86 percent humidity during the heptathlon; then a dangerous, track-slickening rain in the long jump. I won the heptathlon with a score of 7,128 points, some 564 points ahead of Larisa Nikitina of the USSR. But by the end I was severely dehydrated and close to collapsing. Dwight Stones grabbed me for an interview on NBC Sports immediately after the 800 and I was so woozy from the heat that I couldn't comprehend what he was saying. I could hear him and see him talking, but I didn't understand what he was asking me. I have no idea what I said or whether I made any sense at all. I only remember being very dizzy and feeling faint. Bobby was waiting as soon as the interview was done. He handed me a bottle of water and doused me with another, then led me out of the stadium to the first aid area.

It took a day to recover from the effects of the heptathlon. It was tough. Bob Forster, my physical therapist, iced and massaged my legs twice. On the second day, I went out to the warmup track and jogged around at a leisurely speed to keep the muscles loose before the long-jump competition.

Sportswriters speculated that I couldn't come back because I'd been so drained by the heptathlon. But it never entered my mind that I wouldn't. Whenever I compete in two events in one meet, I always try to put the experience of the heptathlon behind me and move into the long jump as if it's my one and only competition. Even if I feel fatigued, I won't give in to it. On that jog, I kept telling myself, "You can do it, you can do it."

The next day, I scampered through the rain to hit

24' 1¾" on my third leap. I thought it was a good, legal jump. But a frowning face appeared on the track's electronic scoreboard, indicating that officials ruled the jump a foul. In the stands, Bobby was frowning, too. And fighting mad.

I did a double-take at the referee. I wanted to say, "Hey, you can't do this! Why do you want to take my jump from me?" But I kept my cool and walked back to the starting area, figuring that if I had to jump again, I could do it. I wanted to focus on the positive, not on being upset and angry. That would only distract me and sap my energy if I needed to jump again. Besides, through their sustained whistles and howls, the boisterous 41,000 stadium spectators were expressing enough outrage for them *and* me.

Fortunately for all of us, instant replay had come to track by then and when a tape of my jump was shown on the screen, it showed clearly that my toe was a quarter of an inch behind the line. Upon reviewing the replay, the officials changed the ruling. No one jumped farther, including runner-up Heike Drechsler of East Germany, with whom I shared the world record. I was the heptathlon and long-jump world champion!

Bobby and I celebrated over pizza, cannelloni and my favorite pasta of all—tortellini—at a restaurant not far from our hotel. I sat on two plastic bags of ice that the waiter had graciously made up for me so that I could ice my hamstrings during dinner.

A photograph of me preparing to heave the javelin during the heptathlon appeared on the cover of the next week's issue of *Sports Illustrated* beside the billing: "SUPER WOMAN." It was my first *SI* cover appearance.

I said *ciao* to Rome with my two gold medals packed safely away. No injuries. No upsets. Everything was falling nicely into place for the final push toward the Games in Seoul, South Korea.

After a few more meets in Europe, we returned to Drake Stadium at the end of the year to prepare for the Olympic Trials. The days were intense and exhausting. Typically I was at the track by 8:00 A.M. for warmups and didn't leave until dusk, at around 6:00. Mornings were devoted to endurance work, including timed, repetitive sprints and stair-climbing drills. The routine began at the end of the indoor season in April and continued until the Trials in July.

One memorable morning in May, I inhaled the aroma of the freshly cut infield grass as I stepped off the last stair at the end of a run through the stadium with Florence, Jeanette, Val, Alice and Al. It hadn't been terribly taxing. Bobby had spared us his usual five-minutes-around-the-whole-stadium sprint. I was slightly winded, but I would recover on the walk to the next drill. We'd all been through the pattern a thousand times before over the past three years.

Suddenly, there in broad daylight, I saw stars. Then I felt my throat closing. I stopped walking and bent over, my palms gripping my knees. I was wheezing. I couldn't get a breath. I was terrified. I started to cry. Al rushed over and asked what was wrong.

"I'm scared," I said, my voice whistling. "I can't breathe!"

Al and Bobby tried to rush me to the car, but I kept grabbing their arms, stopping them. I didn't want to move too quickly. With every step, my throat tightened further. I was sure it would close completely. It was like trying to breathe through a coffee straw.

The doctors at UCLA Medical Center told me I'd just suffered a full-blown asthma attack. A very serious one. They immediately connected me to an IV containing antibiotics and the steroid prednisone, which works to counteract allergies and is frequently prescribed for asthmatics.

The drug poses two problems for me. As a steroid, it is

banned in track competition. It's allowed during training, however. So, I had to stay out of competition while ingesting it and for several weeks afterward, until it was out of my system. But unlike most steroids, prednisone isn't a performance-enhancing drug. On the contrary, it breaks down muscle tissue and makes me weaker. That's the second problem. I feel healthier as an asthmatic when I'm on prednisone, but as an athlete, I feel lethargic and weak. I don't like any of its side effects, really. When the doctors give me high dosages immediately after a bad attack, my bones and joints ache and my eyes and face get puffy, as if I'm retaining water. But I haven't had the severe weight gain that a lot of people experience while taking it for extended periods. I'm never on it for very long and have taken it only when I'm in danger of getting a cold or the flu. My doctors have warned me that having an attack when I have the flu or a cold can be deadly, because an asthma attack while my lungs are congested and inflamed could suffocate me. The doctor prescribes prednisone for limited periods, to go along with whatever antibiotic I'm taking to quickly end the cold or virus.

It wasn't news to me that I had asthma. I'd taken Bobby's advice a few years earlier and consulted a specialist, Dr. Roger Katz, who told me I was asthmatic. Actually, Bobby made me go. "Asthma? What's that?" I asked Dr. Katz, annoyed by the notion that I, a world-class athlete in superb physical condition, might have some debilitating affliction. When he explained the condition and told me I'd have to take medicine regularly to control it, I shrugged. It didn't sound serious to me.

Dr. Katz prescribed several pills, including theophylline, and an inhaler containing Ventolin. But every year after that, particularly in the spring, the shortness of breath became worse and worse. Now, three years later, sitting in the emergency room bed, the doctors told me that my allergies to grass aggravated the asthma and had caused the attack.

I knew this latest incident would make Bobby overprotective. But I wasn't about to let that happen. Things were going too well for me. I was finally at the place I wanted to be in athletics. I was coming off my finest season ever, having settled comfortably into the top ranks of the heptathlon and the long jump. I was right on target for the 1988 Olympics and I hoped that great things were in store for me at Seoul.

The doctor said it was important that I take the medicine he prescribed. No problem, I thought, I can handle it. All I had to do when I felt sick was to stay relaxed, catch my breath, take the medicine. That would take care of everything. I left the hospital determined not to let asthma stop me.

Just before the Trials, however, I had another close call. This time I was at home. Bobby and I were living in Canoga Park, California. He wasn't at home but Val had stopped by. It's a good thing she did. I don't recall what prompted it, but I started getting hot and seeing stars. I began to panic, because I knew it was another attack. I started stripping off my clothes, trying to get air any way I could. I felt like the clothes were restricting my ability to inhale and exhale. I was working so hard to get every breath, my whole body was heaving.

I called for Val, who was in the living room. She found my inhaler, gave it to me, then called 911. The paramedic arrived and asked me questions about my condition that I couldn't answer. I tried and tried to convince him I was going to be okay. But he insisted on taking me to the hospital.

When Bobby arrived, he and the doctors scolded me for not taking my medicine. I promised to reform. And I did— for a few days. But as soon as I felt better, I slacked off.

Later, I stopped taking it altogether, as if I were cured. I just wouldn't accept the idea that I had a serious illness that required constant pill-popping and being chained to an inhaling device. Just like in 1983, the only thing on my mind was Olympic gold.

23

Another Kind of Grace

After Houston and Rome, I thought I was ready for any and all weather conditions at the Olympic Trials in July in Indianapolis. But standing on the track and feeling 115-degree heat rising from the rubber surface was like being inside a barbecue pit.

The heat turned out to be less stressful than what happened to some of my teammates. I watched in horror, my hand over my mouth, as Jeanette screamed and fell to the track halfway through the quarterfinals of the 100 meters, grabbing her ankle. I knew what had happened. Her Achilles tendon was sore coming into the meet. She had ruptured it and run her last race. Oh, my God, I thought. What's next?

It was a roller-coaster Trials. Val just missed making the 200 team. We cried together.

In her quarterfinal heat of the 100, Florence turned heads around the world with her sexy racing outfit, a purple body suit with the left leg cut off, topped off by a pair of turquoise bikini briefs. Then she kept everyone's attention by running a breathtaking 10.49 seconds. It was a new world record, one that probably won't be broken for decades. I was ecstatic for her.

Greg Foster, running with a cast on his broken left arm, bumped his right arm against the left arm of a competitor in an adjacent lane during the 110-meter hurdles. The collision knocked Greg off balance and he had to stop running in the middle of the race to avoid falling on his bad arm. Time for tears again.

Andre Phillips earned a spot behind Edwin Moses on the 400 hurdles team. More celebrating.

Then it was my turn. I felt the heat. But it didn't bother me. I sailed through the hurdles in 12.71, setting an American heptathlon record in the process. I set another one in the high jump, with a 6' 4" leap, just as it started to rain and cool things off a bit. This was fun.

I had to shot-put in a downpour, but managed to heave it 51' 4¼". I set a heptathlon world record and my third American record of the day by running 22.3 seconds in the 200. Final score: 4,367 points. I was on pace to hit 7,300 points! I was in the zone again, clicking on all cylinders.

The next day, I long-jumped 25 feet, but it was a foul. I played it safe from there, dropping down to 22' 11¾" on the next jump. My javelin throwing had improved during training and I hurled it 164' 4", right after Jeanette went down in the 100. Watching her traumatic collapse had yanked me out of my zone momentarily. I had to really bear down and block out the sorrow I felt for her to pull it off.

To beat my own world record, I needed to run the 800 in at least 2:24.95. That would be easy. I had run faster than that to win the Junior Olympics when I was fifteen.

But Bobby had cautioned me the night before about the expectations trap. By posting an extraordinary score, which was now a probability, I might be setting myself up for disappointment and criticism at the Olympics if I couldn't improve on it. "I think you should ease up on the 800 because it's going to be hard to come back and top 7,300 points at the Olympics," he advised me. Once again, I needed to know both how and why in order to reach my goal. I knew how to reach 7,300, and I knew why it was best not to achieve it now.

I stayed off the accelerator during the 800, following Cindy Greiner to the finish line and crossing it in 2:20.7. I finished with 7,215 points. A new world record. One down, one to go.

Cindy finished second. I was delighted for her. But I was heartbroken for poor Jane Frederick. She reinjured her pesky hamstring in the long jump and lost the race for the third spot to Wendy Brown. I gave her a hug and, as I panted, told her I was sorry she wouldn't be with us in Seoul.

I was still doubled over, struggling to get my breath when Bobby reached me. He asked if my asthma was acting up, and I truthfully answered no. He poured two big bottles of cold water over my back and waited for me to recover.

From the track, Bob, Bobby and I walked inside and mounted the stage in the press room. We removed the microphones from the long interview table. I climbed onto the table and lay on my stomach. Bobby placed four hot-water bottles full of ice under me, one on each hip and each thigh. In front of the roomful of reporters, Bob began to massage my leg muscles, while I propped myself up on my elbows, held the microphone and prepared to take the first question.

At that moment, the press box announcer's voice came over the intercom. The men's triple jump was over. I held up my index finger, asking for a minute to listen to the results. "Willie Banks, Charlie Simpkins, Robert Cannon," the voice said.

Al hadn't made the team. I shrugged and forced a smile of resignation. Then I dropped my head and broke down. This news was more disappointing for me than any of the day's other developments because it was about my brother. I wanted so badly for us to return to the Olympics and try again for brother-and-sister gold medals. I also wanted it for him. Al had come such a long way from his wild teenage days at home. He'd really gotten himself together and settled down. His friendship with Florence had grown into a romance, and they had recently gotten married. I knew how much he wanted to make the team after Florence's performance.

Bittersweet. That's what the 1988 Olympic Trials had been for all of us.

From the Trials, the four of us, Al, Florence, Bobby and I, flew to New York to appear on *Good Morning America*. After sitting on the couch in front of the camera and talking about how track was a family affair for us, and how much fun we all had together, Al and Florence headed back to Los Angeles and we flew to Orlando, Florida, for a vacation at Disney World. Bobby's last words to them were: "I'll call you about practice when we get back to L.A."

The next day, we hopped into a cab outside our hotel to go to the Epcot Center. The cab driver recognized us from television. Then he started talking about how sorry he was to hear about what had happened. "Family should stick together, you know," he said.

Bobby said, "I'm sorry. I don't know what you're talking about."

The driver handed him the morning paper.

The article said Florence and Al had announced that they were no longer going to be coached and managed by Bobby. They'd hired a new manager and Al was taking over as Florence's coach.

Bobby told the driver to take us to Epcot. He saw no need to call Florence and Al to discuss it. Bobby said the decision spoke for itself, adding that everyone had the right to move on.

With no contracts or commitments tying them to Bobby, Al and Florence were certainly free to leave. But I was shocked and disappointed. There are appropriate and inappropriate ways to do things. And I think they handled this all wrong. Bobby and I shouldn't have had to find out about something like that by reading it in the paper. I didn't understand why they hadn't told us when we were together in New York. Or called us on the phone.

As for the decision to leave, that was their prerogative. I wished we all could have continued to train together. But, after I got over the initial shock and sadness, I resigned myself to it.

I think the decision hurt Bobby more than he revealed. He had coached Florence for nearly ten years. He thought of her as a daughter, the way he does Gail Devers, the 1992 and 1996 gold medalist in the 100 meters. He's known them both since they were in high school.

The news stunned everyone in our World Class Track Club. But we all just wanted to put it behind us and concentrate on preparing for the Olympics. The media wouldn't let us, though. Before and during the Games, there were articles everywhere about the four of us, inaccurately depicting us as feuding in-laws. A profile of Florence published in *Newsweek* helped ignite the controversy. Quoting Florence, the article claimed Bobby tried to alienate me from Al, which was absolutely false. The article also contained a widely reprinted quote from Florence to the effect that Bobby ran the track club like a cult. A hundred times I have been asked to respond to the quote and a hundred times I've refused because I've never seen the need to do so. People can hold whatever opinion they like about his coaching style, but the results Bobby has produced in international competition, in terms of Olympic medals, world records and world championships, speak for themselves.

Many of the pieces published after that one zeroed in on my relationship with Florence, and our so-called contrasting styles. Invariably they referred to her as glamorous and to me as conservative, and implied that I was jealous of her. I had no reason to envy Florence. I'm very secure with myself. I wasn't as close to her as I was to Jeanette and Val. But we were friendly, and we were teammates who supported each other.

What frustrated and insulted me was the inaccurate characterization of me by the people who wrote those stories. The perception of me as conservative is based on two things: One, I compete in the heptathlon, which is regarded as grueling, whereas the sprint races are considered glamour events. Two, I choose not to put on a lot of makeup and jewelry or wear flashy outfits during competition. But what you see of me on the track is only one facet of my personality. Off the track, I like makeup and nail polish and brightly colored clothes as much as any woman.

When I'm competing, I'm engaged in a battle. And when you're in a battle, things sometimes get untidy. So, if it's pouring rain and the wind is gusting when it's my turn to throw the javelin, I've got bigger concerns than whether every strand of my hair is in place. Likewise, I can't help it if, after running 800 meters in 118-degree heat, I don't look like I just stepped out of a beauty salon.

When I was in high school, some people believed that playing sports would make girls unfeminine. Now, people were trying to categorize certain women's sports as more feminine than others. It's all so nonsensical and irrelevant. I told Tom Callahan of *Time* magazine during an interview before the 1988 Games that "I don't think being an athlete is unfeminine. I think of it as a kind of grace."

As for what or who is truly beautiful and glamorous, I look beyond the superficial. I see beauty, elegance and grace in every female athlete. Selfishly speaking, I believe there's something especially beautiful about the ability to perform seven distinct athletic skills well. I consider heptathletes the Renaissance women of track and field. In my mind, ours is the most glamorous competition of all.

Reporters continued to ask me about Florence and to ask Florence about me. I wasn't stupid. I understood the true agenda. They wanted to pit us against each other so they could portray us as a couple of cat-fighting, egomaniacal women. It was not only sexist, it was untrue. And I wasn't going to fall into their trap.

Florence and I discussed the situation one night on the phone for a long time. We wished each other well at the Olympics and agreed that we couldn't allow outsiders to tear our family apart. Since then, the birth of little Mary Joyner, Al and Florence's daughter, has brought us all even closer.

After the talk with Florence, I pushed the issue out of my mind. I had to stay focused on what I was trying to do. Nothing could distract me from my objective at the Games. One night before we left for Seoul, Bobby and I were on a shopping trip. After pulling the car into the parking spot at Sears, he turned to me with the most serious look on his face. "Let's make each other a promise," he said. "Let's promise to make this Olympic experience fun."

That sounded like a great idea to me.

He had one more request. "In that spirit, I think we should dedicate these Games to our mothers, who aren't here to experience them with us."

Such a sweet sentiment. I nodded and started to weep. We kissed.

Bobby also did his best to keep the bad omens at bay. *USA Today* wanted me to pose for photographs in front of a Buddhist temple in Seoul before the competition began. When we arrived, a service was underway inside. We heard the chanting outside. Bobby thought it wasn't respectful to be taking photos outside while the service was going on inside and insisted the photographers find another location. "I'm not going to start pissing off God now," he said.

The conditions were ideal for a high heptathlon score. It was September in Seoul and the weather felt like Southern California in spring, highs in the seventies, lows in the sixties. Bobby figured I could cut 10 seconds from my 800 times under those conditions. The big East German threat was Anke Behmer. She joined her veteran teammate Ines Schultz. Natalya Shubenkova of the Soviet Union was there, too.

I was startled to see Sabine Paetz, who'd gotten married and was now Sabine John, jogging around the warmup track. She'd given everyone in the West the impression she'd retired. I hadn't seen her at a meet since the 1986 Goodwill Games. Must have been a long honeymoon, I thought to myself as I watched her run. Seeing her annoyed me. Here was a woman who hadn't competed in two years and all of a sudden she shows up at the Olympic Games! No matter, I told myself, I'm ready.

Sabine's presence upset me more than I realized. The first event is the hurdles and she's a superb hurdler. Her 12.64-second performance in 1984 still stands as the heptathlon world record. I didn't know what kind of shape she'd be in. But I knew it would be a fast race. At the starting blocks, I put pressure on myself. "You've got to be strong and tough, Jackie," I whispered. "Don't let her beat you. Don't let her beat you."

I got out of the blocks well, but I hit a hurdle and stumbled. John was charging on my heels and had practically pulled even with me. I remembered Bobby's coaching: "If a mishap occurs, keep your composure and try to stay one step ahead of your competitor." I pulled away and registered a 12.69. I hadn't buckled. I'd kept my composure and recovered. It boosted my confidence. I wasn't going to let her upset my concentration or beat me.

The high jump would be a real test. Here was an opportunity to score big points because my technique was vastly improved. I was finally getting the hang of the flop. I didn't want to squander the chance. But, I was scared. I had a slight case of tendinitis in my left knee and it was killing me. The left leg is my launch leg and I thought my weakened knee was going to let me down. I struggled to get my speed right on the approach and then strained my ailing knee trying to clear a measly 6' 1¼". I couldn't jump any higher. Luckily for me, none of my competitors jumped exceedingly well. Still, I was nearly 100 points off world-record pace.

As Bob taped the knee, I knew it would bother me for the rest of the day. This would be a real test to see if I'd learned anything from 1984.

The shot put requires a right-handed athlete to bend slightly and push off the left leg while tossing the metal ball. It's murder on a strained knee tendon. But I stared down the pain. "These are the Olympics, Jackie," I said. "You're gonna have to block it out."

I put the shot 51' 10". Okay, but not great. I was proud of myself for hanging tough against the pain and staying positive. It spurred me on.

I ran the 200 meters in a so-so 22.56 seconds. By the end of the day, I was 181 points in front of John, but 103 points off the world-record pace. With the shape my knee was in, my primary concern was holding off John and the others to win the gold medal. But I knew the record was well within reach. I knew my knee would hold up if I needed to push it a little to get the record.

Overnight I slept soundly, despite a half-dozen electric wires taped to my left leg that sent electrical stimulation to my aching patellar tendon. The stimulation keeps the muscle from swelling, and contracts and relaxes it to keep it loose. It's like having a physical therapist massage it all night. I also had a gigantic bag full of ice on the leg to keep the blood flowing and to prevent soreness after straining it during competition.

After a breakfast of pancakes, I was off to the warmup track. I felt relaxed. Bobby and I looked around at the other athletes and chatted about nothing important for fifteen minutes. I got up and started a low-speed jog. I didn't want to exhaust myself ahead of time.

I needed a big jump to set the stage for the rest of the day. The gold and the record, if they were to be mine, would be won or lost right here. Fortunately for me, my plant leg in the long jump is the right leg. It was strong and healthy. I could let it rip. That was my intention as I took off from the starting mark. I didn't keep my legs upright through the air as long as I would have liked. But it was a new heptathlon long-jump world record, 23' 10¼", and good for a whopping 1,264 points. No one jumped nearly as far. Just like that, the record was back in hand. And I had pretty much slammed the door on my competitors.

The wonderfully maddening thing about the heptathlon, though, is the way it can jump up and bite you just when you think you've got it under control. That's why I never give up or get too cocky when I have a lead. And so it was with the javelin competition. I needed a strong left leg again for pushing off and mine was sore and achy. Without much of a leg to stand on, I fell into my old habit of arming the throw—not using my legs at all. The result: a disgusting 149' 10". I shook my head after my last attempt. I knew I could have and should have done better.

So, as usual, everything came down to the 800. I wanted so badly to win the heptathlon, I had to calm myself down at the starting line. My adrenaline was pumping. My heart was pounding. I wanted to prove that I was much better than my performance in 1984. The victories in Moscow, Houston, Rome and Indianapolis had been satisfying. But they weren't the Olympic Games. If I didn't turn in a winning performance here, none of those other wins would matter much. This is what they would remember. This is the Super Bowl. The others were just the preseason.

I needed to run a 2:13.67 to break the record. I had so much anxious energy I felt I could run it in 2:10. Keeping in mind Brooks Johnson's targets, I knew I wanted a 62-second pace at the 400-meter mark, halfway. That meant a very fast first lap and a lung-busting second one. I shot ahead at the start with all the power I could muster. Shubenkova overtook me and had a 62.63-second time at the halfway point. I was right behind at 63:60. My stomach started to burn. "Oh no! What's this, Jackie?" I wondered to myself.

The three Germans passed me. I was falling off the pace. I quickly stanched the impulse to dwell on the pain. "Block it out, block it out," I ordered my brain. "If your legs aren't burning, you can still run."

A fresh surge of adrenaline shot through me. With 200 meters to go, I had caught them, and even contemplated passing them. But I still had 200 long meters left. I decided to stay put. I was in fifth place. But I knew I was on the right pace. I could feel it.

At the last turn, I just pushed and pushed and pushed some more. I actually felt good sprinting to the line. I was content to finish fifth in the race, because I knew I was first overall. And first in the world. The clock read: 2:08.51

"Yes!" I screamed silently. I was overjoyed. The 1984 demons were exorcised. After four years of heated arguments, exhausting workouts, strategy sessions, pressure, massages and ice packs, I had my Olympic heptathlon gold medal. And a new world record score of 7,291 points.

Two days later, Ben Johnson shattered the world record in the men's 100-meter finals. Three days after that, the International Olympic Committee announced that he failed his drug test and had to surrender his gold medal. In the span of seventy-two hours, track and field went from ecstasy to agony. Pandemonium reigned. All of the reporting about performances stopped as journalists tried to figure out who would be caught next. Every question, it seemed, was about drugs and test results.

I was shocked. I couldn't believe it was happening at the Olympics. But I still had the long-jump competition and I didn't want to get caught up in the chaos. I prepared myself in case anyone questioned me. Otherwise I kept my mind on my own business.

The speculation, however, got to be outrageous. Suddenly every successful athlete at the Games was viewed suspiciously. Athletes were pointing fingers and whispering about each other. The atmosphere was pure poison. The thinking was, if you'd been a perennial second or third and had started winning, there was reason to wonder. But I'd never believed for a minute that every successful athlete was using performance-enhancing drugs.

The night before the long-jump competition began, I was dragged into the muck. Joaquim Cruz, the gold medalist in the 800 meters in 1984, and silver medalist in 1988, told a television reporter that I looked like a gorilla and that Florence and I "must be doing something that isn't normal to gain all those muscles."

I didn't care about the steroid allegations because I knew I was clean. I had been tested as much as any athlete at the

Games and I'd always passed. But I really took offense at the gorilla comment. Besides being cruelly unflattering, it smacked of racism. I was also offended that the media played up the quote as much as it did. I kept hearing it over and over on the television news the night before the long-jump competition.

"They think this is so cute," I said to Bobby, disgusted as I listened to the story. He was lying on the sofa, munching peanuts. He didn't flinch as he watched the report. "Someone calling me, a black woman, a gorilla. He might as well have just called me a nigger." I didn't think it was at all newsworthy.

The phone started ringing. Reporters wanted a comment from us about the story. Cruz, shamed by my brother and my father when they confronted him in the Olympic Village, denied he'd said those things. Bobby handled it all. I wasn't interested in discussing the matter with reporters and I certainly didn't want to hear anything Cruz had to say. Later, my brother and father watched a tape of the interview in which Cruz did indeed utter those words. They came storming into our room, incensed and talking about what we should do about the lies. Bobby, suppressing his outrage to keep me from getting upset, told them to ignore the whole thing—at least until after the Games were over.

I tried to put it out of my mind. It was another intrusion, a distraction from my appointed purpose at Seoul. I reminded myself that getting upset about it and wasting energy being angry the way Al and my father were would be a victory for the intruders. But I was upset.

I didn't have breakfast the next morning. I just wanted to get away from it all. I went to the track early to find some peace. I also felt I'd be better protected from reporters on the warmup field.

The Inter-Continental Hotel provided bodyguards to all

the athletes who were guests. Those men were the greatest. Every morning at 6:00 A.M. there was a knock on the door and a voice said, "Bodyguards are here." The two men, dressed in khaki pants and white shirts, waited for me to come out of the room into the hall. They weren't the beefy kind of guys I envisioned. They looked more like Secret Service agents—quiet, serious and conscientious. It was a wonderful luxury and it made me feel very secure. They escorted me to my destination and, as a precaution, hung close by as I walked around.

Since the Munich Games in 1972, where Palestinian terrorists killed several Israeli athletes, there was an ever-present fear of attacks at the Games. Those fears were heightened in Seoul because of the hostilities between North and South Korea. The bodyguards drove me around the city in a little van. I didn't have to bother with the regular athletes' transportation. I was dropped off right on the warmup track. Later, when I went shopping for dolls after my events were over, they shadowed me in and out of the shops.

So that morning, I sat peacefully on the grassy infield, beneath one of the tents on the warmup track with my two Korean bodyguards. There were only a handful of people out. Most of them were other long jumpers. I felt completely safe and sheltered from the chaos swirling around the Games. That time alone out there relaxed me and got me back into the right frame of mind after the unsettling events of the night before.

Heike Drechsler showed up after an hour or so. We couldn't really talk because of the constraints imposed by her government. But she congratulated me for winning the heptathlon and smiled. Then we both started our warmup routine. Gradually the track became crowded as other athletes and coaches began filing in. Florence and the other runners in the 200-meter sprints, also scheduled for that day, showed up. The smell of Icy Hot, Ben-Gay and other ointments filled the air as the physical therapists began their morning massages, loosening the tight, sore muscles of their athletes.

After a light jog around the track, I stretched out my legs. My front thigh muscles, the quadriceps, were tight. At about forty minutes before the competition, the officials summoned all the long jumpers to the call room, where our shoes and other equipment was checked to make sure they were legal. After that, we sat around for fifteen minutes until they were time for the ride to the track.

Throughout the competition, I was having trouble hitting the board. Though Heike had jumped 23' 8¼", the best I could do on my fourth jump was foul. Between jumps, Bob Forster massaged my legs. I kept whispering to myself, "You're *not* tired. You're *not* tired." I was starting to feel fatigued and I didn't want those thoughts getting too close to my consciousness.

Bobby, dressed in a blue cap, blue warmup pants and T-shirt, hollered to me, "Accelerate through and hold the extension. Let Sir Isaac Newton drop you out of the air."

At the line before my second-to-last jump, I said out loud, "Think indefatigable." Then I took off. It was a good leap. I sat down in the hole dug by my heels, a sign that I had grabbed every inch that I could out of the jump. The measuring tape extended to 24' 3¼". It was an Olympic record. Bobby let out a blood-curdling scream and lay out on his back on the stadium floor. I ran back to the waiting area with my face in my hands. I was overjoyed. Heike had one jump left. She gave it a good go, but only managed 23' 6¼". The gold medal was mine. Heike came over and hugged me.

Bobby was so excited—more than I was, I think. When I saw him down on the track, my first thought was that he might not have clearance to be there. "Are you supposed to be down here?" I asked worriedly. "I don't want them to take away my gold medal."

He wanted me to take a victory lap, but I resisted at first, feeling it was cocky. I hadn't taken one since an embarrassing incident at a high school track meet.

At that meet, the scores were announced after the last race and the speaker said Lincoln had finished first. All of us Tigerettes chanted, danced and bragged during our victory lap. We carried on for almost a half-hour. Then, the loudspeaker came on again and the announcer said there'd been a mistake. The officials had miscalculated and we weren't the winners. They took back our trophy and awarded it to—of all schools—our crosstown rival, East St. Louis High. We were devastated. The obvious lesson: We never should have behaved so ungraciously. I vowed then that I would never take another victory lap.

Besides, I'd never seen a jumper take one. But Bobby was adamant, "As much hell as I've been through, you'd better get out there and enjoy it." And so, I trotted around the track, waving to the crowd, wearing a big grin, overcome with joy about my second gold medal.

There wasn't much joy at the press conference afterward. It was crowded and chaotic. Reporters and photographers and television cameras jockeyed for vantage points and seats. Others sat or stood in any empty space they could find. They all wanted to know what I thought of the comment made the night before. "I'm not using drugs and I'm not on steroids," I said emphatically.

Then I added something I'd been wanting to say for a long time but had kept to myself. Because of Cruz's comment about my looks, I thought it was the perfect time. I told them that I had read and heard all the disparaging remarks about my appearance. "I never thought I was the prettiest person in the world," I said. "But I know that, inside, I'm beautiful."

As pleased as I was with my performance, I was disheartened about the reception I received. At the press conference and interviews immediately afterward, I felt like the journalists were searching for something that wasn't there and giving short shrift to my achievement. They wanted to talk about Cruz, about Florence, about steroids. Anything except my heptathlon world record, my long-jump Olympic record and my two gold medals.

The final straw was the zillionth question about whether I'd taken steroids during a press conference in New York, a month after the Games. The Women's Sports Foundation had named me Amateur Athlete of the Year and the steroid question was one of the first ones asked. "No, I've never used drugs," I said as convincingly as I could. "I will put my hand on a Bible."

I was so tired of the whispering and veiled accusations and never-ending queries, I broke down in tears. How many times did I have to deny it before they believed me?

"I do not take steroids," I said again. "I never have. It's sad to me that people want to point fingers. I don't do that. That's not me. I wouldn't feel like a human being. I've never thought about taking drugs even in childhood. I see what they have done to my own family. My grandmother was shot to death by the man she married. He was involved with drugs and alcohol. He shot her. Growing up, I lived across the street from a liquor store and near a poolhall. Every day something was going on. Some days, my father would come home drunk."

I wiped my face and continued. "There are a lot of reasons now why I won't even take a drink. I don't feel like putting anything into my body. It took a long time before I would even take an aspirin."

It was so frustrating. Partly, I felt the allegations were a reflection on the fact that I'm from East St. Louis. Some people think it's a corrupt place, so they figure I must be a corrupt person. I know I shouldn't be so sensitive. And I tried not to be. But it finally got to be too much. After the nasty stories following Al and Florence's announcement, to have to deal with these accusations and suspicions was more than I could bear. The whole experience left a bitter taste in my mouth and made me very cynical about the media.

I'd finally reached the pinnacle of my profession. Finally achieved my goals. But I wasn't allowed to enjoy it and feel good about it. Jealous athletes and scandal-hungry journalists were trying to tear me down and make me feel bad. It frustrated and angered me. It wasn't fair. I wanted to quit track and field.

24

Rejuvenation

East St. Louis looked more depressed than I'd ever seen it on the cold, gray January afternoon in 1989 when I visited for a homecoming celebration. A dusting of snow covered the ground, but it couldn't hide the gloomy reality.

I visited my hometown a dozen times or more during the year, so I knew the general condition of things. But the decay I noticed as we drove through my neighborhood disturbed me more than usual.

The rust-colored smokestacks of the manufacturing plant across the street from Parsons Field still belched smoke. But the days of star-making were over for the track and stadium, now hidden and forgotten amid a forest of weeds. The Al and Jackie Joyner Park that was to have been developed by the city was a deserted, unused field, with only a single slide and a set of swings. Across the street, the brick house that was to have been our gift from the city was unfinished and boarded up. Life itself seemed to be boarded up. There were no children running carefree along the sidewalks or playing games in the street the way we had. The place had no laughter, no music, no joy.

233

As our car approached the corner of Piggott and 15th Street, I looked at my childhood home. Some years earlier, lightning had struck it during a bad thunderstorm and it caught fire. My father hadn't lived there since then. The house was nothing but a raggedy, empty shell now. The fragile roof looked as if the next breeze that blew through would cave it in. Bobby and I got out of the car and walked up on the rotting porch. I showed him where I used to jump from the railing to the makeshift sand pit. Standing in the yard, the memories flooded back. I could almost hear my mother's voice calling me in to help prepare supper.

I glanced across the street at the Mary Brown Community Center. The front doors were held shut by a giant steel chain and an oversized padlock dangling on the end. The facility had closed while I was at UCLA, after the funds that kept it operating were cut from the federal budget. It pained me to see the Center like that. The closing symbolized the locking up of hope and the shuttering of ambition in my neighborhood, which I refused to accept.

The year before, I'd established the Jackie Joyner-Kersee Youth Center Foundation to provide enrichment programs for children in East St. Louis and to raise the funds to reopen the Center. The Seven Up Co., one of my sponsors, had agreed to help, donating $700 to the foundation every time I long-jumped 7 meters or accumulated 7,000 points in the heptathlon, and $7,000 for every world record.

It was a heartbreaking sight, all of it. As I'd become more successful, some people even suggested that I should disavow my hometown. "You shouldn't say you're from East St. Louis," someone in sports marketing advised. "It will hurt your image."

A reporter asked whether I was embarrassed to be from the city and whether I worried that it would tarnish my image. Even some people in the neighborhood couldn't understand why I so often came back. Such comments and questions upset me. "What do you mean?" I always countered. "East St. Louis is my home. I think by coming back, I give people there pride and hope. The city has a few problems, but it's a part of me."

As Bobby and I drove up to Lincoln High, the sight of the school was an antidote to the sadness I felt about my neighborhood's decline. Instantly, I felt happy. I got out of the car and read the marquee on the school's front lawn: "CONGRATULATIONS JACKIE JOYNER-KERSEE SEOUL OLYMPICS." I smiled. I was home.

The first thing I saw when I entered the gym to a thunderous ovation was a huge banner bearing the 7UP logo that read, "Congratulations Jackie! A Dream Come True." Several 7UP executives had flown up from Dallas to participate in the school's celebration, which I thought was a wonderful demonstration of the company's commitment. Mr. Fennoy escorted me to the podium, where I looked out on a sea of cheering voices, toothy grins and wide, bright eyes. About forty girls wore T-shirts bearing the words: "Jackie Joyner Kersee Dream Machine." Another sixty students stood along the back wall.

There was so much to tell them about the facts of life. This was my chance to educate, encourage and inspire.

My parents taught us never to hate or to dwell on racism. For Al, Debra, Angie and me, people were either good or bad, not black or white. But as I got older, I learned the harsh reality. The fact is, for black people, life is more of a struggle because we must deal with racist attitudes on an almost daily basis. Young blacks are particularly challenged because of the lack of suitable role models. Standing there, gazing at these kids, I wanted to be a symbol of the potential they all had—to play for them the role that Katherine Dunham had played for me. I wanted them to see me as someone from East St. Louis who, against the odds, had applied herself and used her talents to succeed. They needed to know that although we all start out as raw material, great possibilities lie within each of us.

Someone also had to tell them to expect criticism whenever they grasped for more. Although others might discourage their ambitions, they had to know they wouldn't find a way out without determination and a clear focus. I wanted them to keep their eyes on the prize.

With that message in mind, I stepped up to the podium. "I've been in your shoes. I know how difficult life is around here," I said. "Still, I'm proud to be from East St. Louis. I think about my raggedy old house. It represents what my family is all about and the struggles we went through to make our lives better.

"It's important to set goals and work hard—no matter how many people tell you it's useless or that you won't succeed. Without determination, your dreams of a better life won't come true. And I hope when you all are successful, you'll come back to the community and bring along a piece of your success to inspire others. Because that's the only way life in our hometown will get better."

I knew, however, that I needed to do more than just dispense platitudes. When Macy's invited me to ride a float in its Thanksgiving Day parade in New York, I got an idea. With help from 7UP, some other corporate donors and some of my foundation funds, I shared the experience with a group of boys and girls from East St. Louis, who might otherwise never get to ride a plane or visit New York City and see the parade in person. I chartered a plane to fly them from St. Louis to New York. The group numbered over 100 students, including the entire sixth grade from John Robinson Elementary, the honor roll members from Hughes Quinn Junior High, the honor students and History Club members from Lincoln High, and members of a citywide girls' club.

At lunch the day before the parade, we all sat around eating sandwiches and talking about whatever was on our minds. The night before the parade, I hosted a party for the boys and girls. Terrie Williams, a publicist from New York who was working with me at the time, arranged for Marvel Comic Book characters to entertain at the party. The room erupted with squeals and cheers when Spiderman and Green Hornet walked through the door. The superheroes handed out souvenirs and posed for pictures. The folks at Revlon also gave each girl a shiny red shopping bag full of cosmetics to take home for their mothers.

It was chilly the morning of the parade. But seeing the girls' happy, excited faces when I passed them along the parade route gave me a warm feeling. I run into some of those young women from time to time and they tell me that trip was one of the most memorable experiences of their lives.

Unfortunately, political and bureaucratic obstacles forced me to give up the dream of reopening the Community Center. But in July 1996, my foundation announced plans to build a new youth center at Kenneth Hall Park, not too far from where I grew up. We've already collected several million-dollar pledges. We've also received support from the Monsanto Fund. It won't be easy. We must raise $10 million for the first phase of construction. But I'm excited by the challenge.

Meanwhile, there are bright spots to sustain those who call East St. Louis home. The city built a big, beautiful brick stadium to replace Parsons Field and named it after Clyde Jordan, the powerful township supervisor, school board president and newspaper owner. A few years ago, the annual citywide track meet was moved to the new facility and renamed the Jackie Joyner-Kersee Relays. It's a high honor for me and another opportunity to remain con-

nected to the city's kids. Each spring, I find myself looking
forward to attending the competition.

I also like to spend several days each year working out
with the Lincoln High girls' track team at the stadium, and
indoors at the school during the winter. In 1991, Gail Devers joined our workout sessions. After our running drills
in the hallways, we led the squad into a classroom for a discussion, and I asked them to tell me about their goals. The
team wasn't as successful as it had been when I attended
the school, and I wanted to help Mr. Fennoy figure out
why.

In response to my queries, the kids offered mostly
canned responses—they wanted to be doctors, lawyers, etc.
Immediately, I was suspicious. No one had said anything
about winning a championship, which was always the first
thing out of my mouth in high school when someone
asked me that question.

"You guys are just saying stuff you think we want to
hear, but you don't fool me," I told them. "Jot down on a
piece of paper what's bothering you because I can tell
something's wrong."

Reading some of the notes broke my heart. There was a
lot of dissension on the squad. Several members were angry
that others put their boyfriends ahead of the team's goals.
Some came from families with drug problems and had no
one to talk to. A lot of the girls had similar problems, but
each felt isolated. I started a discussion about it, without
being specific, that brought them all closer together. And
that year, the team won the state championship. I was
pleased about that, liked to think that my encouragement
had played some small part in it, but helping those girls win
a trophy wasn't my ultimate goal. I was more concerned
with helping them get their lives on track.

I was so affected by the experience, I decided to include
an open forum for girls during the annual relay activities.

Each year we gather the 600 to 700 female participants in the meet and encourage them to ask questions and discuss problems with me and the other elite athletes who join me on the weekend. I hope we're making a difference.

25

Adored and Ignored

After the 1988 Olympics, I became everyone's favorite example of the cool reception women, blacks, and track and field athletes received from corporate America when seeking sponsors. I was an all-purpose victim. I was expected to be up in arms about it. But the stories assumed something that wasn't true—that I was dissatisfied with the number of endorsements I'd contracted to do or with my opportunities. As *The Wall Street Journal* correctly pointed out at the time, I was sponsored by Adidas, 7UP and asthma inhaler maker Primatene, and was doing quite well, thank you. At various times, I've also appeared in ads and commercials for Avon, Gap Stores, Procter & Gamble's Secret deodorant and Ray-Ban.

The point I kept making to journalists and others who asked me about endorsements was that more isn't always better. My sponsors have given me a lot of flexibility in fulfilling my obligations so that I have time to train sufficiently. I know a lot of struggling athletes who're caught in a Catch-22 situation. They're so desperate for training funds that they wind up with burdensome sponsorship contracts requiring them to spend many days speaking and traveling, leaving little time for training.

I particularly enjoy speaking on behalf of Nike's PLAY (Participate in the Lives of America's Youth) program, which has goals similar to those of my youth foundation. PLAY supports the Boys & Girls Clubs of America in its efforts to provide athletic, intellectual and social enrichment activities for young people.

I signed on with Nike in 1992, after the Barcelona Games. I first visited the company in 1991 while I was in Oregon with Bobby for the NCAA Championships. Bobby decided on the spur of the moment to drive over to Beaverton to Nike's headquarters, known as "The Campus." I was still under contract to Adidas at the time, but Gail was a Nike client and she had meetings scheduled with the designers about the moldings for her track shoes. While she was with them, Bobby and I strolled the campus walkways, looking at the plaques that honored great athletes. I was self-conscious about being decked out in Adidas stripes from head to toe—sweatpants, shoes, T-shirt and jacket. Had I known we were going to Nike, I would have worn something different. I apologized to one of the company officials, who was very understanding.

We were in the cafeteria having lunch when Nike's chairman, Phil Knight, of all people, walked up to our table and introduced himself. It was so thrilling. Then I remembered what I was wearing. "Oh, my God, this is like a slap in the face to this man!" I thought.

He's the head of the company. We're at the corporate headquarters. And I'm covered in the logo of his chief competitor. But if it bothered him, he showed no sign. He was very warm, and as we talked, I saw a sparkle in his eye that excited me. Here was one of the most powerful men in business and in sports, taking the time to acknowledge me—a female athlete. It meant a lot—made me feel good about him and his company. Bobby didn't approach Nike about sponsoring me for several more months, after my contract with Adidas expired. But, in my mind, that meeting was the real start of my relationship with the company. After that, every time I went to the Beaverton campus, Phil took the time to chat.

Despite my good fortune with sponsorships, I'm not blind to the narrow thinking of many on Madison Avenue and in corporate boardrooms. Companies can come up with all sorts of excuses not to use you to promote their products. If you don't fit into the mold they've already come up with, you won't get the job. And no amount of ranting and raving and complaining will change it. That's why I've always taken the view that as long as I know I've done my best on the athletic field, I've done my job. If endorsements come my way because of it, fine. But if not, it just wasn't meant to be. It doesn't do any good to bad-mouth organizations or people because of it. It's not something I can control, so I don't waste a lot of energy worrying about it.

The combination of my philanthropic work, personal appearances and disillusionment kept me off the track for much of 1989. I needed a break from the rigorous training and the endless sniping and cynicism.

I ran in a few sprint-hurdle contests during the indoor season, but continued to speak before civic and corporate groups and to visit hospitals and schools. Bobby fretted about my schedule, constantly telling me I was overdoing it. But I stubbornly plowed ahead. I enjoyed meeting people and having them greet me like an old friend. In airports or at restaurants, total strangers would walk up with big smiles on their faces and say, "Hi, Jackie!" Some gave me hugs and told me how proud they were. Others asked for an autograph or just wanted to talk.

I also judged the Miss USA Pageant, which I loved. I was a huge beauty pageant fan as a youngster and I still am. I never pass up an invitation to judge one, unless it conflicts with a prior commitment. I've also judged two Miss America pageants, the last one in September 1996. Some people criticize pageants. But they're very serious business for the contestants and the organizers and I always earnestly evaluate each young woman according to the established criteria. Sitting in the front row of the auditorium, decked out in an evening gown, makeup and jewelry, is also a lot of fun. I used to fantasize about doing such things when I was growing up. It's a great escape from the pressures of track and field.

As much as I enjoyed the limelight and charity work, however, it began to take a toll. I was constantly exhausted, dragging myself from hotel to airport and back again. In spring, I divided my time between the track and my personal appearances. The training, coupled with the strain of traveling, slowly wore me down. I lost almost twenty pounds and was physically and mentally spent.

Then I contracted a cold that hit me hard. I felt faint and weak in practice. I had no energy at all. One morning, I was so tired I couldn't get out of bed. Bobby took me to the doctor, who said I was on the verge of a mental breakdown. I argued with him, telling him he was exaggerating. But he insisted on keeping me in the hospital for two days. On the third day, he walked into my room and said, "I'll release you on one condition—that you take a vacation."

Bobby and I packed our suitcases and flew to Maui for a week. It was the honeymoon we'd never had. I went shopping while Bobby went sightseeing and spent hours on the beach. He was itching to go snorkeling, but I begged him not to. I was terrified that he'd have an accident underwater. He agreed to stay on land with me. It was kind of schmaltzy, but we couldn't leave Hawaii without seeing Don Ho perform and hearing him sing "Tiny Bubbles."

I was back on the road by the early part of 1990 however. That year was only slightly less taxing than the previous one had been. At the end of the year, Bobby sat down and calculated that I'd been away from home 284 nights. In one ten-day period that year, I went from Los Angeles to Phoenix, to St. Louis, to New York, then back to Los Angeles, according to his records. "That's still way too much, Jackie," he said. "You've got to cut back or you'll wear yourself down again."

In addition to cutting back, I needed help handling the bags of fan mail coming in every week and responding to the stack of requests for appearances. People gave me presents, schoolchildren wrote me poems and sent photographs and posters to be autographed. Civic groups wanted to honor me or have me address their organizations. The crush of attention eventually overwhelmed us.

My aunt Della was traveling with me at the time and trying to help out. But the travel and the workload were too much for her alone. She tells a story about the morning we left New York, stopped in Indianapolis for a drug test and then went to New Orleans. Three states in one day. We both woke up the next morning not quite sure where we were. Della was married, had a young son and wanted to spend more time at home. Soon after that whirlwind trip, she gave up the job as my assistant and became the bookkeeper and office manager at JJK & Associates.

Greg Foster's sister Valarie, who has boundless energy and an unfailingly cheery disposition, took over for Della as my assistant. Though I've tried to cut back on speeches and appearances, the volume of invitations and requests for pictures and autographs has continued to grow, particularly before and after Olympic Games.

I'm still amazed by the reception I get and some of the

places I'm recognized. Val Foster and I were riding on the interstate in Richmond, Virginia, in 1996 when we kept hearing a truck horn. I looked over at the next lane and saw a huge Brink's truck. The uniformed driver and his colleague in the passenger seat started waving furiously at me. Reading their lips, I could tell they were saying, "It's Jackie! It's Jackie!" I smiled, waved back and said "Hi!"

A few years ago an employee from Wal-Mart came running after me in the parking lot after I left the store. She was out of breath by the time she reached me. I thought something was wrong. "I couldn't see you, but I heard your voice and I knew it was you," she said while trying to regain her breath. "I just had to get your autograph." When I think back to those incidents it makes me laugh. But it also touches me.

The outside activities took my mind off track temporarily, but my attitude didn't really improve. When I returned to competition in 1990, I tried to let things roll off my back and to remain upbeat. But my skin was tissue-paper thin.

I know that some wonderful things have been written about me over the years. And I appreciate all the kind journalistic words. But that didn't stop me from feeling that, by and large, my accomplishments were given short shrift, taken for granted or overlooked altogether. Maybe I was overly sensitive, but in my opinion, many sportswriters were overly *insensitive* to my accomplishments. Once I surpassed the 7,000-point milestone, anything less by me wasn't good enough for them. It was as if the bar was higher for me than it was for other athletes.

I'd played by the rules. I'd become the best. I expected to be acknowledged, if not appreciated. But there was always some reason I wasn't. First, the excuse was that I hadn't competed enough internationally. Then, once I'd dominated the international field, set world records and won the Olympic gold medals, I became a bore. Bobby helped fan the flames of expectations by always talking about reaching the 7,300 plateau. He actually told one reporter, "The 6,700 or 6,800 she could win it with isn't our style."

I knew Bobby was trying to motivate me. And, believe me, I wanted to see myself score 7,300 points as badly as he did. But statements like that did more harm than good because when I didn't meet those expectations, it gave the media a reason to criticize.

Dating back to the 1984 Olympics, I'd won every heptathlon I entered and finished. Yet, if I didn't score at least 7,000 points in a competition, I was treated like a failure. A story published just before the 1991 U.S. Championships was typical of the kind of press I was getting. It suggested I hadn't done anything worthwhile since the 1988 Olympics. Furthermore, the writer said, there wasn't any reason to expect that I ever would. The article referred to me in the past tense, using phrases like "the indomitable force she once was." The article belittled my efforts in the long jump and hurdles. Although I was ranked third in the U.S. in the 400-meter hurdles and eighth in the 100-meter hurdles at the end of 1989, and had followed that in 1990 by finishing first in the world in the heptathlon, first in the U.S. and seventh in the world in the long jump, and fourth nationally in the 100-meter hurdles, the writer remained unimpressed. The article contended that "in no event was she especially imposing." The writer was also bored by the 6,783 points I scored at the Goodwill Games in Seattle to win by more than 500 points. But, if all of that wasn't especially imposing, I don't know what is.

Nothing irks me more than being underestimated and taken for granted. But I was too disgusted to fight back. For the first time in my career, I wasn't motivated. I was just sick and tired of it all. After the first day's events at the 1991 U.S. Championships, I was on pace to score 7,000 points. That night, Bobby tried to pump me up to do it, calculating the numbers I needed in the remaining three events. I looked at him with disdain and asked, "Why should I do it? Someone will just find a reason to criticize."

When I was younger, I competed in track and showed up at practice every day because I knew if I worked hard I'd be the best. Being the best meant I had become a success at something and had accomplished something important.

As I got older and the competition intensified, so did my need to excel. The challenge of being the best in the world, of breaking records, of winning Olympic gold medals energized and motivated me. I was like a musician on the track. Every dash down the runway toward the sand pit, every stride around the track, every heave of the javelin and shot, every jump over the high bar, and every step over the hurdles was an expression of that urge inside me to be a virtuoso.

Coach Fennoy and my mother told me I could look forward to some wonderful fringe benefits of excellence— chiefly, prosperity, and a feeling of accomplishment and self-fulfillment. They were right about the prosperity and the sense of accomplishment. I was financially secure and had proven that a poor black girl from East St. Louis could rise above meager circumstances to become the very best at something.

But I still didn't feel fulfilled. As gratifying as the trophies and gold medals were, they didn't satisfy my deeper hunger. It may sound shallow, but I wanted people to appreciate and acknowledge the real extent of my accomplishments. I think it's a very basic, very human desire.

For me, after the world records were set and the gold medals won, the ultimate prize became acceptance and approval. I had to wait until 1984 to get it from my hometown. In 1991, I was still trying to find it within my sport. The frustrations I felt were making me bitter and self-pitying.

As I struggled to cope with the situation, I tried to imagine what my mother would want me to do. She wouldn't have wanted me to lash out at anyone or walk around with a bad attitude. She'd expect me to handle the situation with good cheer. "Today might look gloomy," she would have said, "but tomorrow will be bright." At my lowest moments, I've tried to remember that and keep the faith.

By the time the World Championships rolled around in the late summer of 1991 I was in better spirits. In fact, I drew strength from the experiences of 1988 and used them as motivation. Even if people slandered me and denigrated my accomplishments, I would just continue competing and trying to excel.

26

Asthma and Other Annoyances

My new attitude couldn't keep heartbreak, adversity and controversy away. But it did give me the strength to overcome them.

Twice in the span of eight days in January 1991, I opened my front door to find an overnight delivery envelope from The Athletic Congress (TAC), the track and field governing body. Each time, the envelope contained a letter telling me I had forty-eight hours to report for random drug testing unless I had a compelling excuse. Notices for a third and a fourth test arrived a few days later, forty-eight hours apart. The overnight delivery person visited my house once more in February with another TAC testing notice. In all, I was called for random testing five times in five weeks, on January 10, 18, 22, 24 and on February 14.

It was hard to believe my name came up that many times in that short a span during what was supposed to be a random selection process. I suspected I was the target of a witch hunt—that someone at TAC suspected me of doing something wrong and was determined to catch me red-handed. I didn't want to believe our own governing body could be that malicious, but what else was I to think after so many tests in so short a time?

Bobby had ruffled a lot of feathers and inspired jealousy over the years in the track and field community. He was a black man who'd been very successful as a coach of black athletes, training as many, if not more, Olympic track and field medalists in 1984 and 1988 than any other coach in the country, and I think some other coaches were envious and suspicious of his success.

Also, TAC prohibited personal coaches of American athletes from standing on the field during international meets and consulting with their athletes. TAC only wanted national team coaches, such as Brooks Johnson in 1984, on the field. Bobby had lots of athletes competing in those meets and he thought it was absurd that, while individual coaches from East Germany were down there with their athletes in addition to the national team coaches, he had to either buy a ticket to the meet and sit in the stadium or settle for a limited-access pass and linger near the track entrance behind a fence. Often, he'd just bolt past the security officers, walk onto the field and stay there all day. I thought he had a valid point. Nevertheless, I always worried that Bobby's defiance would get me disqualified from a meet. When the notices started piling up, I wondered if this also might be the governing body's way of harassing Bobby.

There were other circumstances that made us think there was a hidden agenda. Through the track grapevine, we learned that almost none of the other heptathletes and long jumpers had been tested during the same period—an indication that I was being singled out. Also, a TAC official snidely remarked to Bobby that I "shouldn't be so good in all those events," implying that I'd invited the scrutiny by excelling. I'm happy that track and field has drug testing. Ordinarily, I don't mind taking the tests, because I have nothing to hide. I just didn't appreciate being singled out or punished for doing my job well.

The bigger frustration for me was how little faith there was in test results among journalists, athletes and coaches. No matter how many tests I took and passed, doubts persisted. When allegations were made about me at the 1988 Games, it didn't seem to matter that I'd never failed a drug test. People were eager to speculate about my taking steroids, insisting that the test isn't foolproof, that it can be beaten by ingesting other drugs that mask the presence of steroids in the urine. I've never understood that logic. If no one had ever been caught by the testing officials, the skepticism would be understandable. But if the sport is conducting tests and athletes are being snared, that should prove that the testing procedures were effective in uncovering problems. Conversely, the fact that under the same rules and procedures I'd never failed a test should also prove something. It still perplexes and frustrates me.

I'm hardly the lone victim of such cynicism. At every summer Olympics since Seoul, the same old questions have come up, with reporters, coaches and athletes alike pointing fingers and whispering about athletes who were successful, unfairly casting clouds over their performances.

I don't know how to solve the problem because I'm not an expert in drug testing. But I wish the people running our sport would find a way to inspire more confidence in their testing policies and procedures. While I know it's easy to make the media the scapegoats in controversies like this, I think they do bear some responsibility, too. I wish journalists would demand concrete proof of wrongdoing when accusations are made, rather than just repeating unsubstantiated and slanderous allegations and envy-inspired gossip.

Despite my misgivings, I dutifully reported to the testing lab each and every time I was notified, no matter how burdensome it became. The last thing I wanted was for someone to say I wasn't complying with the rules or that I was trying to hide. But I dreaded the process because it disrupted my whole day. Often I had to cancel appointments or reschedule appearances. Also I hated having to tell the organizers that I had to take a drug test because I didn't know how they would react. They didn't know how random testing worked. It probably made some of them think I had a drug problem or had previously failed a test.

When I received the notices at home in Canoga Park, I immediately called the doctor who was certified by TAC to administer the test and made an appointment to meet him either at a hospital in Long Beach or his office. He was very accommodating, often agreeing to meet me at 6:00 A.M. so that Bobby and I could avoid the heavy freeway traffic and not disrupt our daily schedules.

So I woke up really early and drank a lot of water. Then, Bobby and I began the hour-and-a-half drive from our home in the San Fernando Valley, past Westwood, Beverly Hills and the airport, to Long Beach. My bladder was so full and the drive so long the first time we did it, that I had to stop to use the bathroom four times and drink more water before reaching the hospital. The next time I had to prepare for the test, Bobby told me not to drink anything until fifteen minutes before we left home.

At the hospital, I worried that my urine would be too diluted and the testers wouldn't be able to get a reading because I'd flushed out my bladder and refilled it so many times. During track meets in very humid conditions where the risk of dehydration was high, after drinking water and relieving myself all day, I would sometimes have problems producing a usable sample for the drug test after the meet. Or if the testers threw out the first 70 ccs and asked for a second sample, as they sometimes did, if I was empty, I had to drink more water and sit around the waiting room until I could produce another sample. Sometimes I only spent twenty minutes at the lab. Sometimes I was there for several hours.

After going through that drill so many times in January, Bobby blew his top when I received that fifth letter in February. "It's a witch hunt and I don't think you should go," he huffed. "Track and field expects you to forget you have rights."

I tried to calm him down. "It's better to just do it and avoid any controversy later on," I said. "If I do what they ask, they can't come back and say I have something to hide."

But I was ticked off, too. During an appearance in Dallas, I raised questions about the system by making light of my situation. "Is it really random or a conspiracy?" I asked the journalists rhetorically. "I really don't know how the process works. But if my number is going to keep coming up that many times, I ought to start playing the lottery."

My comments sent the reporters running to TAC with a notebookful of questions about the testing policies and procedures. The responses were vague and unresponsive. But after I publicly complained, the notices became less frequent. That only made me more suspicious of the process.

After living in California for a while, I greeted spring with trepidation. The season wreaked havoc on my asthma and my allergies, the list of which seemed to grow daily. From Dr. Katz, an allergist at UCLA Medical Center, I'd discovered that I was allergic to nuts, shellfish, fruit, dust, grass, pollen, ragweed, feathers and animal hair. Digesting or encountering any of them could prompt a seizure and bring on a severe asthma attack. The words "seizure" and "severe," however, didn't faze me. I still regarded my condition the way I did an East German heptathlete or any other foe—it could be defeated if I stayed relaxed and didn't panic.

The threats were becoming increasingly serious however. Bobby knew it. He'd accompanied Jeanette Bolden to a seminar in Colorado on asthma and learned to detect the warning signs of an attack and the proper preventive measures and care in emergency situations.

When he returned from the meeting, he habitually called me off the track during practice to study my eyes, my breathing and my complexion. If I looked drowsy, or my eyelids seemed to be constricting or my breathing was labored or my face was flushed, he lightened the workouts and took me to the hospital for an examination. And he badgered me about taking my medicine.

In March 1991, we were preparing for the World Championships to be held in Tokyo. It was nearly dusk on the track. As I said good-bye to Bobby before walking off the track to Al's waiting car, he looked into my eyes and told me to stop by the hospital for a check-up. He walked with me to the car and gave Al the same instructions. I felt fatigued, but once we drove away, I told Al to take me home to Canoga Park, saying I preferred to rest there. He obeyed his sister.

When Bobby came home I was lying on the bed. Al had gone to the store for me. Bobby asked if I'd been to the hospital, and when I told him I'd decided to come home and rest instead, he stomped upstairs.

Less than fifteen minutes later, I saw stars in front of my eyes. I started wheezing and a surge of intense heat ran through my body. I took off my jog bra, which seemed like a vise grip around my chest. Fighting for air, I put on an oversized T-shirt. I was starting to get really nervous now, because I was taking in less and less air with each breath. I realized I had to get to Bobby. He was upstairs talking on the phone with Greg Foster.

I was trying not to panic, but I knew it was a bad attack. I needed to get to the hospital. I didn't have the energy to get up and walk. So I slid off the edge of the bed and crawled to the staircase in the hallway.

I raised my head and called out.

"Bobby. Help."

He didn't hear me. I could still hear him talking on the phone. I didn't have much strength left to yell, but I gave it all I had.

"Bobby! Help!"

He appeared at the top of the stairs holding the cellular phone. When he saw me at the bottom on the floor, he dropped the phone and ran down. Al walked in the house at that moment and ran to us. They carried me to the car and the three of us drove to the hospital. My breathing was still labored, but my lungs had relaxed a bit when we pulled into the parking lot at the emergency entrance. Bobby and Al tried to rush me inside but I couldn't walk that fast. "Relax, Jackie," I said out loud. I bent over, trying to calm down and catch another breath. They were moving me too fast.

Bobby said, "Let's carry her in!"

They picked me up and ran toward the door. As soon as the glass doors parted, Bobby darted inside and yelled to the nurse, "Her name is Jackie Joyner-Kersee and she's as—"

"Oh, yes, I remember," the nurse said, motioning for Bobby to put me in a wheelchair she rolled over. "Asthma, right?"

After sitting with the IV and the breathing machine in a room inside the emergency ward, my system calmed down. I begged the doctors not to admit me. I begged Bobby, too. It was no use. I spent the night in the hospital and was released with another warning about taking my medicine.

I was diligently taking my medicine when I accompanied

Bobby to Eugene, Oregon, for the NCAAs a month after the episode. But nevertheless I had another attack. The problem was the thick pollen in Eugene. I'd been out at the track all day, watching Bobby's team compete for the collegiate championship. The pollen was so thick, we could see it floating in the air, like dust pellets. My anxiety about the UCLA team's performance heightened my stress level, which exacerbated everything. I was talking to Bobby when the wheezing started. I grabbed the inhaler and started breathing into it and pumping it. The attack subsided, but he took me to the hospital anyway, where I stayed overnight for observation.

When an attack hits, my chest tightens and my body overheats in a matter of seconds. I feel as if I'm on fire and everything inside my body is closing up. My first impulse is to take off anything I'm wearing that's tight. I want to free myself of all confines and constrictions to get air, and let my body breathe and cool off. After an attack is over, my chest and back muscles are sore for several days, as if I've been lifting heavy weights. That's how hard I have to work to breathe.

Shortly before the Worlds, I accompanied Bobby to Houston, where he spent a week working with tennis player Zina Garrison while I trained for the World Championships. We were all out at the Rice University track, when an attack hit me. I started wheezing and my body got hot. I yanked my T-shirt over my head in the middle of the track, in front of everyone. Then I started pulling down my jogging pants, which fit like leggings. Zina's eyes widened as she watched me. She bolted down to the other end of the track and alerted Bobby that I was breathing hard and taking my clothes off.

She and Bobby came sprinting over to me. They grabbed two big towels and stood in front and behind me while I stripped off my pants and bra and put my T-shirt on over my panties. I grabbed my inhaler and pumped it several times before I could get enough air to relax. It was a tense moment and poor Zina was freaked out. She kept asking me and Bobby if I was okay. She'd never seen anyone have an asthma attack. Later that year, Zina and her husband, Willard Jackson, spent New Year's Eve with us in St. Louis. The four of us laughed long and hard about the day I did a striptease at the track.

Despite it all, I stopped taking my medicine and carrying my inhaler around as soon as I felt better. I didn't want to be a prisoner to medication or some inhaling device. Amazingly, I was still in denial about my condition. In a desperate attempt to convince the emergency room staffs that it wasn't serious enough to warrant an overnight stay after an attack, I often said things like: "You don't understand. I'm not your typical asthmatic. I'm an athlete."

One doctor just laughed at me. He told Bobby, "I think we'll have to put your wife on the psychiatric ward."

Once I left the hospital, my thoughts immediately turned to the next competition. In 1991 it was the World Championships in Tokyo. Performing well on the track reinforced the notion in my head that there was nothing seriously wrong with me. But in the back of my mind, I knew how serious my asthma was getting. Each time I had an attack, it was more violent and scarier than the last.

27

Heike

For the first time since I began entering the heptathlon and long jump in international competition, the long jump was scheduled before the heptathlon at the World Championships in Tokyo. Learning about the unusual scheduling jolted Bobby and me. Competing in that order meant four consecutive days of pounding my legs on the track with little time to rest. We hadn't prepared for that in training. Ordinarily, I did the two-day heptathlon and then had two, three or four days of rest before the long jump.

In Tokyo, I would have nine rounds of jumps, three to qualify and six in the finals, in two days. All that jumping would be followed the very next day by sprint hurdling, high jumping and the 200-meter sprint. The fourth day involved more long jumping and finished with the 800. Not the ideal situation. But there was nothing to do but give it my best shot.

As it turned out, I hit 24' ¼" on my first jump in the long-jump finals, good for first place. My second attempt was a foul but no one eclipsed my mark, not even Heike Drechsler of East Germany, my archrival and good friend.

258

With no one threatening, I decided to rest my hamstrings and pass on the third attempt. On my fourth jump, I missed the board and my foot touched down on the plasticine just beyond it. Plasticine is a gushy, claylike substance. It grabbed the spikes on my right shoe and yanked my right ankle around as I tried to launch in the air. I felt something twist. I shrieked as I went down, head first into the sand. I was crying as Heike ran over to me and knelt down in the sand beside me.

"My leg! It's my leg!" I cried.

She picked up my head and held it in her lap and dusted the tear-soaked sand from my face. Tears welled up in her eyes.

I couldn't move my leg. I thought it was broken. I was terrified. Bobby and Bob Forster, my physical therapist, ran over and kneeled on either side of us.

"It's my leg! It's my leg!" I cried to them. Bob started to examine my knee.

Heike asked if I was okay, and I calmed down.

"Yeah. I'm okay," I said, nodding. She blinked her eyes at me, her signal that she wished me well. She got up and walked back to the athlete waiting area, as Bobby and Bob continued to poke around my leg.

"No, it's my ankle," I told them. Bob examined and touched it. A doctor had arrived and he also examined it. It was a slight twist. He asked me to try to get up and stand on it. With Bobby and Bob's help I gingerly stood up in the sand. I put my weight on the ankle and felt okay, just a slight twinge of pain. I walked to the infield.

I sat on the grass with my legs stretched out in front of me. The doctor examined it some more, while Bobby and Bob crouched beside him at my feet. He said it wasn't serious. No broken bones. That's when Bobby told Bob to tape it up if it wasn't broken because he wanted me to take the last jump. I tried running gingerly at first. No pain. I put more pressure on the leg. Still no problem. I ran back and told them it felt okay.

Bob scrambled furiously to wrap the leg, but discovered he didn't have an Ace bandage with him. Ever resourceful, Bobby pulled a 5,000-yen bill out of his pocket and handed it to him. "Here, use this," he said.

Bob wrapped my ankle with the yen bill, then, as an added prevention against swelling, put a bag of ice on it and secured it with tape, which I kept on until my next jump.

At the line, my ankle was still wrapped with the yen bill. I didn't improve on the last jump and neither did Heike. She needed only 1¼ inches to beat me, but she couldn't pull it off. She didn't use it as an excuse, but I knew she had a knee injury. She came over and congratulated me with tears in her eyes. "You're the best," she said. I started crying and we embraced.

I prevailed that day at the Worlds. But Heike took home the gold medal a year later at the Barcelona Games and I received the bronze. After my last attempt came up short at the Olympics, I got up, dusted myself off, shook my head once and walked to Heike with a big smile on my face. "Congratulations. Today was your day," I told her. "*You're* the best."

As the episode in the sand pit showed, I was closer to Heike than I was to any member of the American long-jump team. We first met in 1985 at a meet in Zurich. Bobby pointed her out to me on the warmup track. I knew she was the young East German long jumper who'd set the world record at the age of eighteen in 1983. Bobby told me she was the best he'd seen and the one to beat. He marveled at her sprinting and jumping ability.

"You're going to have to work hard to beat her," he said as we stood on the edge of the track, watching her run around, her blond curls and long legs flapping in the breeze as she trotted past us.

Heike was one of the few friendly athletes in the East German track delegation. I knew how careful the athletes from the Eastern Bloc had to be because their coaches and chaperones were watching every move they made and expected them to keep their game faces on at all times. I wouldn't have blamed her if she kept her distance. The only other member of that team who ever behaved civilly to athletes from the West was heptathlete Anke Behmer.

In 1986 at Gotzis, Anke and I had struck up a friendship and she wanted to exchange uniforms with me. She talked to me about it away from the prying ears and eyes of her coach. We made a secret plan to do it at the athletes' banquet that night. Back at my hotel room, I stuffed my uniform in my purse and headed to the dining room. Before dinner, Anke snuck over to me and whispered, "We can't let the boss man see us. I'll go to the bathroom first. Then you come. We'll do it there."

I kept one eye on her and one on my meal all night. We were sitting across the room from each other. She got up and went to the exit. I waited until she'd disappeared. Then I followed her. In the bathroom, we greeted each other with mischievous smiles and giggles. We quickly pulled the bunched-up uniforms out of our purses, made the switch and shoved them back inside. Anke left first. I waited a minute or two and then walked out. We were never seen together and no one ever knew what we did.

At the Zurich meet, Heike came over and said hello on the warmup track. She had a nice smile. She asked whether Carol Lewis was competing in the long jump. I guess my ego got the best of me, because I thought to myself: "You should be concerned about whether I'm competing!"

Heike was three years younger than me, but she was a world champion before I was. I admired her versatility, her incredible athletic ability and her staying power. She'd dabbled in the sprints and made her Olympic team as a sprinter, posting some of the best times in the world. In fact, she was the one competitor Florence worried about while preparing for the 1988 Olympics.

Our friendship grew through the years and we chatted whenever we could steal a few minutes out of the view of her coaches. On the track, she used eye signals—blinks and winks—whenever she passed me. I'd acknowledge her by smiling or winking back. It added fun to the competition and kept me relaxed. I always knew what her eye signals meant. "Hi! How are you?" or "Nice to see you," or "Good jump." In the sand pit that night in Tokyo, the blinks told me she was concerned about me and was relieved I was okay.

Some reporters suggested we'd become friends because we both came from underprivileged backgrounds. Some said Bobby and I sympathized with her because the East German track coaches forced her to compete in too many events. But Heike and I never discussed any of that. We became good friends because we admired each other as athletes. I think, too, that we're both caring people. After the fall of Communism and she was freer to talk, we shared several plane rides together to meets throughout Europe. She pulled out the latest picture of her baby son. Then she started prodding me to have kids. We also talked about visiting each other once we retired and didn't have to worry about rushing back home to resume training.

When she got injured just prior to the 1996 Olympics, Bobby and I sent her a telegram. In it, I told her I could imagine what she was going through and I knew how difficult it must be not being on the Olympic team. She sent me a letter before the Games wishing me luck and told me she was looking forward to our competition in Europe shortly after the Olympics. She made it there, but I didn't, because of my hamstring injury.

28

Anointed

Despite the twisted ankle from the long jump, I felt fine by the start of the heptathlon the next day at the World Championships. I'd slept with electrical stimulation on my hamstrings the night after the long jump and I was raring to go on the first night of competition.

I had a comfortable lead after three events, heading into the final event of the first night, the 200-meter sprint. But in the 200 meters, as I tried to round the curve, my right leg went crazy. There were 130 meters to go. I was in the middle of the turn, at the stage in the race where I needed to really accelerate. I tried to explode around the curve. Instead my leg exploded. A sharp pain crept up my thigh, as if someone was dragging a needle from the back of my knee to my buttock. Then, suddenly, I felt a ball build up in the back of the thigh. An instant later, the ball burst. I screamed. The sensation was so painful and so jarring, it lifted me off the ground. I came down and fell face-first onto the track. The other runners were passing me. I reached out and grabbed the red rubber track in front of me with my fingernails and tried to crawl to the finish on my left hip. My mind wasn't processing what had just happened to my leg. I wanted to finish the race so that I could come back the next day and compete again.

Bobby leaped over the stadium railing and ran to me, with Bob Forster right behind, carrying his shoulder bag full of therapist's supplies. Two paramedics brought over a stretcher. I was screaming and crying and trying to crawl. Bobby knelt down beside me and held me down with his hand on my hip to keep me still. He put his other hand to my cheek. "Jackie, it's over. It's over," he said to me.

He picked me up and placed me onto the stretcher on my back. As they rolled me off the track to the medical area, I covered my face in my hands and continued to sob. Why did this have to happen now? I'd withstood the painful ankle and won the long jump. I was trying to be tough, but my leg had let me down. I was so disappointed.

I was also in a great deal of pain. In the first-aid shelter, it hurt every time Bob and the doctors touched any part of my leg. I thought the hamstring was torn. A big, dark red spot had already appeared on the back of my leg, which was swelling by the minute. The spot was the bruise mark where the muscle had pulled and the blood had seeped out of the end of the frayed tissues and fibers. Bob hurriedly packed the leg in ice and wrapped it with an Ace bandage to prevent further swelling, then I was wheeled out of the stadium on the stretcher, surrounded by photographers, cameras and reporters. An official ordered the medics to move the stretcher from the entrance, where we'd stopped so that I could answer the reporters' questions. I tried to talk through my tears as I replayed the events. Meanwhile, the camera lights nearly blinded me in the dark Tokyo night.

Soon the cab showed up to take me to the hospital. When the paramedics rolled the stretcher off the curb, the wheels banged onto the street, jarring my leg. I winced.

The cab driver, Bobby and Bob waited while I answered the last question. Then they lifted me off the stretcher and loaded me into the back seat. My Worlds had just come to a painful end.

The physical rehabilitation of the hamstring was routine. After a couple of days, I was walking. Six weeks later, I was running at full speed.

The emotional rehab was more complicated, though. The injury had been more traumatic than I realized. I found myself flashing back to the moment of injury in Tokyo each time I reached that point on the track during practice. In the middle of a sprint, I'd literally slow down at the spot the muscle had yanked, terrified that it would happen again. I thought I actually felt my leg tighten. But it was all in my head. "I don't know why this is happening," I told Bobby after one flashback.

"It's okay, it's all part of the healing process," he said.

He asked Alice Brown, my former training partner, an expert curve runner and silver medalist in the 100 meters in 1984, to teach me to negotiate the turn properly. "I want her to have confidence, instead of fear as she approaches that curve," he told her.

Before I worked with Alice, I was like a car out of control coming around there, entering it at too fast a speed and hugging the left edge too tightly. Alice moved me to the center of the lane. From there, she said I could run as fast as I wanted, with better control.

The end-of-the-year rankings by *Track & Field News* disappointed me once again. I'd looked forward to being number one in the heptathlon and the long jump and possibly being Female Athlete of the Year. I had the top score in the heptathlon internationally. But because I got injured and withdrew from the World Championships, the magazine ranked me second in the event, behind Sabine Braun of West Germany, who'd won the world title. Ditto the long jump. I had the longest jump in the world that year and also won the World Championship. But I was placed second to Heike. The editors said I hadn't competed in enough events to earn the top spot. I didn't begrudge the other athletes their awards, particularly not Heike, but I couldn't suppress the feeling that the editors already had other athletes in mind and were forced to come up with excuses to rank them ahead of me.

I tried not to, but I took the slights personally. The more I gave, the more they withheld. Telling me those performances weren't good enough made me feel as if I wasn't good enough. But I gamely tried to take it in stride and wait for brighter, happier days.

Bobby gave me a reason to smile early in 1992. I never had birthday parties growing up. But he always gave me a nice present and made a fuss. Uncharacteristically, when my thirtieth birthday arrived on March 3, 1992, he said nothing and gave me nothing. We spent all day at the track without the subject coming up. I was disappointed. But I tried to hide it.

On the way home from the UCLA track, Bobby went through Beverly Hills for some strange reason, instead of heading for the freeway. Then his pager went off. He pulled into a restaurant parking lot and went in to use the phone. He came out and said Della was calling from St. Louis and wanted to talk to me. "Somebody stole your car from the house," he said casually.

"What?" I flung open the door and ran inside.

I spotted the phone and dashed toward it, past a big room filled with people. I got to the phone, turned around and they were all staring at me. Suddenly I realized they were all of our friends. They yelled, *"Surprise!"*

I pride myself on not letting anything get past me. But

Bobby pulled this surprise party off without my having the slightest notion. I was really happy he had. It was a much-needed boost to my flagging spirits.

We always arrived in Europe at least two weeks before a meet to give our bodies time to experience jet lag and recover from it. In the midst of packing and traveling to Barcelona for the 1992 Games, I contracted a cold. Then, an asthma attack hit. Both Bobby and my inhaler were nearby and I was able to quickly get it under control. After a visit to the hospital, the doctor prescribed an antibiotic for the cold, which we scrambled to find. I didn't dare go near prednisone. It was just ten days before the start of the heptathlon competition and I didn't want any drug test complications.

To pass the time and motivate us, Bobby took Gail and me to a bullfight. The outdoor arena surrounding the bullfighting ring was beautifully rustic. While Bobby rattled off the gory details of what the contestants had done to the bulls, I tried not to listen, focusing instead on how cute the matador's costumes were. To Gail and me, it seemed so barbaric. Exciting, but barbaric.

Bobby said the bullfight was a metaphor for what we had to do at the gorgeous Estadi Olimpic across town. He wanted us to go for the kill, which I thought was a bit much. "I don't need to act mean," I told him. "I'll just do what I'm capable of and the rest will take care of itself."

I did take his other insights to heart, however. "Everyone in that stadium has talent," he pointed out. "It's going to come down to who can concentrate, maintain focus and make the fewest mistakes. If the matador doesn't concentrate, his life is gone. If you don't, your gold medal is gone."

The Olympic stadium stood majestically atop Montjuic, a mountain range outside the city. To get there, spectators rode a long escalator that rose past waterfalls and pinewoods. As the staircase ascended, riders had a breathtaking view of the Olympic flame burning just above the treetops. At night, floodlights illuminated the scene. It was magnificent.

Instead of a hotel, we roomed in a dorm-room-sized cabin on the gigantic cruise ship *Sports Illustrated* rented for the Games and docked at the Barcelona seaport. Ann Moore, who had been publisher of the magazine's sister publication, *SI for Kids,* arranged for us to stay there for the entire two weeks. It was fabulous. It was such a scene, with movie stars, models and athletes, including Arnold Schwarzenegger, the original Dream Team members and Kathy Ireland mingling among the crowd at mealtime. I met George Foreman and had a nice chat with him.

The ship's staff catered to our every need. The rooms had color TVs. The food service staff knew what I liked to eat and had turkey and bagels ready for me. The staff even handled our transportation to and from the stadium. It was the best thing anyone could have done for us, because with all those details taken care of, I could concentrate on my performance.

I never trailed in the heptathlon. However, Irina Belova of the Unified Team of athletes from the former Soviet Union kept things interesting until the end. She needed to run 20 seconds faster than me in the 800 to overtake me. But I stayed within 7 seconds of her and won by 199 points with a total of 7,044.

Bobby greeted me with a dozen roses and hugged me twice, all before I could sufficiently catch my breath. I was also allergic to flowers. I had to walk away from him. The NBC cameras caught him looking hurt and sounding jilted. I didn't mean to reject him; but I was about to choke. It was a muggy night. I'd just run 800 meters. I was exhausted and out of breath.

One thing about our relationship is that we're always ourselves, even when the eyes of the world are watching. Whether Bobby's screaming at me to "Come here, right now!" when I'm in the middle of an interview, or I'm telling him to stop kissing me because he's suffocating me, it's always candid camera. With us, what you see is the way it is.

I stood on the medal stand wearing a strand of pearls and my brand-new gold medal. I held my flowers close to my chest, but away from the allergy alarm bells inside my nose. I was both gratified and relieved. What a four years it had been. I'd shaken myself out of 1988's dejection, forgotten 1991's disappointment, overcome physical and emotional exhaustion, and survived another scary hamstring injury. No matter what anyone else thought, I was very proud of myself.

At the end of the contest, during a walking victory lap, I saw Tracy Austin and ran over to hug her. Out of the corner of my eye, I saw Bruce Jenner trying to get my attention. When I walked to him, he told the crowd of journalists, friends and fans gathered near him that I was "the greatest multi-event athlete ever, man or woman."

I beamed. His words warmed my heart. Here was the very athlete whose performance in the 1976 Games had inspired my Olympic aspirations—a decathlete who himself had held the title of world's greatest—anointing me. Such compliments from a superstar male athlete to a female counterpart are rarely bestowed. It said a lot about what a generous person Bruce is. It meant more to me than any magazine ranking. I was momentarily transported from that mountaintop high in the Barcelona sky onto Cloud Nine.

29

Human Relations

Sometimes my sensitivity brings me joy, rather than grief. When I hear about or see another person in pain or in trouble and I can do something to help, I'm happy to do it. That's when a thin skin comes in handy.

I think compassion for your fellow man is a very undervalued trait. Acting on it to bring comfort to someone who needs it makes me feel great. And I appreciate it when others do the same for me.

I remember how my heart broke for Chris Webber of the Michigan Wolverines during the final game of the 1993 NCAA basketball tournament against the North Carolina Tarheels. The last seconds were ticking down and the game was close. Caught in a bind on the court, Chris called a timeout the team didn't have. The Wolverines were assessed a technical foul and had to surrender the ball to the Tarheels, who went on to win the game and the national title.

The TV camera froze on Chris's face as the North Carolina players, coaches and cheerleaders celebrated around him. He looked so dejected and sad. I knew he was probably blaming himself. I thought he could use some cheering up.

"I'm going to send him some flowers," I said to Bobby, who was sitting beside me on the bed watching.

I'd never met Chris. He probably didn't know who I was. I just wanted him to know that someone was in his corner. In the note accompanying the flowers, I told him to hang in there because he had a promising career ahead of him. I didn't want him to let that one moment spoil the rest of his life.

A year or two later, I was in Connecticut to participate in a program honoring heroes. Chris, who was by then an NBA star, was also speaking. His eyes lit up when I walked into the room. He walked over and hugged me.

"I want you to know how much I appreciated those flowers and your note," he said. "When I received them I was still feeling depressed about what happened. They really cheered me up."

I was so pleased to know I'd helped him. I knew firsthand that when you're in the public eye, people have no reservations about harshly criticizing you or saying things that hurt your feelings, without concern for how it will affect you. At those times, it's nice to hear comforting words or to have a shoulder to cry on.

At that point, I was in the midst of my own search for comforting shoulders and encouraging words. I'd lost most of my on-track support system when Al, Valerie Brisco and Jeanette Bolden stopped competing after 1988. My other good friend, Sandra Farmer-Patrick, was still competing, but she was married with a baby, and her family needed her attention.

Gail Devers, whom Bobby also coaches, has been my teammate, friend and training partner since 1986. But her serious health problems and intense competitions have demanded her full attention. Gail suffered from a severe case of Graves' disease, a thyroid disorder, for nearly two years after the 1988 Olympics. Then, the radiation treatments for the thyroid played havoc with her body and caused her feet to ache and bleed. Her doctors were considering amputation when they realized the radiation therapy was the cause. Gail never gave up. By 1991 she was back on the track, running and winning. I admire and applaud her determination. Her single-minded focus is one of the big reasons she was able to overcome Graves' disease and win gold medals in the 100 meters in Barcelona and Atlanta.

I wasn't completely abandoned, though. Bobby has always been a great listener and my biggest supporter. Also at especially grim moments, I drew strength and inspiration from my mother's spirit. Still, I sorely missed the camaraderie I'd felt with other athletes over the years.

During the thirteen years I've been competing on the world-class level, track and field athletes have become less collegial and more self-absorbed. Even during the Olympic Games, there's no feeling of "we" among team members, just "me." It's the attitude in every sport, I guess. But in track and field, it bothers me to see people treat their competitors like sworn enemies and act as if every race is a matter of life and death.

To be sure, the competition has always been intense. And gamesmanship has always been a part of our sport. I remember a girl at a college meet stepping into the blocks beside me before the start of a hurdle race. She whispered to me that her girlfriend was sleeping with my boyfriend, in an attempt to rattle me. I almost lost my concentration, but not because she'd distracted me or upset me. I thought it was such a silly thing to say, I wanted to burst out laughing. I saw right through what she was trying to do.

Occasionally someone would elbow me out of their way during a race and, once or twice during the long jump, girls would move each other's starting marks to screw up their runs, but that was about as bad as things got.

In the old days, we were all able to turn it off and on. I was able to compete against Heike, Anke, Jane and Cindy, and still laugh and talk with them. We were fierce, but friendly rivals.

People were colleagues, not enemies. Athletes and coaches formed track clubs to share a pool of sponsorship money, facilities and training advice, and to work out together. A few clubs still exist around the country—including the Santa Monica Track Club, which includes sprinters Carl Lewis, Mike Marsh and Leroy Burrell, who work out together, despite the fact that they regularly compete against each other. But for the most part, such arrangements are an anachronism. That sense of team spirit in track and field went out of style with- baggy running shorts.

Nowadays, it's every athlete for him- or herself. Money is the chief reason, I think. Athletes feel they're chasing the same small pot of endorsement money and the only way to get it is to knock their competitors out of the race and out of the public's consciousness. I'm always happy to see other track and field athletes get endorsements and do commercials and I hope the spots are a hit so that the next time a company wants a spokesperson, it will think about using another track and field athlete. The only way our sport will prosper is if we all prosper. But many people don't see it that way.

A few overly aggressive agents, I think wrongly, tell their clients that they have to look out for their own best interests and ignore the best interests of the sport. The result is the selfish, cutthroat, contentious atmosphere that exists at meets. With so much pressure, it's little wonder people sometimes say things they wish they hadn't in the heat of the moment.

At the Barcelona games, Gwen Torrence caused an international incident when, after finishing fourth in the 100 meters behind Gail, Juliet Cuthbert of Jamaica and Irina Privalova of the Unified Team, she blasted her competitors and accused them of using steroids. "I think three people in the race were not clean," Gwen said. "As athletes, we just know who's on drugs. Everybody knew about Ben [Johnson]."

Later, when she repeated the allegations, she amended her comments to say that "Gail won it clean."

In fact, Gail repeatedly denied ever using performance-enhancing drugs. Bobby nearly had an aneurysm, he was so mad about Gwen's comment. He angrily told reporters, "Anyone who believes Gail Devers has taken performance-enhancing drugs can kiss my ass."

What a mess it was. I felt caught in the middle. Gail was my teammate and my friend. Bobby was my husband. I wasn't a close friend of Gwen's, but we'd been friendly since she joined the international circuit after a successful career at the University of Georgia. I knew she was going to accomplish great things in track. When she was just out of school, during the Millrose Games in Madison Square Garden, I offered her some friendly free advice, as one black female track athlete to another. "Make sure you're always prepared when you face the media," I told her. "Be ready for the harsh questions. Don't let them catch you off guard or make you say something you'll regret later."

Gwen's remark didn't directly involve me. But when she started pointing fingers at other sprinters—even though she excluded Gail—my teammate and my husband were caught in the undertow of suspicion. I felt like, indirectly, I'd been attacked, too. Nevertheless, I tried to stay out of it. But several weeks after the Games I knew something had to change. Gail and Gwen weren't speaking. Bobby and Gwen weren't speaking. We'd pass each other in the hotel hallway, ride elevators together or jog past each other on the warmup track without so much as a "Hi, how are you." I couldn't stand it. Gwen and I had always been cordial.

During a ceremony at a meet in Zurich, I walked over to Gwen and told her it was time for everyone to bury the hatchet. "This is silly. We have to get beyond this," I told her. "It makes no sense for us to be on the circuit together and not speak to one another. I'm not going to let it happen."

I also told her I admired her and all that she'd accomplished but that the whole situation was bad for her, for women, as well as for track and field in general. As I talked, I saw her facial muscles relax and the tension leave her face. She smiled and said she was glad I had come over to talk.

Incidents like that one sadden me because I think the behavior is destructive to the sport. Basketball, football and baseball players can get away with saying and doing controversial things because the public already embraces them. But track and field athletes aren't held in the same esteem. We should be looking for ways to lift up our sport, rather than tear each other down.

I know I'm part of a dying breed. I realized it a few years ago, after the coach of an American heptathlete told her I was only being nice in order to "steal her energy" and keep her from winning. I shook my head.

I've never felt more alone on the track than I did during the 1993 World Championships in Stuttgart, Germany. I was struggling through the heptathlon competition in a way I hadn't since the 1984 Olympics. I didn't know what was wrong with me.

The weather was hot and muggy, and at the start of the hurdles, I felt really tired. Usually I'm bouncing around in front of the blocks, blood and adrenaline pumping. That day, I stood flat-footed, looking down the track, wondering where I'd find the energy to step over all ten hurdles. I lost the race and recorded a pitiful time. Right off the bat I was behind.

I felt so sick and lethargic. I was hot one minute, then shivering with chills the next, during the high jump. I put the back of my hand to my forehead. I was burning up. Bob Forster kept handing me cold towels, telling me to wipe them over my body to stay cool. Waves of nausea came and went. Several times I got up to run to the bathroom, because I thought I was about to throw up. Then it was my turn to jump. I couldn't clear 6 feet. Now, I was really miserable. I started crying. Out of the corner of my eye I saw Bobby approaching. I quickly wiped away the tears and cleared my throat. I knew if he saw me crying he'd get on me.

I tried to pull myself together at the shot put, which didn't go so well either. I was well below my target scores. After the shot put I was in third place, behind the leader, Sabine Braun of Germany.

Braun and I had a little feud going. Actually, she had a feud with me. I hate mind games and think they're a waste of energy. But I'm not going to be intimidated or back down from a challenge, either.

She'd won the 1991 World Championships in Tokyo after I withdrew. On the victory stand, she'd raised a finger, declaring herself number one. That was fine. But in Barcelona in 1992, she'd gone too far. It was my turn to long-jump. I walked toward the starting line and she stepped in front of me and wouldn't get out of my way. I held my ground and we bumped shoulders. "Okay, so that's how you want to play? Fine," I said to her in my mind. I jumped 23' 3¼", scored 1,206 points and clinched the gold medal in one fell swoop.

Now, I wanted to win back the World Champion title. After the way she acted at the Olympics, the thought of losing a second consecutive world title to her was unbearable.

But if I didn't do something fast, the contest would be over. I had to summon the energy to prevail in the 200. Sandra Farmer-Patrick came over to me and tried to make me laugh.

At the gun, I just charged forward out of the blocks and kept charging until I got to the finish. I won the race in a pretty good time, which put me back in the lead, by a very slim margin, over Braun.

But I still felt weak and uninspired at the end of the first day. One reporter thought he'd figured out the problem. At the press conference after the first day, he asked me if I was pregnant! I laughed out loud and said, emphatically, "No." I told him I'd been hot and then cold out there and I was fatigued. At least he didn't ask me if I thought I was past my prime or if it was time to retire. I later found out that I had a slight fever that day, but Bobby and Bob didn't want me to know because they were afraid I'd blow it out of proportion, dwell on it and lose my focus.

The next day, while preparing for the last three events on the warmup track, the fever was gone, but my blue mood was still clinging. I felt sorry for myself. I looked around the track at everyone warming up. I saw Gwen Torrence, Michael Johnson, Butch Reynolds, Quincy Watts, Carl Lewis, Mike Marsh and Jon Drummond. Each person was in his or her own little shell. No one mingled. Some people wore headphones as they jogged around the track stone-faced, looking straight ahead, making eye contact with no one. I'd have to fend for myself, find my own motivation and inspiration.

I thought about all the times I'd cheered up other athletes when they were down or given them pep talks when they were nervous or struggling. And about people who'd done the same for me. I missed the old days, when Cindy Greiner and Jane Frederick and I chatted between events and during warmups. No one had come over to encourage me except my old friend Sandra Farmer-Patrick.

Just then, Gwen jogged up behind me. "How you feeling today?" she asked.

"Not so good, but I'm gonna try to get it together," I said.

"You can do it," she said. "Remember, you're still JJK."

"All right, Gwen. Thanks a lot," I said. It was the first time I'd smiled since that reporter asked me if I was pregnant.

Then Quincy Watts, who'd won a gold medal in the 400 meters in Barcelona and was being coached by Bobby, walked over with Jon Drummond to check on me. Quincy and Jon are sweet guys. Quincy was suffering from a sore back after falling in the shower a few days earlier. We ended up consoling each other. The show of concern from Gwen, Quincy and Jon touched me and pumped me up. It was as if they'd all heard my silent wish. They did more to cure me than any medicine could have. It turned around my whole outlook. It also gave me hope that sportsmanship lives.

The heat was suffocating and the humidity was draining. I'd lost over five pounds the day before and it showed. I was so gaunt I'd been startled that morning when I looked in the mirror and saw my sunken cheeks.

I nailed the long jump, 23' 1¼". Braun couldn't reach 22 feet. Then I gave it all back on the javelin. Braun's throw sailed 175' 4"; I couldn't do better than 143' 7". She led by seven points. During the three-hour break before the 800, I went back to the hotel and sat in a bathtubful of cold water. And I drank water constantly. Sitting in the tub, I thought about what I had to do. I had to beat Braun in the 800 by 0.6 seconds. I had to risk dehydration, exhaustion, asthma, cramps, a muscle pull—everything—to win that race. She didn't seem to be nearly as tired as I was, but I had to run like it was the first event of the meet.

I was relieved when I stepped out of the hotel to board the van to the track and felt a cool breeze. The sun had set and the night air was energizing. Sandra came out to the warmup track with me and talked the entire time. She had an endless supply of funny stories. I loved her for it. Finally, it was time to run. "Sandra, I have to give this 800 everything I have," I said.

"Then go do it," she said.

The crowd was very partisan, waving German flags and screaming wildly for Braun.

I moved to the inside lane after the start. Braun was right behind me, just over my shoulder. I played it cool, trying to make her think I was tired. After the first lap, I charged out. She didn't follow. She was tired. I got so excited I almost went out too fast. I started wheezing on the backstretch. The asthma was kicking in.

"Okay, Jackie. Here it comes," I thought. Immediately I began feeding my mind one positive thought after the other. "Just keep pumping your arms. It's not that bad, so keep going. You can make it. You're not going to have a full-blown attack. You have enough air. You've got this thing won. Don't lose it now."

Braun was gaining on me with 300 meters left. This was it, now or never. "Just run as hard as you can in this last 200 meters, Jackie," I said. "If she comes up and catches you, she deserves to win."

As I reached the line, in fourth place, I took a quick glance over my shoulder to see if Braun was still shadowing me. I didn't see her. I turned sideways and bent over to try and control my asthma and saw her coming up to the finish line. I'd won. She was 3 seconds behind me. Bobby rushed to me and handed me the inhaler. He and Bob stood around me, along with a doctor, as I tried to catch my breath. It took ten minutes for my body to calm down. Meanwhile Braun and her German teammate took a victory jog around the track.

I was still recovering when Braun came over, hugged me and raised my right arm toward the crowd. They jumped to their feet and cheered wildly for me. I was ready to collapse from exhaustion. But I relished the moment. I was delighted about the way I'd fought for that victory.

In the press conference afterward, I was determined to write my own headline for this story. I wasn't going to let the journalists be the judges this time. "I have to say this is my greatest triumph, considering the competition and the ups and downs I was going through. It was a test of strength, a test of character, and of heart. If I really wanted it, I had to pull it together. I will enjoy this one."

Back at the hotel I ran into Wilma Rudolph in the hallway. She kissed and hugged me and told me how proud she was. We agreed to talk the next day. Wilma and I had met a decade earlier at a Women's Sports Foundation Awards dinner in New York. That night, we embraced and began talking and laughing as if we'd known each other all our lives. From that moment on, she was no longer just a role model, she was one of my closest friends and like a second mother.

The next day in Germany, I sat on the sofa in her room and unloaded all the frustration and sadness that had been building inside me since 1988, the same way I used to do with Momma. "I don't know, Wilma, I just feel sometimes that winning isn't enough for people anymore when it comes to me," I said. "If I don't break a world record, it's a disappointment. If I don't score over 7,000 points, it's mediocre."

She smiled sympathetically. "That's what happens when you're on top," she said. "People are gunning for you. You can't let it get to you, though. You have to turn a blind eye and a deaf ear to it."

"I'm doing the best I can. Why do they have to be so harsh?" I asked.

"Forget about trying to please them," Wilma said. "Remember why you're doing this. You have to want this for yourself."

I always enjoyed our talks so much. Wilma was so wise. I wish we'd had more years together. Sadly, she died of brain cancer a year after I saw her in Stuttgart.

That advice—so obvious in a way, yet so meaningful, coming from Wilma—was her priceless, final gift to me. She'd given me the new perspective I was seeking, a way to cope with the pressure of expectations. She also reminded me of something very important that I'd forgotten. I'd become so wrapped up in earning everyone's respect and approval, I'd lost sight of the reason I started jumping and running in the first place—because it satisfied something within me. My performance in the heptathlon the night before had pleased me because I had to fight for it. I didn't care what the papers said. I knew it was special.

30

At Death's Door

The asthma attack I suffered at the World Championships should have set off alarm bells. My condition was getting worse. The attacks were coming with increasing frequency. That year alone, I had three serious attacks, including the one in Stuttgart during the 800 meters.

I'd anticipated an attack in the spring of 1993, when I returned to Eugene—the site of a 1991 attack during the NCAA Championships—for the U.S. National Championships. But fortunately I didn't have one. We'd taken a lot of precautions. I was taking my medicine. Also, Bobby and I consulted with a doctor there, who told me to wear a mask over my face while competing to protect my lungs from the thick pollen.

People teased me about the mask. Someone called me Darth Vader. Another athlete asked me if I'd become a surgeon during the off-season. Even though I knew the consequences of not wearing the mask were grave, I actually toyed with the idea of not putting it on because of the ribbing I was getting. It was probably the only thing that could protect me from a severe, perhaps even fatal attack, but I foolishly felt embarrassed and self-conscious about wearing it.

But I knew I needed to do it. I also knew Bobby would kill me if I didn't. So I wore it. *Track & Field News* ran a photograph of me in the mask in 1993. I wore a similar one at the 1995 Championships and again was pictured in the magazine.

On Mother's Day that same year Bobby and I visited his best friend, Dave Harris, and his family at their home in Whittier, California. We all went out to eat Chinese food that night and I ordered the corn soup. It was scorching hot that day, but I was in the mood for soup. With every spoonful I swallowed, I got hotter and hotter. I gulped down several glasses of water during the meal and by the time the check arrived, I felt awful. I was so hot. I used the inhaler several times in the car on the drive back. Back at Dave's house, I went to sit by the pool hoping that I could ward off an attack if I cooled off. But after a few minutes I realized I wasn't getting better. I started wheezing. I got up and tried to make my way into the house, when the heat wave surged through me. I inhaled several shots of Ventolin through the inhaler. It wasn't helping. In fact, it seemed to make my chest and throat close even faster. I could feel my windpipe shrinking by the second.

I tried to call Bobby. But I couldn't summon my voice— the only thing coming out of my mouth was a whisper. I don't know why it came to mind, but in a speech class at UCLA, the professor told us that it's not always the loudest person who gets heard; sometimes, it's the quiet voice that people hear. I thought if I just kept saying Bobby's name in a whisper, he'd eventually hear.

"Bobby, Bobby, Bobby, Bobby, Bobby . . ."

Dave's son heard me and came to find out what the noise was. He ran inside and got Bobby, who rushed me to

the hospital. The doctors made me stay overnight for observation again. I tried to get them to release me. But
Bobby insisted that I stay. He was getting tired of my irresponsible behavior, the episodes and the close calls. "This
is the best thing for you," he said. "You're hardheaded and
you don't take your medicine."

I didn't change my ways until November, after I returned from Germany. I don't think I'd completely recovered from the attack at Stuttgart or the exhaustion. Yet, I
hit the ground running. We flew back to L.A., stayed there
a few days, then flew to St. Louis. For the next few weeks,
I was engrossed in planning the annual fund-raising dinner
for my foundation. I always invited celebrity athletes to join
me at the dinner. Monica Seles, whom Bobby and I had
known for a year before her stabbing, had agreed to attend.
It would be one of her first public appearances since the attack. We hoped her presence would generate excitement
about the event and the foundation's work. But for Monica's sake, we tried to minimize the hoopla.

There were a million details to finalize the day before the
dinner. Monica and her father were due to arrive at my
house, where they were staying for the weekend. Val Foster had driven me to the radio station to do a promotional
spot for the dinner. I'd been struggling to adjust to the
constantly changing climates, first the humid, then breezy
conditions in Germany, then the warmth of L.A., and now
the chilly temperatures in St. Louis. When we came out of
the radio station, the cold air hit me and I told Val, "Whoa,
I can't keep going like this or I'm gonna get sick."

From there I went to the Regal Riverfront Hotel, the
site of the dinner, to do a TV interview. During the taping,
I started making whistling sounds every time I took a
breath. I knew it was a signal that the wheezing would be
next. I apologized and told them I had to leave because I
was getting sick. On the way home, I remembered I had to

go to the mall to buy some presents for the people who helped me plan the dinner. I devised a plan. I would go home, take some medicine and then drive to the mall. I don't know what I was thinking.

When I walked into the house, I said hello to Bobby, Monica and her father, who'd just arrived from the airport. Even then, I could feel the attack coming on. I ran into my bedroom to take some medicine, all the while telling myself, "Okay. It's gonna be all right. Just stay calm."

I was preparing to walk out of the bedroom when my chest tightened suddenly, without warning. I screamed for Bobby. Everyone came rushing down the hall. I was sitting on the bed gasping for air. He found my inhaler and handed it to me. It wasn't helping. Monica and her father looked scared to death. Bobby was calm, though. He lacked familiarity with the St. Louis roads, so he asked me how to get to the doctor's office. Shaking my head, all I could manage was a breath to say, "No time."

He picked up the phone and dialed 911 and told them it was an asthma attack, an emergency. I just lay on the bed, staring at Bobby and holding his hand. I was terrified. My chest was heaving violently, but I was only getting tiny bits of oxygen. My air supply was practically shut off. I couldn't keep my eyes open. I thought I might be dying.

"The ambulance is on the way. Just take it easy," Bobby said. He went to the bathroom and came back with a syringe and needle and a bottle of adrenaline, just in case I lost consciousness.

Monica kept asking him, "Can I do anything? Is she going to be all right?"

The ambulance arrived within minutes. The paramedics brought in oxygen and placed the clear plastic mask over my mouth. I started breathing better. One of them checked under my fingernails. He looked at Bobby and said, "It's a good thing we got here when we did. The skin beneath her nails had started turning blue."

They lifted me onto the stretcher and wheeled me out of the house. All I thought about was Monica, who was still recovering from the trauma of her stabbing seven months earlier. I hated the fact that she had to go through this because of me. I was so embarrassed. I kept apologizing to her and her dad. She was crying as the medics wheeled me out the door. I told her not to worry.

I was terrified of that ambulance. They'd put my mother in one the morning she died. When the attendants opened the doors and began pushing me inside, I became hysterical. I screamed for Bobby. "I don't want to die, Bobby," I cried. "I don't want to die in here!"

He climbed in with me and sat next to the stretcher. When the door closed, I panicked again. I felt claustrophobic. "Oh, my God, I can't breathe! I can't breathe!"

The attendant working on me was so nice. He kept telling me everything was going to be okay. But I was a basket case. I was still convinced I was dying.

At the hospital, the nurse gave me an injection of epinephrine to open my lungs. But after several hours and several tests of my lung activity, the results weren't satisfactory. Dr. John Best, the pulmonary specialist who treated me for asthma, said they had to admit me.

"Oh, no!" I said. "I have to be ready by tomorrow because I have my dinner for my foundation. I can't have a dinner and not be there. Monica Seles came all the way here for it and she's at my house—"

"You must be kidding!" he said, listening to my pleas. "After what you've been through? You have to be hospitalized."

"Will I be out by tomorrow?"

"I don't see how that will be possible."

As I started to cry, Bobby and Dr. Best looked at me incredulously.

Several hours before, I'd been nearly unconscious, with blue fingernails, fighting to breathe. But with the seizure past and my normal breathing restored, I was already putting it out of my mind. Just that quickly, I'd shifted my focus away from my health problem. I know now that it was a dangerous attitude. But at the time, I couldn't help myself. It was an instinct, a bad, bad defense mechanism I'd developed.

As I lay in the hospital bed that night, I reviewed the day's events. I kept seeing the terrified look on Monica's face. She and I had become very close friends after knowing each other for just a few months.

Her father was a track and field fan and he asked her agent to contact Bobby about helping her train. Monica was the number one ranked player at the time, but she wanted to improve her conditioning. She was trying to become more fit, more agile and stronger. She and Bobby arranged to meet after the Australian Open in 1993. She came to California and worked out with me on the track and in the weight room at UCLA for about a week. Her father told me he liked having me out there with her because some of the strength work for the heptathlon would be beneficial for her in tennis. Bobby put her through the wringer. She started out with a warmup run, short sprints and then longer endurance runs. In the weight room we lifted, did squats and rode stationary bikes together.

We bonded very quickly, comparing our experiences as female athletes. She, too, had been stung by critical stories in the press. It upset her when writers called her shallow or talked about her weight. I didn't think she was shallow at all. With great insight and compassion, she talked about the cultural differences in America and Eastern Europe, and about the political and racial strife in the former Yugoslavia, where she was born and raised.

She worked as hard on the track as most world-class track athletes. I most admired, though, her ability to concentrate for long periods of time. I understood how she'd become the best tennis player in the world. You could see the determination in her face as she ran those sprint drills and struggled with the heavy weights. It was really hot out there and it was hard work, especially with Bobby breathing down her neck. But she never complained, never asked to take a break. I think she's a first-rate athlete.

She's a first-rate person as well. She enjoyed her workout in California so much that she invited us to Florida for more workouts the following month. Her assistants had set everything up for us in Sarasota. But when she reviewed the arrangements, she said, "Oh, no that won't do!" She took over the job, driving around the area and personally evaluating the hotels. She told me that we'd been so nice to her in L.A., she wanted to make sure we had the best of everything. She put us up at the Colony Beach and Tennis Resort, a swank resort on Longboat Key, near Sarasota.

A few weeks later, in April, Bobby was driving to the airport to pick me up when the news bulletin aired on the radio: Monica had been stabbed at a tournament in Germany. We were both shocked into silence on the drive home. We cried while watching the report on the news later. Bobby tried contacting her through her agent, but Monica was already on her way to Vail, Colorado. We finally reached her there and had a long, tearful conversation. During her recuperation, we kept in touch and arranged another workout.

She and Bobby worked together several times during that period. There were plenty of stories in the papers and magazines suggesting that she didn't really want to come back. They were dead wrong. Monica was working diligently toward her comeback. She was very committed to returning to tennis. At the time, I don't think anyone, not even I, could comprehend what she must have been going through.

The hard part wasn't physical, she told me. She recovered from that fairly quickly. The mental aspect is what took longest, which I understood completely. To be in the place where you think you're safe—the arena where you do what you enjoy and where people enjoy and appreciate what you do—only to have someone attack you, is the most frightening thing I could ever imagine. I thought about how easy it would be for someone to do the same thing at a track meet and how it would traumatize me. It was a horrible ordeal for Monica to have to go through. For people who didn't know anything about it to speculate and conclude that she didn't want to come back was insensitive. It took a lot of courage and strength to come back from something like that.

I was so excited when she accepted my invitation and agreed to travel to St. Louis for my dinner so soon after the attack. It showed me how comfortable she was around Bobby and me. I didn't want anything to happen during her stay to upset her—like my collapsing and having to be rushed by ambulance to the hospital! Fortunately, the doctor agreed to release me the next morning, in time to host my dinner and spend time with Monica and my other friends. But he gave me a long, stern lecture before he did. He told me I could have died that day in my house. If I didn't start taking the disease seriously and taking better care of myself, he said, it probably would kill me. That got my attention.

Then Bobby sat on the side of the bed to talk with me. He'd been calm the day before at our house and in the emergency room. But now he was upset. He told me he couldn't keep going through episodes like that. It was too frightening. "You've just had a very close call, Jackie," he said. "Now, do you realize your attitude is putting your life in danger?"

I did. I finally did. I knew I had to take the illness seriously or there would be serious consequences. I started thinking of the asthma regime as part of my training. I had to attack it with the same commitment and discipline. If I didn't, I wouldn't be able to run or long-jump. I viewed it as a threat to my ability to continue competing in athletics. I wasn't going to lose the ability to do what I most enjoyed just because I was stubborn. I had to learn to control the disease, instead of letting it control me.

When I talk to asthma sufferers, I try to help them understand what it took me too long to learn—asthma won't keep you on the sidelines if you follow doctor's orders and take your medicine properly. But if you don't, the condition will take you out of the game—permanently.

31

The Lesson

For many athletes the word "farewell" might as well have four letters. They see it as the end of their glory days, of their turn in the spotlight, of their very lives. I don't have that attitude. I've always known that my time on top would end someday, that someone would come along and eclipse me. I wanted to prepare myself for it and, to the extent I could control it, start walking away before being pushed aside.

The moment I decided the 1996 Games would be my last Olympics, I started planning the next phase of my life. After the Games ended, aside from selected long-jump competitions and personal appearances on behalf of my sponsors, my calendar would be virtually empty. For the first time since I was ten, the bulk of my time would be spent on something other than running, jumping and competing.

Suddenly, a world of opportunities was available to me. I wanted to dive into the unfinished work at my foundation, including raising the remaining $6 million to start the first phase of construction on the youth center in East St. Louis.

I also was eager to focus more on my personal life. Since our wedding day, I've been buying baby clothes and stashing them away inside a drawer until Bobby and I started a family. Biologically speaking, it's time. In March 1997, I turned thirty-five. I'm ready emotionally, too. Bobby has been talking about having kids for years, but I wanted to wait until I could give our children my undivided attention. I know how single-minded I am when I'm training. To raise a child in those circumstances would have been unfair and irresponsible.

The night before the long-jump qualifying in Atlanta, still burdened with thoughts of whether I'd be risking grave injury by competing, I went to a women's basketball game between the U.S. and Japan at the Georgia Dome. Tara VanDerveer, coach of the U.S. team, sent me a note, asking me to help her fire up the women at halftime if they weren't playing well. But the Americans amassed a 15-point halftime lead and went on to beat the Japanese by the same margin. The Dome was packed, the crowd was enthusiastic and the U.S. women's team played so spectacularly, it was thrilling to be in the arena. I stopped by the locker room afterward, greeted my old friend Teresa Edwards, who played guard, and wished the rest of the team luck. "You've worked and sweated to get to this point—fifty-eight games without a loss," I reminded the eventual gold medalists. "Just two more to go. It's what you've dreamed about. Go get it."

The episode made me nostalgic. I'd made an almost identical speech to my basketball teammates at Lincoln High when we were undefeated and one game away from the state championship. It also shifted my thoughts briefly to overtures I'd received *before* the Olympics, from both the about-to-be-established National Basketball Association women's league and its competitor, the newly formed American Basketball League (ABL). Both organizations wanted me to trade in my track spikes for basketball sneakers. It was a tempting notion, particularly since I've always enjoyed blazing new trails, and since the existence of a financially healthy women's pro basketball league would give female athletes so many more options.

Eventually, after the Olympics were over, I would take the ABL up on its offer. But first, I had some unfinished business on the track.

It had been five days between my withdrawing from the heptathlon and leaving the stadium in tears, and my returning for long-jump qualifying. I was hoping to dispense with the preliminary round quickly, without unduly straining my leg, so that I'd be in competitive shape for the finals the day after.

What a relief it was to jump 21' 11¾" and make the finals on the first leap. I was on the field for less than thirty minutes. Someone walked up to me as I was putting on my warmup jacket and asked if I'd made it. "Yeah," I said smiling. "Thank God!"

The afternoon of the long-jump finals, I could feel every single eyeball in the place when I walked onto the field at the warmup track. My therapist, Bob Forster, and I tried to rearrange the beige bandage on my right leg to make it more comfortable. Carl Lewis, who'd already won the men's long jump in spectacular fashion on his last attempt, came over and gave me a hug. "Come on," he said. "Now it's your turn." He flashed a thumbs-up signal as he walked off.

Inside the tent, Leroy Burrell was lying on a massage table getting a rubdown. I climbed onto the table beside him and said hello while my therapist began wrapping my ankles. Leroy looked over, saw my right thigh and my ankles and laughed. "Gosh, Jackie," he said. "You're all bandaged up. You look like the walking wounded."

I was pretty worried, so the repartee and good wishes helped calm me. As soon as I got down off the table and tried to jog around, though, my leg went into spasms. I thought the bandage might be too tight. I asked Bob to rewrap it. As he finished, it was time to get on the bus and ride to the stadium. Inside the bus, the other athletes sat on the seats, while I stretched out on the floor. I wanted to keep the leg extended and loose. At the stadium entrance, the officials checked our bags, equipment and shoes and lined us up to walk onto the track. I took a deep breath. This was it.

Just that week, Kenny Moore had written an essay for *Sports Illustrated* about the Centennial Park bombing. The piece recounted his experiences as a member of the U.S. marathon team during the 1972 Olympics in Munich, where Palestinian terrorists killed several Israeli athletes. He discussed the indomitable athletic spirit and what he called the essential lesson of sports:

> *Everyone suffers. It's what you do with the suffering that lifts and advances us as a species. . . . Athletes turn pain into performance.*

I was certainly suffering now. Not just physically, but emotionally. I so badly wanted this Olympic experience to be joyous. I wanted to give my best performance in front of an American audience on American soil. I was so disappointed, so heartbroken that it wasn't turning out the way I'd envisioned. Here was one last chance—six jumps—to salvage something from these Games.

I instinctively grasped the essential lesson and applied it to my predicament. I didn't care if my leg blew up. I wasn't going to quit on myself because of a hamstring problem. I'd told Bobby that morning, "I won't leave the track on a stretcher like I did in Tokyo in 1991. If I have to shed blood out there, I will; but I'm staying until I take all of my jumps."

When I walked onto the field that night, a thunderous ovation began. I studied the arena for the first time. It was vast, with three tiers of seats. Beneath the darkened sky, thousands of camera flashes illuminated the stadium like so many twinkling stars. The crowd of 80,000 was standing and cheering for me now. I couldn't stop smiling as I looked and listened. My heart was pumping. A flood of adrenaline shot up from my toes to my fingertips. It gave me goose bumps. The affection from the crowd flowed into my pores and turned to pure energy. I felt courageous. I wanted to get out there and give it my all because I knew they were on my side. They were pulling for me as hard as I was pulling for myself. It was the most invigorating experience I've ever had on the athletic field.

I loosened up on the runway after putting on my spikes. After locating the spot I wanted to start from on the runway, I nailed my marker into the ground next to it. The painful throbbing in my leg matched, beat for beat, the pleasant pounding in my chest. I sat down and banged on the bandage with my hammer, trying to beat the spasms into submission and loosen up the tightening muscle. I mixed some Powerāde and water together and took a few sips. Then I dipped two fingers into a jar of Icy Hot and tried to slide some of the ointment under the bandage to keep the leg warm. I got up, walked around and shook the leg out, blocking out the feeling of desperation creeping up on me.

The first jump was terrible. I don't know how far I went, but it was nowhere near long enough. "It's going to be a long night," I thought. Then I caught myself. "Don't get down on yourself. You have six jumps. If it means you're going to have to slowly work your way through it, then that's what you'll do. Let's just take it one jump at a time."

After the third jump, I was in sixth place at 22' 6¼". Three tries left.

The fourth jump felt pretty good and I was hopeful, until I saw the line judge raise the red flag signaling a foul. I don't know what happened on the fifth jump. When I landed and got up, all I could do to keep from being frustrated was to laugh. It was pathetic. "Oh my God, Jackie!" I said to myself, trying to shake things up. "Is that all you have to show the world?"

I walked over to the fence to get some guidance from Bobby before the last jump. He was way up in the stands and had to walk down to a tiny railing that was still a long way from me. We had to shout to hear each other.

"Is it too fast?" I asked.

"Yeah, slow it down. Build in the middle and accelerate at the end," he said.

He turned and climbed the long flight back to his seat. I was struck by how calm he was. Not a trace of excitement or panic. Al was sitting near the railing where Bobby spoke to me. He held his breath each time I stood on the runway, terrified that my leg would blow up at any minute. Mr. Fennoy sat in one of the four far corners, in what would be the end zone in a football stadium. He'd been clocking my runs with a stopwatch to monitor my timing down the runway. But he put it away to watch the final attempt.

As I walked toward my marker, I was oblivious to the crowd's gathering roar, the flashbulbs going off all around me, the camera lenses pointed in my direction, the thousands of live eyeballs and the countless millions of others staring at me through TV screens.

I saw only the strip of Mondo in front of me and the pit of sand beyond it. All I heard was the conversation I was

having with my soul. "Well, Jackie. This is your last jump
in the Olympics. The ultimate test of everything you believe athletics is about. You have to bear down and focus on
the execution. The pain is going to come, but you have to
block it out and persevere. Here's where you show them
your character and your heart."

I tapped my right foot behind me and whispered,
"Come on Jackie." I gathered my hands, put my legs in
motion to run. I was racing down the runway, bringing my
knees up. As I prepared for the last four strides, I told myself, "If this leg pulls, then it just pulls!" I attacked those
last four steps, planted my right foot and launched. I tried
to hold myself in the air as long as I could.

For the first time in my career, when I landed in the pit
I didn't know if the jump was good enough. The judge at
the foul line raised a white flag, signaling it was fair. Then,
the electronic scoreboard flashed 22' 11¾". I had leaped
into third place and a spot on the medal stand.

I had to wait a few moments for the rest of the competitors to take their final jumps. But I thought my leap would
hold up because the three athletes who were also vying for
third place each looked at me wearily after my jump as if to
say, "I can't believe you jumped that far!"

When the final results were posted on the scoreboard,
the crowd went nuts. I was so overcome with emotion, I
wanted to personally thank each person in the stadium. I
was so grateful for their support. I went over to Al and
hugged him. He was elated, simultaneously laughing and
crying. Then, as we left the track, the line of athletes swung
past Mr. Fennoy's section and I ran to his open arms and
hugged him. I looked at him just the way I had after finishing near the back in my first race as an eleven-year-old,
and said the same thing I had that day.

"I tried."

He clutched my head in his hands, pressed my forehead

to his and said, "As far as I'm concerned, that was a gold medal performance."

I felt the same sentiment from the cheering fans as I walked around the stadium. They were treating me like a record-breaker and a world-beater, even though I was neither, simply because they knew how hard I'd tried. So many times in my career I'd been made to feel that because I didn't win and didn't win big, nothing I did mattered. But this time, every inch of it mattered. This time, third best was just fine. Those ovations that night in Atlanta fulfilled and satisfied me more than any others I ever had. I left the stadium waving to the crowd, with tears streaming down my cheeks. Bobby was waiting at the edge of the track, as always. We hugged for a long time.

"That was the most courageous thing you've ever done," he said. "I know you were in pain, but you didn't give up. This is a medal to be proud of."

I was proud. As the bronze medalist, I led the procession to the awards stand. When the medal was placed around my neck, I felt I'd received the highest honor of the competition.

While the national anthem of Nigeria played in honor of the gold medalist, Chioma Ajunwa, I realized that the essential lesson of athletics has also been the essential lesson of my life. The strength for that sixth jump came from my assorted heartbreaks over the years—the loss of my mother, the disappointing performances, the unfounded accusations, the slights, the insults and the injuries. I'd collected all my pains and turned them into one mighty performance. And I had, indeed, been uplifted by the result. I showed the world that the little girl from East St. Louis had made something of herself. She was a woman, an athlete, with character, heart and courage.

I shall forever cherish my beautiful bronze medal from the 1996 Games. It is my reward for having learned the essential lesson and passing the tough test. It had been a most joyous Olympic experience after all.

32

Dear Momma

Dear Momma,

As I've sifted through my memories and organized my thoughts for this book, you've been constantly on my mind. You were so important to me when I was growing up, and your influence on me continues—in ways I'm not sure I can fully express. It seems that everything I've ever done somehow relates back to you, to something you once said or did.

I've felt your spirit with me during both happy and sad times. On graduation day at UCLA, I heard you applauding as I received my history degree. You were somewhere in that crowd on the streets of East St. Louis during Al's and my victory parade. I bet you cried at the sight of Al escorting me to the altar to exchange wedding vows with Bobby. And yours was the voice I heard as I walked to the line that final time in Atlanta, telling me to have faith in myself.

So many times I've tried to imagine what you would say about the things I've done, the life I'm leading and the person I've become. Since you aren't here to tell me, I decided to write this letter and share some of my thoughts with you.

I know I sometimes muttered at you under my breath and resented your rules. But I'm so grateful now for the way you raised me. Without the discipline you taught, the wisdom you imparted and the sense of hope you instilled, I wouldn't be where I am.

When I was just a little girl, you planted the seed that even though I was black and a female and from a family for which nothing came easy, I could achieve great things in this world. The key to success, you said, was to set goals, and not be deterred by hardship or distracted by temptations.

I realize now that I owe a big part of my success in the heptathlon to you. It's a lot like life, that event. It's a seven-piece puzzle that must be put together, even on days when the pieces aren't falling neatly into place. You, Momma, gave me the three most important tools I needed to contest that event successfully: fierce determination, an appreciation of hard work and unwavering faith.

On the personal side, I've been very fortunate to have Bobby in my life. I think you'd like him. He's a good Christian man. We have a very happy, very comfortable life together. But it's not money or cars or houses that I care about. It's the love that Bobby shows and the support he's given regardless of where I place in the standings— whether I'm the world record holder or the sixth-place finisher at the World Championships or even just Jackie the Joker, a girl from East St. Louis. He is my security, always looking out for my best interests and protecting me—at times, even from myself. I feel blessed to have him as my husband.

All in all, I'm happy with who I am and with what I've accomplished. And I'd like to think I'm a success.

My biggest fear is that I haven't lived up to your expectations. The one thing I've never wanted to do was let you down. That's why whenever I feel lost or perplexed about something, I try to think of what you'd want me to do. Some people who've judged me—as a person and as an athlete—have made me feel like I wasn't pretty enough or that I wasn't good enough. Each time, I thought, "Am I good enough for Momma?"

I hope that every time you look down on me from heaven, that—no matter how I look on the outside—you always see beauty within me. If you do, Momma, then I'm a success.

Thank you for everything. I miss you.

Love,
Jackie

Index